Am I Still
My Brother's Keeper?

Biblical Perspectives on Poverty

Robert Wafawanaka

UNIVERSITY PRESS OF AMERICA,® INC.

Lanham • Boulder • New York • Toronto • Plymouth, UK

Dedicated to my parents
Tafios Mafuba Wafawanaka and
Shuvai Chara Wafawanaka

Table of Contents

Foreword

I have known Robert Wafawanaka for over twenty-five years. He was among the first students to enroll in the first Biblical Hebrew course that I initiated and taught at the University of Zimbabwe in 1984. Not only was he diligent in Hebrew; but he also finished among the top students in Hebrew Bible courses that he took. I was not amazed that he subsequently displayed his intellectual ability at both Harvard Divinity School and Boston University where he obtained the Th.M. and Th.D., respectively. I am quite familiar with his research interest in the area of poverty in Africa as the backdrop of the biblical teaching on poverty. Being a fellow Zimbabwean, I am familiar with the area of the country where he was born. It was rustic, segregated and labeled as African or native reserved areas by the whites who owned the lush agricultural parts of the land. He and I know poverty not from what is reported about it; but because we both experienced it growing up. Our relatives are still grappling with it thirty years after blacks achieved majority rule from a white and oppressive minority government. Robert is writing his book not only based on the study he has done, but more so from the heart.

The monograph that is before us is the culmination of several years of Robert's relentless investigation of poverty. As a display of his research acumen, Robert has gleaned information from the texts of the ancient Near East in order to compare modern day poverty with what the Bible teaches about poverty, and the consequences of humans' failure to be our brother's (or sister's) keeper. He noticed that in the ancient Near East and in the Bible, it was the duty of the government and the community leaders to care for the poor. In his study of the Torah, the Prophets and the Writings, Robert has found that exploitation of the poor ranged from the improper distribution of the resources to stark oppression and exploitation of the poor by the rich and powerful landowners. He prophetically contends that if modern societies, like the Israelites, continue to ignore the lessons of the past, and continuously fail to play the role of brother's keeper, there will be created a society that is increasingly disenfranchised and inequitable.

Before turning on to the New Testament, Robert looked at rabbinic literature where he found a significant shift regarding the cause of poverty from the community to individual responsibility. The rabbinic debates with each other on the questions of poverty focused on who the poor were and what to do with the poor. These debates did not reach a consensus; but their influence continues to impact our responses to modern varieties of poverty.

Robert has provided a broad review of literature on the subject of poverty from ancient times to the contemporary period. He has also helped the reader with a preface and abstract of his book which, in turn, is divided in clear sections that aid the reader to follow the trend of poverty diachronically. That alone is a significant achievement, especially his summary of what various authors have written on poverty.

I am greatly honored to present this book as a comprehensive study of poverty. It is a welcome resource for those who wish to pursue this topical subject of poverty that is unbridled in the world today.

Temba L.J. Mafico
Professor of Old Testament/Hebrew Bible
Associate Vice President for Academic Affairs/Associate Provost
Interdenominational Theological Center
Atlanta, Georgia

Preface

This book deals with what the Bible says about poverty and our responsibility toward the poor. It is an examination of the meaning of the concept of
brother's keeper from the ancient Near Eastern context through the biblical
period and our own times. My interest was to research and understand the
problem of poverty in different contexts and also evaluate the human response to poverty on a historical continuum. My ultimate goal was to discern
what we can learn about poverty from the biblical world and how we might be
able to appropriate some of those insights to fight poverty in our own modern
communities. While this research covers an extensive area, it is my belief that
I have herein presented a variety of biblical perspectives on poverty which
will enhance our attempts to wrestle with this timeless and endemic issue in
today's world.

My contention is that Israel failed to play the rightful role of brother's
keeper and we too have strayed far from the traditional conception of being
our brother's keeper. Failure to revisit this concept is likely to create a society
that is increasingly disenfranchised and inequitable. Conversely, by returning
to this basic biblical mandate, we have a chance to rectify many of our social
and economic problems on a global scale.

This work is divided into three parts. The first part introduces the problem
of poverty by examining the nature of the biblical mandate regarding the poor
especially as found in the book of Deuteronomy. Essentially, this mandate
states that there should be no poor people among the Israelites as long as
they take care of the poor and needy persons among them. Intended for those
with power and resources, this requirement challenges these groups of people
to assume their responsibility for the poor. With a brief focus on poverty in
Africa, I argue that the spirit of the biblical mandate is equally relevant and

applicable to the modern context where poverty continues to increase while some continue to prosper in the same context. The subject of poverty is a global problem which requires a global response from the human family.

The second part shifts attention to the three divisions of Hebrew Bible and analyzes each section in detail. Here I focus on the Law Codes, the Prophets and the Writings with particular attention to the status of slaves, resident aliens, widows, fatherless minor children, and other groups of poor people designated by specific Hebrew words. To expedite our understanding of these groups and why they are classified among the poor, I also examine the structure and causes of poverty in these sections and explore how the poor coped with their predicament. Using the hermeneutics of suspicion and the insights of ideological criticism, my research here focuses on why so many laws were legislated yet the poor continued to exist throughout the biblical period. Why did the prophets rant and rave so much about those who oppressed the poor? What had happened to the biblical mandate with its obligatory and imperative tone? Herein I contend that these very laws masked an underlying social problem due to the disregard of the divine mandate on the part of Israel. The increase in oppressive tendencies during the monarchical period especially at the height of Israel's political and economic success is evidence of the plight of the poor and the abandonment of the nation's responsibility toward its poor citizens. Consequently, I seek to demonstrate that the practicality and observance of many of the laws regarding the poor is highly questionable. This scenario possibly explains the prophetic critique of the oppression of the poor in both Israel and Judah.

The third part attempts to pull the work together by summarizing our findings and making some recommendations in our struggle against poverty. The failure to eliminate poverty in the ancient world parallels our own global experience where the poor continue to increase everywhere. Drawing some pertinent lessons from the ancient world, I seek to determine how we might appropriate them in our own contexts. Ultimately, I seek to demonstrate that the Bible is a minefield of information and perspectives on poverty which we can successfully unearth to illumine our quest for understanding poverty in our contemporary settings. For if we are going to be our brother's keeper, we need to pay close attention to the successes and failures of a people who received that mandate and chronicled their story for posterity and for our benefit as well.

Robert Wafawanaka
Richmond, VA
June 2011

Acknowledgments

This book has materialized as a result of much support that I have received. I wish to thank all those who have directly or indirectly assisted me in the writing and completion of this project. Unfortunately I can only mention a few individuals in this space.

My foremost thanks go to Samantha Kirk, my original editor at UPA, for her interest in my work and constant encouragement throughout the writing process. I thank her for her boundless patience and understanding as I labored to complete this book. I am also grateful to Brian DeRocco for his tireless efforts and prompt responses to my questions at the final stages of manuscript preparation. Thanks are also due to Lida Ramsey, Lindsey Porambo, and Laura Espinoza for their editorial assistance, as well as the rest of the staff at UPA. Special thanks to Beverly Shellem and Yung Suk Kim.

This project would not have been completed in a timely fashion had I not been granted teaching relief by my dean, Dr. John W. Kinney. For his unwavering support, encouragement, and faithfulness, I thank him. I also wish to thank the entire faculty and staff of Virginia Union University School of Theology, past and present, for providing a collegial atmosphere out of which this work could be developed. In particular, I wish to thank Dr. Boykin Sanders and Dr. James Henry Harris for their friendship and mentoring. A word of appreciation also goes to my students including those from Chicago in the CAATS program, who reflected on some of this material in my courses on poverty and wealth in the Bible. These classes have generated some of the most stimulating and memorable discussions of my teaching career.

Special thanks are due to Professor Temba L. J. Mafico, my first mentor and academic father in whose footsteps I continue to walk. Dr. Mafico instilled in me the interest and appreciation of Biblical Hebrew and the Hebrew

Bible. He has continued to be a constant source of support and encouragement throughout my academic and professional career. Dr. Mafico also graciously agreed to write the foreword to this book. I can never fully repay the intellectual debt that I owe him.

My thanks and appreciation also goes to Katheryn Pfisterer Darr at Boston University for her interest in my work and competent guidance through much of the research material that comprises this book. She served as my major advisor and helped me to complete my doctoral program in a timely fashion. I also fondly remember professors Simon B. Parker and J. Paul Sampley for their competence and erudition in the classroom. I must also thank my Harvard professors who have impacted my life, in particular, Paul Hanson, Frank Moore Cross, Theodore Hiebert, Patrick D. Miller, Jr., James Kugel, Elisabeth Schüssler Fiorenza, and Bernadette Brooten.

I cannot forget to thank those who have offered suggestions to strengthen this work. For his unique insights and perspectives on the Bible, I thank Randall C. Bailey for encouraging me to study the subject of poverty from the perspective of ideological criticism. He enabled me to understand how the system of oppression works, power dynamics, and other ideological underpinnings of the text. He also pointed me to some pertinent texts concerning this subject. I also wish to thank Dale Patrick for enabling me to comprehend the nature of poverty in the social world of ancient Israel.

For his friendship, sense of humor, and constant support, I am grateful to Professor Hugo A. Kamya of Simmons College. I also extend my thanks to the Salzman family for their interest in all my work. This family has truly become my extended family in America. My family in Zimbabwe deserves my heartfelt gratitude for their patience and support of my work. I especially thank my parents, Tafios Mafuba and Shuvai Chara, for initially instilling in me the love of the Bible that has now become my life's work.

Last but not least, this book could not have come to fruition without the constant love and support of my wife Ellen. I am blessed to have a life partner who is far more precious than jewels. She is the one who suggested the title of this book after seeing me wrestle with this subject matter over the years. To my children, Justin and Eleanor, thank you for providing that balance in my life and for giving me space to work on my computer even past the midnight hour. To this extended family of mine, I dedicate this book.

Abbreviations

AB	Anchor Bible
ABD	D. N. Freedman (ed.), *The Anchor Bible Dictionary*
AEL	Miriam Lichtheim, *Ancient Egyptian Literature*
AfricaJEvTh	*Africa Journal of Evangelical Theology*
AJBS	African Journal of Biblical Studies
ANE	Ancient Near East
ANET	J. B. Pritchard, (ed.), *Ancient Near Eastern Texts Relating to the Old Testament*
ARC	*ARC: The Journal of the Faculty of Religious Studies, McGill University*
ARE	*J. H. Breastead (ed.), Ancient Records of Egypt*
AsiaJTh	*Asia Journal of Theology*
ATLAPro	American Theological Library Association: Proceedings
AusBR	*Australian Biblical Review*
AustinBul	*Austin Bulletin: Faculty Edition*
AV	Authorized Version
BA	Biblical Archaeologist
BAGD	W. Bauer, W. F. Arndt, F. W. Gingrich, and F. W. Danker, *Greek-English Lexicon of the New Testament*
BAR	*Biblical Archaeology Review*
BASOR	*Bulletin of the American Schools of Oriental Research*
BCE	Before the Common Era
BHS	*Biblia Hebraica Stuttgartensia*
Bib	*Biblica*
BiBh	*Bible Bhashyam: An Indian Biblical Quarterly*
BSac	Bibliotheca Sacra

BTB	Biblical Theology Bulletin
BZ	*Biblische Zeitschrift*
CalThJ	*Calvin Theological Journal*
CB	The Century Bible
CBC	The Cambridge Bible Commentary
CBQ	*Catholic Biblical Quarterly*
CC	Covenant Code
CDS	Centre for Development Studies
CE	Common Era
CEV	Contemporary English Version
Chap(s).	Chapter(s)
ChrCent	*The Christian Century*
ChrSchR	*Christian Scholar's Review*
ChrT	*Christianity Today*
ChSoc	*Church and Society*
CMHE	F. M. Cross, *Canaanite Myth and Hebrew Epic*
Colloq	*Colloquium: The Australian and New Zealand Theological Society*
Commentary	*Commentary*
ConcorJ	*Concordia Journal*
Crux	*Crux: A Quarterly Journal of Christian Thought and Opinion*
CurTM	*Currents in Theology and Mission*
DC	Deuteronomic Code
DH	Deuteronomistic History
Dialogue	*Dialogue (Mormon): A Journal of Mormon Thought*
DownR	*The Downside Review*
EcR	*The Ecumenical Review*
Enc	*Encounter*
EpworthR	*Epworth Review*
EvQ	*Evangelical Quarterly*
EvRTh	*Evangelical Review of Theology*
ExpTim	*Expository Times*
Foundations	*Foundations*
Frontier	*Frontier*
Furrow	*The Furrow*
GNB	Good News Bible
GraceThJ	*Grace Theological Journal*
HALAT	L. Koehler and W. Baumgartner, *Hebräisches und Aramäisches Lexicon zum Alten Testament*
HALOT	L. Koehler and W. Baumgartner, *Hebrew and Aramaic Lexicon of the Old Testament*

HAR	*Hebrew Annual Review*
HB	Hebrew Bible
HC	Holiness Code
HDB	*Harvard Divinity Bulletin*
Hermenia	Hermenia
Horizons	*Horizons: The Journal of the College Theology Society*
HS	Hebrew Studies
IBT	Interpreting Biblical Texts
ICC	International Critical Commentary
IDB	G. A. Buttrick (ed.), *Interpreter's Dictionary of the Bible*
IDBSup	*IDB Supplementary Volume*
IDS	Institute of Development Studies
IEJ	*Israel Exploration Journal*
IliffR	The Iliff Review
Int	Interpretation
IntBulMissR	*International Bulletin of Missionary Research*
ISBE	G. W. Bromiley (ed.), *The International Standard Bible Encyclopedia, rev.*
JB	Jerusalem Bible
JBL	Journal of Biblical Literature
Jeev	Jeevadhara
JETS	Journal of the Evangelical Theological Society
JNES	*Journal of Near Eastern Studies*
JPH	*Journal of Presbyterian History*
JPOS	*Journal of the Palestine Oriental Society*
JSNT	Journal for the Study of the New Testament
JSOT	*Journal for the Study of the Old Testament*
JSOTSup	JSOT Supplement Series
JTSA	*Journal of Theology for Southern Africa*
JTS	*Journal of Theological Studies*
Judaism	*Judaism: A Quarterly Journal of Jewish Life and Thought*
KB	L. Koehler and W. Baumgartner, *Lexicon in Veteris Testamenti libros*
KJV	King James Version
LCBI	Literary Currents in Biblical Interpretation
LXX	Septuagint
MethR	*Methodist Review*
MissSt	*Mission Studies*
MQ	*McCormick Quarterly*
MQR	*Methodist Quarterly Review*
MT	Masoretic Text

n(n).	note(s)
NAB	New American Bible
NBDB	F. Brown, S. R. Driver, and C. A. Briggs, *The New Brown, Driver and Briggs Hebrew and English Lexicon of the Old Testament*
NCB	New Century Bible
NCBC	New Century Bible Commentary
NEB	New English Bible
NIB	L. E. Keck (ed.), *The New Interpreter's Bible*
NICOT	The New International Commentary on the Old Testament
NIV	New International Version
NJB	New Jerusalem Bible
NRSV	New Revised Standard Version
NT	New Testament
OBT	Overtures to Biblical Theology
One World	*One World*
OrAnt	*Oriens Antiquus*
OT	Old Testament
Other Side	*The Other Side*
OTL	Old Testament Library
P(p).	page(s)
Par.	Paragraph
PastPsych	*Pastoral Psychology*
PDL	Poverty Datum Line
Per	*Perspectives: A Journal of Reformed Thought*
QR	*Quarterly Review (Methodist)*
RB	*Revue biblique*
REB	Revised English Bible
RHPR	Revue d'histoire et de philosophie religieuses
Risk	*Risk*
RSV	Revised Standard Version
SBL	Society of Biblical Literature
SBLDS	Society of Biblical Literature Dissertation Series
SBLMS	Society of Biblical Literature Monograph Series
SBLRBS	Society of Biblical Literature Resources for Biblical Study
SBLSP	Society of Biblical Literature Seminar Papers
SBT	Studies in Biblical Theology
ScEs	*Science et esprit*
Scriptura	*Scriptura: Journal of Bible and Theology in Southern Africa*
SEDOS	*SEDOS Bulletin*
SJOT	*Scandinavian Journal of the Old Testament*

Sojourners	Sojourners
ST	Spirituality Today
StMarkR	St Mark's Review
SWJT	Southwestern Journal of Theology
Tanakh	Torah-Nevi'im-Ketuvim
TBT	The Bible Today
TDNT	G. Kittel and G. Friedrich (eds.), *Theological Dictionary of the New Testament*
TDOT	G. J. Botterweck and Helmer Ringgren (eds.), *Theological Dictionary of the Old Testament*
THAT	E. Jenni and C. Westerman, *Theologisches Handwörterbuch zum alten Testament*
Transformation	Transformation: An International Dialogue on Mission and Ethics
TrinityJ	Trinity Journal
TS	*Theological Studies*
TWAT	G. J. Botterweck and H. Ringgren (eds.), *Theologisches Wörterbuch zum Alten Testament*
TWOT	R. L. Harris, G. L. Archer, and B. K. Waltke (eds.), *Theological Wordbook of the Old Testament*
TynBul	*Tyndale Bulletin*
v(v).	verse(s)
vol(s).	volume(s)
VT	*Vetus Testamentum*
Witness	*The Witness*
WW	*Word and World*
ZAW	*Zeitschrift für die alttestamentliche Wissenschaft*
ZIDS	Zimbabwe Institute of Development Studies
ZJE	*Zimbabwe Journal of Economics*

Introduction

Are we still our brothers' keepers? Do we need to be our brothers' keepers in our global context? Who is our brother? These questions lie at the heart of this study. While we live in a world that is increasingly interconnected due to the wonders of technology and the benefits of modern travel, we seem to be drifting further and further apart as human beings. My quest is to assess whether we are still our brothers' keepers given the rich legacies of care we have inherited.

The concept of brother's keeper is one we find in many contexts. Moral philosophy obligates us to care for one another because it is the right thing to do. The notion of care and responsibility for one another is introduced at the very outset of the Bible. After Cain kills his brother Abel, we read about the conversation between Cain and the Lord. The text reads as follows: "Then the LORD said to Cain, 'Where is your brother Abel?'" He said, "I do not know; am I my brother's keeper?" (Genesis 4:9). Cain not only lies about the whereabouts of Abel, but he seems to confess ignorance as to his obligation concerning his brother's wellbeing. However, we know that the same text calls upon the reader to care for others and protect them. It obligates us even in modern times, to be our brother's keeper, unlike Cain.

My contention is that we have moved away from the traditional concept of brother's keeper. Failure to revisit this concept will create a society that is increasingly disenfranchised and inequitable. Conversely, by returning to this basic biblical mandate, we have a chance to rectify many of our social problems.

This book wrestles with the problem of poverty from antiquity to the present. It seeks to argue that human beings, both ancient and modern, have fallen short of the biblical mandate to take care of the poor and needy in their midst.

Taking as its point of departure the text of the Year of Release (*šĕmiṭṭâ* שמטה) in Deuteronomy 15, the book argues that this text provides readers with a seminal teaching on the proper response to poverty, not only in ancient Israel, but also in the modern world. The text of Deuteronomy 15 essentially argues that the poor should not really have existed if Israel had been obedient to the biblical mandate and had taken care of the needs of the poor in its communities. However, it is evident that this law was not strictly followed because the poor continued to exist. Consequently, this contributed to widespread poverty that can be traced throughout the scriptures, suggesting that the nation was not obedient to this mandate in the strictest sense.

On the basis of this biblical mandate, the book takes a survey of the Hebrew scriptures in the three legal codes, the Covenant Code (Exodus 20:22 - 23:33), the Deuteronomic Code (Deuteronomy 12 – 26), and the Holiness Code (Leviticus 17 – 26) to determine Israel's response to this challenge. In all cases, it is apparent that the poor existed at different periods of Israelite history. While still aware of this divine imperative, Israel was somehow unable or unwilling to stem the cycle of poverty. Despite the heavy legislation to care for the needs of the poor, the requirements of this mandate were not fully met.

This argument that ancient Israel failed the test of brother's keeper is still relevant in our times. A brief look at human history and the progress we have made indicates that we too have not been our brother's keeper as were the ancient Israelites. While we have made some significant achievements, we have failed to eradicate the problem of poverty in our societies. The irony of human progress seems to be the increase in levels of poverty around the globe. Even in more advanced societies such as the United States of America, poverty is an increasingly common phenomenon. With the current economic crisis in the United States, more and more people will become poor as people lose their jobs, savings, or homes. While an unemployment rate of 10% in the United States is a scary scenario, an unemployment rate of 90% in some developing countries such as Zimbabwe is simply unimaginable.

Research by social scientists and economists indicates that the vast majority of people on earth who live in the developing world survive on one to two dollars a day. In most cases they have no basic necessities of life that many people in the Western world take for granted. In addition, they are victimized by preventable diseases such as malaria, tuberculosis, or cholera due to lack of education or protective equipment and medicines. Despite the effects of globalization, the absolute poor continue to fare badly. They live in extreme poverty even as some pockets of the world seem to prosper. On a global scale, this scenario simply means that we as human beings have failed to effectively play the role of our brother's keeper.

While the separation of the rich and the poor may seem to be a natural consequence of our economic enterprises and competitive market economics, the problems of poverty and wealth are not mutually exclusive. In reality, poverty and wealth are two sides of the same coin and we are better off by addressing them together. While wealth may indicate a society's industry and advancement, it may also be symptomatic of an unequal world. By the same token, while poverty may signify one's lack of industry or acquisition of resources, it may also show a nation's lack of responsibility for the poor in its midst or the unequal distribution of resources.

The biblical mandate clearly calls us to be responsible for each other. It addresses those members of society who have the means and the power to ensure that there would be no needy person among them. Indeed, this is a challenge that many have struggled with from ancient to contemporary times. This book will explore the reasons why Israel failed to meet the divine mandate and also why modern societies are unable to fulfill this requirement. By drawing parallels with the biblical world, we can grasp the relevance and timelessness of this problem.

I hope this book contributes to the discussion of a global phenomenon that seems to be worsening despite human achievements and advancement. By surveying the biblical world and our own, it is my hope that we can draw useful lessons that can help us to be better keepers of our brothers and sisters in our global context.

Jesus' discourse about the great judgment reminds us, once again, what it means to be our brothers' and sisters' keepers:

> Then the king will say to those at his right hand, 'Come, you that are blessed by my Father, inherit the kingdom prepared for you from the foundation of the world; for I was hungry and you gave me food, I was thirsty and you gave me something to drink, I was a stranger and you welcomed me, I was naked and you gave me clothing, I was sick and you took care of me, I was in prison and you visited me.' Then the righteous will answer him, 'Lord, when was it that we saw you hungry and gave you food, or thirsty and gave you something to drink? And when was it that we saw you a stranger and welcomed you, or naked and gave you clothing? And when was it that we saw you sick or in prison and visited you?' And the king will answer them, 'Truly I tell you, just as you did it to one of the least of these who are members of my family, you did it to me' (Matthew 25:34-40, NRSV).

Part I

OVERVIEW OF STUDY

Chapter One

The Biblical Mandate

PRELIMINARY REMARKS

This book wrestles with the problem of poverty from ancient to modern times. It seeks to make a survey of the Hebrew Scriptures and also reflect on the problem of poverty in contemporary times. Due to the ubiquitous nature of poverty throughout human history, this book seeks to understand the reasons for the continued existence of poverty even in modern advanced societies.

The text of Deuteronomy 15:4 provides us with a useful vision of the proper response to poverty in ancient Israel. Essentially, this fifth book of Moses argues that there shall be no poor people among the Israelites. The reason is that if the Israelites were to be obedient to the Torah of Moses, then the poor would not have existed because community members would be bound to take care of needy members among them. This vision of ancient Israel seems idealistic, but nevertheless, it would have eliminated poverty among the Israelites, had it been adhered to.

The problem of the persistence of poverty according to this text seems to stem from a fundamental disobedience to the Law of Moses. In fact, Deut 15:11 seems to anticipate disobedience on the part of Israel, for the text states that the poor will never cease out of the land. However, read in its proper context, the essence of Deut 15 is that the poor ought not to exist in Israelite society. This explains why verse 11 goes on further to state how Israel should address this problem, "Since there will never cease to be some in need on the earth, I therefore command you, 'Open your hand to the poor and needy neighbor in your land.'"[1] This is the biblical mandate, to take care of the poor, and the book of Deuteronomy and indeed other biblical books go to great lengths to demonstrate specifically how Israel was to take care of poor and needy members in the community.

The biblical mandate to care for the poor is evident throughout the biblical period. In fact as we shall see below, the injunction to care for the poor was ingrained in ancient Near Eastern cultures of Babylon, Canaan, and Egypt. It was the particular duty of the good ruler or king to provide for the welfare of the poor and powerless by ensuring that justice prevailed in the land. We see the same care and concern for the poor in both testaments, as well as the intertestamental period. Translated into modern terms, the duty to care for poor members of society falls upon human governments and community members who are in a position to ameliorate the situation of the poor. These ancient concerns are still relevant in our modern societies, if not more.

In light of the ancient concern for the welfare of the poor, what is evident throughout much of the scriptures is a violation of this basic biblical mandate. The poor existed for various reasons that shall be explored in this book but the requirement is still the same. It is apparent that in the Bible are various responses and perspectives on the problem of poverty. In very general terms, the Mosaic Torah views the problem of poverty as a result of the improper distribution of resources. By and large, the prophetic literature blames the existence of poverty on the exploitation and oppression of the poor and powerless by the rich and powerful landowners of the time. While both sentiments are retained in the Writings, we also see a shift toward the question of individual responsibility as a causal explanation of poverty. Rabbinic literature of the intertestamental period is filled with much debate among the rabbis about the question of poverty. The rabbis debated each other on such question as what poverty was, who was poor, and what to do about the situation of the poor. Interestingly, they always came to different conclusions about these questions. Their questions and responses continue to shape our responses to modern situations of poverty.

Despite many perspectives about the poor in ancient and modern times, the evidence suggests that the problem of poverty was not solved in ancient times, neither has it been solved in modern times. What is obvious in modern times is a worsening of the situation of the poor despite human progress and development on many fronts—social, scientific, and economic. How are we to explain this persistent human situation? What can we learn from the ancients and how can we improve the human condition?

It is the argument of this book that the biblical text gives us a useful paradigm with which to address poverty at all times. While the book of Deuteronomy argues that the poor should not really exist in Israelite society, we see consistent disobedience to the Mosaic Torah throughout Israel's history. The problem of poverty continued to exist such that by the time of Jesus, it had not yet been eliminated. This explains Jesus' memorable statement that "you always have the poor with you" (Mt 26:11; Mk 14:7; Jn 12:8) which seems like an antithesis to the letter of the law. What is implicit in this remark is that Israel had continued to disobey the Mosaic mandate such that Jesus recognized the continued existence of the poor many centuries after Moses wrote the words in Deuteronomy. While Jesus recognized the persistence of poverty in his first century society, it is significant what he said after these words. He tells those who were complaining about the wasted expensive oil that they could show kindness to the poor whenever they needed to. As a Jewish Rabbi, Jesus was well aware of the biblical mandate to care for the poor. His response is a stinging criticism of the lack of obedience to this basic command.

By viewing these two positions about the poor in biblical times (that the poor should not really exist and that the poor will always be there), this book seeks to argue that the poor will always be there as demonstrated by ancient biblical paradigms and contemporary situations of the poor. At the heart of the problem is a fundamental disobedience to the Torah of Moses which legislated taking care of poor and needy members among the Israelites. The history of poverty is so extensive that it is difficult to conceive if there will ever truly be no poor people among us. While the basic vision of the lack of poverty in Israelite society is utopian and idealistic, the reality is that the poor continued to exist due to inattention to this idealistic vision of society. The negation of this vision explains why the poor are always present even when the desire is to do away with their situation. The existence of poverty in both biblical and modern societies has other explanations which we will address as this book unfolds. One general explanation is that the poor will always exist because someone else is benefiting from their condition. The prophetic critique of social injustice opens a window into the oppressive social world of ancient Israel. Reading the biblical text from an ideological perspective, Randall C. Bailey argues that poverty was not wiped out because "the system" that created it is in place and the system benefits from the existence of the poor.[2]

When we consider this problem in modern twenty-first century societies, we see increasing cases of poverty in both developed and developing countries of the world. Indeed, there seems to be a greater irony in the existence of poverty in the very affluent societies of the developed world. While resources could be shared more equitably, the reality is that there is great disparity between those who have and those who don't. While the few rich grow richer and richer, the majority poor grow poorer and poorer and by larger margins. The notion of free enterprise and competitive economics fosters a spirit of individualism and consequently a disregard for the welfare of the other.

In our global context and economy, the differences are quite striking. The great majority of individuals in the developing world is poor and survives on only one to two dollars a day.³ There are cases of "extreme poverty" in Africa, Latin America, and other parts of the globe. Despite progress in technology and other areas, the poor of modern times die of poverty, preventable diseases, and a host of other causes.

What this modern situation of the poor demonstrates is the continual human disregard for each other's well-being as in the biblical world. If only we were able to share the resources of the earth more equitably, or have the well-off members of the human community supply the basic needs of the poor, or enable them to be independent, poverty would be greatly reduced. In global terms, if the rich countries could only use their resources to take of the poor in the developing world, extreme cases of poverty would not exist. In his book *The End of Poverty,* Jeffrey Sachs boldly argues that the global condition of extreme poverty could be ended by 2025 if only the rich nations of the world could play their rightful role to assist poor nations achieve economic independence.⁴ Like the biblical mandate, this is a visionary statement of what it means to extend one's hand to a needy member of the human community. This modern prescription for solving global poverty is not unlike Israel's vision of social reform. In both cases the challenge is radical transformation of the human tendency toward self-care without regard for the other. We ought to seriously wrestle with the implications of a world of extremes—extreme wealth on the one hand, and extreme poverty on the other. The two are not mutually exclusive either.

In both ancient and modern times, it is clearly evident that human beings are called upon to exercise a great deal of selflessness by considering the well-being of other members of the community. In both cases the onus is upon those members of the community who have the resources and who are able to positively impact the situation of the poor. A disregard of this mandate will result in the continued existence of poverty. The fact that poverty has existed from ancient to modern times is a testament to the violation of a basic biblical mandate. Without doing something drastic about the situation of the poor, it is evident in both biblical and contemporary times that the poor will always be there.

While there are many other reasons why the poor will always be there, at the very basic, this is the crux of the matter. The major question is, what did the ancients do to address the situation of the poor and how successful were they? For our modern context, the question is what are we to do with regard to the poor among us? Both ancient and modern research indicates that the poor need a social response to their plight. In the 1970s, liberation theologians talked about a "preferential option for the poor" and four decades later, the option for the poor is still relevant as it was then.[5]

Noting that poverty (since the option for the poor was pronounced by Roman Catholic theologians back in the 1960s) has reached "scandalous proportions," Gustavo Gutiérrez, one of the major architects of this concept writes, "The ideal, what we should strive for, is that there be no poor; if there must be some, the conduct of the believer should be that of opening one's heart and one's hand to the poor."[6] Indeed, in Gutiérrez's articulation of the ideal for the human community, is a sad realization that poverty has continued to increase despite the biblical mandate and the modern preferential option for the poor. In a nutshell, poverty will always be there unless we as human beings do something drastic about it.

POVERTY IN HISTORICAL AND MODERN CONTEXTS

As mentioned above, the problem of poverty in ancient Israel and the modern world is timeless. It has occupied the attention of biblical scholars in a variety of ways, such that a number of perspectives are represented in their work. While modern writers tend to view poverty primarily as an economic or socio-political problem especially in our global context, the Hebrew and Greek scriptures see it as fundamentally a result of a breakdown in the biblical mandate especially as expressed in the book of Deuteronomy. Gerhard von Rad is correct when he argues with regard to Deuteronomy 15 that "this sermon is a summons to meet the poor *at all times* with an open hand and an open heart. *It is just the appeal to the heart which is characteristic.*"[7] This text also adds a motive clause for why Israel should help its needy members: the Lord will bless them if they follow this command. While both economic and political perspectives are necessary for explaining the existence of poverty, they can be better understood in light of the biblical mandate to take care of the poor in human communities. Whether poverty is due to the lack of economic opportunity or because of political oppression, the biblical paradigm assumes both and argues for a more just and equitable society. Essentially, denying economic opportunity to individuals or oppressing and exploiting citizens are both guaranteed to produce a society where some are rich while others are poor. While social stratification may serve the needs of some in society, it may very well adversely affect others at the same time.

As we navigate the Hebrew Scriptures, we will discover a plethora of perspectives on poverty. For example, scholars of ancient Israelite law point to laws which were apparently designed to prevent poverty, or at least to protect the poor. Scholars of prophetic literature highlight the problem of oppression in their analysis of the prophetic critique of social injustice. As for wisdom literature, scholars point to a variety of attitudes toward poverty which are evident in, for example, the book of Proverbs.

This book is inspired by the persistence of poverty in both ancient and modern societies. If poverty has existed for that long and there seems to be no end to it, then something must be drastically wrong about the human condition. The disparity evident between the rich and poor of all times is a testament to something that has gone awry with regard to human nature. The evidence also suggests that human beings need to engage in radical approaches to the problem of poverty. If history has not taught us lessons and if we are not motivated to change anything about the status quo, then we guarantee that the poor will always be among us. But we may ask, should the poor continue to exist in our world? We may offer different responses from our perspectives and social locations, but the biblical mandate is clear. Those members of the society who are economically better off are mandated to help those who are poor and disenfranchised. Obviously, poverty has continued to exist at all times despite efforts to ameliorate it because something is fundamentally wrong.

Many biblical scholars have engaged different problems from a variety of perspectives. For example, Robert R. Wilson applied a sociological model to the phenomenon of prophecy in ancient Israel with some groundbreaking results.[8] In light of his work, it becomes clear that biblical scholars can benefit from a comprehensive study of the social dimensions of the problem of poverty in ancient Israel. Some of the relevant questions to be addressed are: What are the sociological aspects of the problem of poverty? What is society's role with regard to poverty in ancient Israel? Who are the poor, and how do they become poor? What is the nature of the economy of the poor? How do the poor survive? What is the role of the family with regard to poverty? What lessons about poverty in antiquity are applicable to modern cases of poverty? Given this extensive historical chronicle of the existence of poverty, the critical question to ask is what have we learned and what can we do differently to break the cycle of poverty?

This book takes a wide-ranging approach and social analysis of the problem of poverty in different contexts. By studying the problem of poverty in ancient biblical society, we can gain a better understanding of the same phenomenon in our modern context. A biblical understanding of poverty may shed significant light on the problem of poverty in modern times. In addition, this approach will suggest useful questions to ask of the biblical text and consider their relevance for modern societies.

Although ancient Israel and modern society are different cultures, there are enough strong parallels to warrant a serious cross-cultural comparative study. Besides identifying similarities and differences, a comparative study also presents familiar issues in a new light. As such, it has the potential to broaden our horizons and perspectives, raise awareness, provoke thinking, and inform our approaches and perceptions. While poverty has changed its form and shape over the years, the reality of its existence and negative effects on human societies has remained constant. Poverty is still poverty, whether it existed in antiquity or in the twenty-first century.

While recognizing the implications of comparing cultures that are separated by centuries, my interest, however, is in the similarity of issues, rather than the specific content of those issues. My goal in writing this book is to show these similarities in cultures that are traditional, rural, and agrarian and their implications for modern societies. I shall emphasize the social, ethical, and religious dimensions of the problem of poverty in both ancient and modern societies. These approaches will help us realize that the poor will always be with us unless we adhere to the biblical mandate regarding them. In its strictest form, the biblical mandate, rather than being an idealistic vision, is a call to action. This call to action is equally appropriate to us since the poor have continued to exist among us. The care of the poor and needy involves "a theology of activism" that exhorts us "to be *doers* and not just *hearers* of God's word."[9]

IMPLICATIONS OF STUDYING THE HISTORY OF POVERTY

This book is intended to provide biblical scholars and interested readers with a fresh perspective on the problem of poverty in ancient Israel and modern times. While many perspectives have been pursued, few scholars have seriously studied poverty as a social, economic and ethical issue. Moreover, the predominantly Western/European approaches have not sufficiently considered poverty in ancient Israel from a cross-cultural perspective. This book pays particular attention to the problem of poverty in ancient and modern cultures.

I intend to draw attention to the subject of poverty in ancient Israel as primarily a socio-economic and moral issue. My main interest is in discovering how the poor dealt with the reality of poverty and endured it. The significance of this study has implications for our global context. I will show how biblical injunctions on poverty have relevance for contemporary situations of poverty especially in Africa and other developing parts of the world.

Poverty in Africa has existed from antiquity to the present. In fact it is the major irony of Africa's postcolonial period that the continent is poorer than it was during the colonial period. How do we explain the attainment of independence vis-à-vis the extreme poverty that plagues much of the continent today? Has something been lost that we need to recover? I think the biblical paradigm, despite its failures and inadequacies, still has relevance for the modern world. This research demonstrates that poverty existed in ancient Israel and throughout the entire biblical period. Our basic contention that the violation of the Mosaic standard contributed to the continued existence of poverty in Israel is also relevant in our modern context. Consequently, measures to relieve the suffering of the poor are still relevant now as they were then. History has shown that the abandonment of these measures has contributed to the ironic increase of poverty especially in modern and advanced societies. My hope is that if we can learn some of the lessons of the past (both good and bad), we can use them as guides for the future. We need to ask ourselves a critical question, how long shall the poor continue to be among us?

The research in this book demonstrates that poverty continued to be a feature of ancient Israelite society and the poor survived in a number of ways. Central to their survival were the institution of the extended family, communal spirit, and social solidarity. However, the writers of ancient Israel continued to call the nation to remember its divine mandate. This call for concern to members of the human community is still relevant in our modern global economies. Moreover, if we should view our world as a "global village," then the call for global social responsibility is even greater. In the ancient context, the primary call for social responsibility was upon kings to ensure that the poor and needy were provided for. This responsibility was passed on to local leaders and eventually to all members of the community. Translated into modern terms, this means that the primary responsibility for care and concern about the poor lies with human governments, local leaders, and finally every member of society. Ironically, some of our leaders seem to care more about their own welfare than that of their citizens. The biblical mandate is to care for *others* first and foremost.[10] With this book, I hope to contribute to the ongoing debate about a very important subject. The urgency of this problem is self-evident in the modern world, in which there is a dearth of traditional values. Poverty is an increasingly significant problem in both developed and developing nations of the world. My hope is that when we look at poverty in the biblical world from a fresh perspective, we can draw some useful lessons and models relevant to our time. These paradigms can be used to suggest ways of alleviating the problem of poverty in modern societies.

SOME USEFUL MODELS: STRUCTURAL AND CONJUNCTURAL POVERTY

The major problem with previous studies on poverty is that they do not fully address its social implications. A sociological analysis of attitudes and perspectives on poverty in ancient Israel will enhance our understanding of poverty in modern societies.

Useful categories for understanding poverty have been proposed by John Iliffe in his study of African poverty. He makes an important distinction between "structural" and "conjunctural" poverty. According to Iliffe, structural poverty is "the long-term poverty of individuals due to their personal or social circumstances," and conjunctural poverty is "the temporary poverty into which ordinarily self-sufficient people may be thrown by crisis."[11] Another distinction is between the characteristics of structural poverty in societies with ample resources like land and those without much land. He argues that:

> In land-rich societies the very poor are characteristically those who lack access to the labour needed to exploit land - both their own labour (perhaps because they are incapacitated, elderly, or young) and the labour of others (because they are bereft of family or other support). In land-scarce societies the very poor continue to include such people but also include those among the able-bodied who lack access to land (or other resources) and are unable to sell their labour power at a price sufficient to meet their minimum needs.[12]

We can draw on this model to understand the situation of the poor in biblical times. Using this model, we can safely deduce that the bulk of the poor in the Bible were the structural poor, whose poverty was due to personal and social circumstances. Moreover, we can argue that the poor of the pre-monarchic or early monarchic period were not landless; rather, they were the structural poor whose poverty was mainly due to personal circumstances. With the rise of the monarchy and the practice of latifundia in general, we can also deduce that the landless poor increased; hence their poverty was due to social circumstances. These are the poor for whom the prophets so passionately advocate. Although the Bible does not say much about those who were poor due to physical incapacitation, three groups of people closely fit the criterion of the structural poor due to personal circumstances. These are the widow (due to lack of a husband and provider), the fatherless (being a minor child), and the resident alien (without full rights). These persons, as well as the poor, did not own property or possess ownership rights. Although they may have been able-bodied, their livelihood depended on the "beneficence" of others or their superiors, as well as the social structures designed to protect them.[13]

POVERTY IN THE ANCIENT NEAR EASTERN CONTEXT

The problem of poverty in ancient Israel only began to receive serious attention in the 1960s and continues to be debated. Not until Charles Fensham's excellent article[14] did biblical scholars start to focus seriously on comparative methodology and the structure of social relations in the study of poverty in ancient Israel. Fensham identifies the widow, the fatherless, and the poor as persons in need of divine protection. Evidence from the surrounding cultures of Mesopotamia, Egypt, and Ugarit shows many similarities with the Hebrew Bible, where Yahweh is depicted as the supreme protector of the weak. He argues that the forsaking of this responsibility to the poor by later Israelite kings (Yahweh's representatives on earth), was the major source of the prophets' ethical and moral preaching.[15] It is evident the poor had continued to exist through the times of the prophets, prompting their virulent response to those who oppressed them. H. Eberhard von Waldow's 1970 article makes the case for the need of social responsibility in ancient Israel.[16] These studies constitute a turning point where the focus is seriously on sociological analysis and the coping mechanisms of the poor. While this is a good beginning, further study of early Israel's social structures as they pertain to poverty is needed.

Scholars of prophetic literature focus on the traditional issues of justice and righteousness in their analysis of the problem of poverty.[17] Inferring from Iliffe's thesis, it is apparent that at this time in Israel's history, the poor are largely the landless, as the wealthy have amassed land and resorted to oppressing the poor. For these structural poor, poverty is mainly due to social circumstances.

Other scholars take a different but related approach by focusing on the question of social justice and morality in the Hebrew Bible.[18] For example, Scaria shows the bankruptcy of Israel's morals when he states: "Blinded by material prosperity, Israel lost the sense of morality; social justice, oppression and extortion abounded . . . yet they had no remorse or conscience."[19] This remark again shows the consequences of departing from the divine mandate and explains why poverty continued to exist despite prophetic critique and advocacy for the poor. It is fair to argue that the unabashed political rhetoric of liberation theologians is motivated by a strong socio-ethical conviction. Faced with glaring inequities in today's world, they relentlessly attack what they deem to be the root cause of the problem.

Recently, several books and articles have attempted to deal much more seriously with the question of ethics in the Hebrew Bible.[20] Bruce Birch revives the traditional approach with an interdisciplinary work seriously addressing the question of ethics in the Hebrew Bible. He views the Hebrew Bible as a "moral resource" and God as "the source and basis of morality in the Old Testament witness."[21] He discusses a wide range of issues encompassing the major areas of the Hebrew Bible and interprets them from a consistently ethical perspective. He sees justice and righteousness as central to prophetic ethics, and "these qualities are rooted in the character of God who has acted in justice and righteousness toward the people."[22] Birch points out that the violation of these moral precepts of the covenant community provokes the prophetic confrontation so evident in the Hebrew Bible. In other words, Birch views the persistence of poverty in biblical times as a violation of a fundamental biblical and ethical principle.

Waldemar Janzen's takes a more comprehensive approach to the question of Old Testament Ethics. He uses five paradigmatic stories that are models of ethical behavior. The major paradigms he identifies are the familial paradigm as demonstrated by the stories in Genesis, Ruth, and Judges; the priestly paradigm exemplifying the holy life; the sapiential or wisdom paradigm exemplifying the wise life; the royal paradigm exemplifying the just or righteous life, and the prophetic paradigm exemplifying the serving, and if necessary, the suffering life. For Janzen, these paradigms model God-pleasing or ethical behavior. The familial paradigm, however, "represents the comprehensive end of all Old Testament ethics . . . the primary ideal of the Old Testament's ethics."[23] He views the other four models as subordinate to the familial paradigm and working together to uphold it. They "promote and support the familial paradigm as their ultimate end."[24] This paradigm has serious implications on the existence of poverty from ancient to modern times. Viewing humanity as a global family challenges our individualistic propensities. We need to keep asking along with Janzen, "What are the things that model God-pleasing behavior?"

By using the insights presented here, I hope to embark on a cross-cultural comparative study and social analysis that goes beyond previous research and enriches our understanding of the primary biblical texts on poverty. I will also consider their relevance as paradigms for socio-ethical behavior in contemporary times. This brief survey of the Hebrew Scriptures has already demonstrated that the poor were a constant feature of biblical times and beyond. Yet it also points to the need to rethink our responses to this problem especially as poverty continues to rise in modern times.

POVERTY IN MODERN SOCIETY: THE CASE OF AFRICA

The various biblical perspectives on poverty may help us to elucidate poverty in contemporary society. We will consider poverty in global perspective but with special reference to Africa which has been most ravaged by extreme cases of poverty even in the modern age of technological advancement and global economics.

Representative early investigations of poverty in southern Africa were Poverty Datum Line (PDL) studies of the 1970s.[25] These were studies attempting to provide short-term solutions to the problem of poverty. The proponents of PDL sought to identify the basic minimum consumption needs of poor African families in urban areas. However, such studies left much to be desired. For example, PDL arbitrarily determined what a family's needs were. Moreover, PDL did not provide families with any significant form of security for the future. Finally, the study of only urban families gave a false picture of the true nature of poverty in Africa. Historically, the majority of poor Africans have been found in rural areas.[26] Therefore, in Africa, poverty was largely a rural phenomenon. However, in the twenty-first century, urban poverty has worsened tremendously due to massive unemployment and disease, particularly HIV/AIDS.[27] Despite the lack of development in Africa, there were social structures that mitigated poverty. Yet these structures are strained by the worsening cases of poverty throughout Africa, for example, the strain on the extended family as more and more members succumb to disease and death.

In a 1980 paper, Charles Elliott[28] attempts to distinguish between "absolute" and "relative" poverty. He has difficulty defining absolute poverty in a society where human relationships transcend material wealth.

More recent studies focus on the historical picture and its relevance to poverty in Africa. An interesting study on the causes of hunger in Zimbabwe provides some pertinent information.[29] The three Zimbabwean authors locate the origin of hunger in Zimbabwe in the colonial political economy and the resulting agrarian structure. They argue that this has caused problems such as unemployment, underemployment, low incomes, and shortage of land, among others. They also stress the importance of the family in the fight against hunger. The family is the main pillar of support, as we shall see, and women have an important role to play.

Since women have been traditionally dependent on men for economic sustenance, a group of authors analyze their relationship to poverty in the Third World.[30] They point to the inequities caused by sexism and discrimination in education and the job market. Usually, women's power is the result of family ties to men with political power.[31]

Although men have traditionally been the breadwinners and excluded women from decision-making processes, women are not simply waiting for handouts. In fact they are at the forefront in the fight against poverty, since it affects them most. Theirs is an even tougher battle against sexism, discrimination, powerlessness, and ultimately poverty.

Perhaps the most thorough work on the history of poverty in Africa has been written by John Iliffe.[32] This book essentially deals with the effectiveness of the social structures of the poor. Iliffe chronicles the history of the African poor from thirteenth-century Christian Ethiopia to southern Africa in the 1980s. It is a history of continuities and discontinuities. Above all, it is a sociological study of the poor and their coping mechanisms.

Iliffe argues that because of the lack of institutions and organizations to support the poor, "families were and are the main sources of support for the African poor."[33] He notes that this intimate connection between poverty and family structure, which has been overlooked by European historians, may be Africa's unique contribution to the comparative history of the poor.

He argues that since pre-colonial Africa was a land-rich continent, its very poor were not landless but mainly the incapacitated (structural poor, due to personal circumstances). During the colonial era in Africa, new categories of the poor were created by colonial rule and the different economic situation. As colonial governments acquired land from the Africans, new groups of the poor were added to the traditional poor. These were mostly homeless and landless people (structural poor, due to social circumstances).

By the end of the colonial era, Iliffe notes, the situation of poverty in Africa was changing. The "traditional poor" were still there, but new categories of poor people joined them in the overcrowded cities. These were unemployed youths, unmarried women, and old women. As he puts it, structural poverty in Africa "has been a cumulative phenomenon."[34] It is also notable that colonial intervention did not solve the problem of poverty in Africa but rather worsened it.

On the other hand, conjunctural poverty exhibited greater change on the African continent. During the pre-colonial era, the chief causes of conjunctural poverty were climatic changes or political insecurity resulting in mass famine mortality. This form of poverty changed its nature during the course of the twentieth century due in part to effective administration, better transportation, and wider markets.[35]

The coming of independence to Africa did not mean the end of poverty either. Instead, the number of the very poor continued to increase. Iliffe asserts that the growth of poverty in independent Africa was largely due to the fact that "conjunctural poverty had changed its nature during the twentieth century . . . structural poverty had not changed at all."[36]

By the late twentieth century, Iliffe argues, the story of African poverty had come full circle. In the past, large families meant wealth because, while land was abundant, labor was scarce and lack of labor meant poverty. By the 1980s, the positions had been reversed—land was scarce and labor plentiful, so large families meant poverty.[37]

Iliffe's contribution to the discussion of poverty in Africa is of great significance. Most relevant are his use of the models of "structural" and "conjunctural" poverty, and his emphasis on the family. While his study concludes with the late twentieth century, the period after that leading into the twenty-first century has seen dramatic rises in the situation of the poor in Africa and other parts of the globe. I think it can be argued that at this time both structural and conjunctural poverty had coincided thereby exacerbating the situation of the poor. Africa entered the twenty-first century with a history of increased landlessness, war, famine, social strife, and disease.

An eye-opening assessment of poverty in contemporary Africa is given by Jeffery Sachs who writes: "By the start of the twenty-first century Africa was poorer than during the late 1960s, when the IMF and World Bank had first arrived on the African scene, with disease, population growth, and environmental degradation spiraling out of control."[38] Sachs proceeds to chronicle the leading historical causes of poverty in Africa:

> Little surpasses the western world in the cruelty and depredations that it has long imposed on Africa. Three centuries of slave trade, from around 1500 to the early 1800s, were followed by a century of brutal colonial rule. Far from lifting Africa economically, the colonial era left Africa bereft of educated citizens and leaders, basic infrastructure, and public health facilities. The borders of the newly independent states followed the arbitrary lines of the former empires, dividing ethnic groups, ecosystems, watersheds, and resource deposits in arbitrary ways.[39]

Many experts on Africa agree that this arbitrary partition of Africa and the colonial masters' divide and rule tactics among Africans contributed not only to poverty, as Africans were pushed to poor agricultural areas, but also to the genocide among the Hutus and Tutsis in Rwanda and Burundi in 1994. Sachs continues to chronicle even deeper causes of poverty in Africa, such as its landlocked geography, depleted soils, corruption, lack of technological infrastructure, and especially the ravages of diseases such as HIV / AIDS, tuberculosis, and malaria. All these factors contribute to Africa's extreme poverty and create "the worst poverty trap in the world."[40] Despite this grim assessment, Sachs remains optimistic that Africa can still be saved if only the international community can do its part to reverse some of these trends such as combating disease and providing basic technological infrastructure especially in rural areas where most Africans live. His documentary study of poverty on every continent reveals how it can be reduced on a global scale. He cites successful examples from Bolivia in Central America, Poland, Russia, China, and India to demonstrate how poverty can be reduced through the work of the United Nations and the countries in need of help. Sachs demonstrates that in all these cases, poverty was reduced due to the efforts of the global community working together.

Such successes can also be translated to Africa if the global community can focus on Africa and its needs, and work with countries on how best to attack cases of extreme poverty. His suggestions are reminiscent of the biblical mandate in which the Israelite community is required to extend its hand to the poor and needy. The same prescription is relevant for Africa if the poor are to cease from the land. Attention to the biblical mandate and Sachs' prescription for ending poverty in this century hold great promise for the poor in a global context. Sachs' economic prescription for ending global poverty is truly reminiscent of the biblical mandate for the poor.

CONCLUSION

From our survey, we can conclude that extreme poverty truly exists in Africa and other parts of the developing world. Traditionally, African families dealt with poverty in a communal way. Poverty was often mitigated by survivalist creativity on the part of the poor, communal spirit and social solidarity, sharing of resources, and above all, the care and support of the extended family. However, more recently, poverty has threatened to wipe out the family and entire generations of people especially due to the ravages of preventable diseases. What can the human community do about poverty? African novelist, Chinua Achebe sums up the case for us to respond to fellow human need:

> The poor of the world may be guilty of this and that particular fault or foolishness, but if we are fair we will admit that nothing they have done or left undone quite explains all the odds we see stacked up against them. We are sometimes tempted to look upon the poor as so many ne'er-do-wells we can simply ignore. But they will return to haunt our peace, because they are greater than their badge of suffering, because they are human.[41]

From this brief analysis, we can conclude that there will always be poor people in Africa and around the globe unless the global community does something drastic about it. Just as in the case of ancient Israel, poverty continued to exist because the nation violated their divine mandate to care for the poor and needy in society. Similarly in the African context and other parts of the developing world, poverty is bound to increase if the developed world does not extend its hand to them. Just as ancient Israel was faced with a national problem, a national solution was needed. The same is true for us. We are faced with a critical global problem which demands a global solution. The lessons from ancient Israel and traditional Africa are extremely relevant for the modern generation wrestling with the problem of poverty on a global scale.

NOTES

1. NRSV. Unless otherwise noted, biblical quotations will be taken from the New Revised Standard Version.

2. Randall C. Bailey, private communication, January 6, 2010.

3. See Jeffrey D. Sachs, *The End of Poverty: Economic Possibilities for Our Time* (New York: Penguin Books, 2005), 21-22.

4. Ibid. Sachs argues that the Millennium Development Goals agreed to by all 191 UN member states in 2002 to cut global poverty in half could be achieved by 2015 and extreme poverty ended by 2025.

5. For the different perspectives on poverty, see J. David Pleins, *The Social Visions of the Hebrew Bible: A Theological Introduction* (Louisville, KY: Westminster John Knox Press, 2001); Leslie J. Hoppe, *There Shall Be No Poor Among You: Poverty in the Bible* (Nashville: Abingdon Press, 2004). See also Gustavo Gutiérrez, *A Theology of Liberation: History, Politics, and Salvation* (Maryknoll, NY: Orbis Books, 1972). For an update on the option for the poor, see Daniel G. Groody, ed. *The Option for the Poor in Christian Theology* (Notre Dame, IN: University of Notre Dame Press, 2007). The authors of this volume argue that the option for the poor is still needed in our global economy. See also Jeffrey Sachs, *The End of Poverty.*

6. Gutiérrez, "Memory and Prophecy," in *The Option for the Poor,* ed. Daniel G. Groody, 23, 27.

7. Gerhard von Rad, *Deuteronomy: A Commentary.* OTL (Philadelphia: The Westminster Press, 1966), 106. Emphasis mine.

8. See Robert R. Wilson, *Prophecy and Society in Ancient Israel* (Philadelphia: Fortress Press, 1980). In this landmark study, Wilson considers the social dimensions of the problem of prophecy in ancient Israel. He accomplishes this task by studying the comparative modern and ancient Near Eastern anthropological evidence on the phenomenon of prophecy, and uses it to interpret biblical material. This methodological approach is one that I think will benefit biblical scholars wrestling with the problem of poverty in ancient Israel and modern societies.

9. Elizabeth J. A. Siwo-Okundi, "Listening to the Small Voice: Toward an Orphan Theology," *Harvard Divinity Bulletin,* Vol 37, Number 2 & 3 (Spring/Summer 2009): 33-43, esp. 39. I find Siwo-Okundi's discussion of what she terms "orphan theology" quite relevant and applicable even in a larger context of poverty since "orphan children" were traditionally part of the poor in both the Ancient Near East and the Bible.

10. This statement does not deny the necessity of self-care in order to be in a position to care for others. The emphasis, however, is on putting concern on the other, rather than on the self and self alone.

11. Iliffe, *The African Poor,* 4. Iliffe cites this distinction from French author Dr. Jean-Pierre Gutton, *La société et les pauvres: l'exemple de la généralité de Lyons 1534-1789* (Paris: privately printed, 1971), 51-53, [p. 280, n. 21].

12. Iliffe, *The African Poor,* 4.

13. See the interesting dissertation by Harriet Katherine Havice, "The Concern for the Widow and Fatherless in the Ancient Near East: A Case Study in Old Testament Ethics" (Ph.D. diss., Yale University, 1978). In this study Havice explores the "hierarchical ethic" in ancient Near Eastern societies. It is expressed in two basic duties: the inferior owe the duty of loyalty and obedience to their superiors, and in turn the superiors owe the duty of beneficence and support to their inferiors.

14. F. Charles Fensham, "Widow, Orphan, and the Poor in Ancient Near Eastern Legal and Wisdom Literature," *Journal of Near Eastern Studies* 21 (1962): 129-39.

15. Ibid., 139.

16. See H. Eberhard von Waldow, "Social Responsibility and Social Structure in Early Israel," *Catholic Biblical Quarterly* 32 (1970): 182-204. See also Peter Darwin Miscall, "The Concept of the Poor in the Old Testament" (Ph.D. diss., Harvard University, 1972). Miscall argues that the four words for poor (*'ebyôn, dal, 'ānî,* and *rāš*) describe the "Israelite concept" of the poor, i.e., its socio-economic meaning.

17. For example, James Limburg, *The Prophets and the Powerless* (Atlanta: John Knox Press, 1977). Limburg sees the prophets as the defenders of the powerless. J. Emette Weir, who also views the poor as powerless, supports Limburg's argument. See J. Emette Weir, "The Poor Are Powerless: A Response to R. J. Coggins," *Expository Times* 100 (1988): 13-15; Other scholars, however, view the poor as powerful. For example, see David Edward Jenkins, "The Power of the Powerless," *Risk* 6, no. 3 (1970): 35-38; and Gustavo Gutiérrez, *The Power of the Poor in History: Selected Writings,* trans. Robert R. Barr (Maryknoll, NY: Orbis Books, 1983).

18. For example, K. J. Scaria, "Social Justice in the Old Testament," *Bible Bhashyam* 4, no. 3 (1978): 163-92; Bruce V. Malchow, "Social Justice in the Israelite Law Codes," *Word and World* 4 (Summer 1984): 299-306; idem, *Social Justice in the Hebrew Bible: What is New and What is Old* (Collegeville, MN: The Liturgical Press, 1996); and León Epsztein, *Social Justice in the Ancient Near East and the People of the Bible* (London: SCM, 1986), especially chap. 7.

19. Scaria, "Social Justice," 187. In the last few decades or so, some scholars have approached the problem of poverty in the Hebrew Bible from the perspective of liberation theology. Elsa Tamez's small but powerful book defends the thesis that "for the Bible oppression is the basic cause of poverty." She argues that the poor have become poor in the first place because they have been oppressed. See *Bible of the Oppressed,* trans. Matthew J. O'Connell (Maryknoll, NY: Orbis Books, 1982), p. 3, and Thomas D. Hanks, *God So Loved the Third World: The Biblical Vocabulary of Oppression,* 2d printing, trans. James C. Dekker (Maryknoll, NY: Orbis Books, 1984). Leslie J. Hoppe argues that poverty is basically caused by the rich who ignore God's laws of equality. See *Being Poor: A Biblical Study* (Wilmington, DE: Michael Glazier, 1987). See also the following works: Gustavo Gutiérrez, "Preferential Option for the Poor," *SEDOS Bulletin* 24 (June-July 1992): 176-81; idem, "Option for the Poor: Assessment and Implications," *ARC* 22 (1994): 61-71; Norbert Lohfink, *Option for the Poor: The Basic Principle of Liberation Theology in Light of the Bible,* trans. Linda M. Maloney, ed. Duane L. Christensen (Berkeley, CA: Bibal Press, 1987); R. S. Sugirtharajah, ed. *Voices from the Margin: Interpreting the Bible in the Third World,* (London: SPCK, 1991); Virgil Elizondo, "Unmasking the Idols," *SEDOS* 24 (May 1992): 131-40.

20. These are James L. Crenshaw and John T. Willis, eds., *Essays in Old Testament Ethics* (New York: Ktav Publishing House, 1974); O. M. T. O'Donovan, "Toward an Interpretation of Biblical Ethics," *Tyndale Bulletin* 27 (1976): 54-78; John Barton, "Understanding Old Testament Ethics," *Journal for the Study of the Old Testament* 9 (1978): 44-64; idem, "Approaches to Ethics in the Old Testament," in

Beginning Old Testament Study, ed. J. Rogerson (Philadelphia: Westminster Press, 1982), 113-30; Walter C. Kaiser, *Toward Old Testament Ethics* (Grand Rapids, MI: Academic Books, 1983); Christopher J. H. Wright, *An Eye for an Eye: The Place of Old Testament Ethics Today* (Downers Grove, IL: InterVarsity Press, 1983); Bruce C. Birch, *Let Justice Roll Down: The Old Testament, Ethics, and Christian Life* (Louisville, KY: Westminster/John Knox Press, 1991); Temba Levi Jackson Mafico, "Ethics (Old Testament)," in *The Anchor Bible Dictionary*, vol. 2, ed. David Noel Freedman (New York, London, Toronto, Sydney, Auckland Doubleday, 1992), 645-52; and Waldemar Janzen, *Old Testament Ethics: A Paradigmatic Approach* (Louisville, KY: Westminster / John Knox Press, 1994).

21. Birch, *Let Justice Roll Down,* 37.

22. Ibid., 260.

23. Janzen, *Old Testament Ethics,* 2-3.

24. Ibid., 3.

25. See Verity S. Cubitt and Roger C. Riddell, *The Urban Poverty Datum Line in Rhodesia: A Study of the Minimum Consumption Needs of Families* (Salisbury: Sebri Printers, 1974); Roger C. Riddell and Peter S. Harris, *The Poverty Datum Line as a Wage-Fixing Standard: An Application to Rhodesia* (Gwelo: Mambo Press, 1975); Verity S. Cubitt, *Supplement to: The Urban Poverty Datum Line in Rhodesia: A Study of the Minimum Consumption Needs of Families (1974)* [Salisbury: University of Rhodesia, 1979]. Cubitt and Riddell defined PDL as "the income required to satisfy the minimum necessary consumption needs of a family of a given size and composition within a defined environment in a condition of basic physical health and social decency." Cubitt and Riddell, 5.

26. See Paul Harrison, *The Third World Tomorrow: A Report From the Battlefront in the War Against Poverty* (New York: Penguin, 1980). Harrison reports that the World Bank has estimated that 85% of the very poor in the Third World live in rural areas (p. 85).

27. Unemployment figures in some African countries such as Zimbabwe are reported to be 90%, coupled with the highest inflation rate in the world, and HIV/AIDS particularly in Sub-Saharan Africa.

28. Charles Elliott, "Rural Poverty in Africa," Occasional Paper No. 12, Centre for Development Studies (Swansea, United Kingdom: University College of Swansea, 1980), 1-43. See also Max T. Chigwida, "Wealth, Poverty, and Justice: The Relationship between Traditional Understanding and Christian Teaching," *Transformation* 6, no. 1 (1989): 1-2.

29. See Sam Moyo, Nelson P. Moyo, and Rene Lowenson, "The Root Causes of Hunger in Zimbabwe: An Overview of the Nature, Causes and Effects of Hunger, and Strategies to Combat Hunger," Zimbabwe Institute of Development Studies Working Papers, No. 4 (Harare: ZIDS, 1985), 1-89.

30. See Mayra Buvinić, Margaret A. Lycette, and William Paul McGreevey, eds., *Women and Poverty in the Third World* (Baltimore and London: The Johns Hopkins University Press, 1983).

31. Ibid., 13, 29, 232-33, 299. See Joanne Leslie and Michael Paolisso, eds., *Women, Work, and Child Welfare in the Third World* (Boulder, CO: Westview Press, 1989).

32. See John Iliffe, *The African Poor: A History,* African Studies Series 58 (Cambridge, New York, New Rochelle, Melbourne, Sydney: Oxford University Press, 1987). Iliffe has also written a shorter book entitled *Famine in Zimbabwe: 1890-1960,* Zambeziana vol. XX (Gweru: Mambo Press, 1990).

33. Iliffe, *The African Poor,* 7.

34. Ibid., 6, 192.

35. Ibid., 6, 230, 259.

36. Ibid., 230, 259.

37. Ibid., 277. While Iliffe's categories are very useful, other authors point out that there are categories of the poor within the poor in Africa, as the study by H. Coudere and S. Marijsse shows. See "'Rich' and 'Poor' in Mutoko Communal Area," *Zimbabwe Journal of Economics* 2, no. 1 (1988): 1-25. There are also what we may call "rich" poor people among the poor. That is, those people who are considered rich in a particular setting like a village may appear very poor in a different context. In fact, the criterion for determining who is rich or poor depends on the culture, the value systems, and the nature of social relations. Hence, "rich" and "poor" are very fluid terms.

38. Jeffrey Sachs, *The End of Poverty,* 189.

39. Ibid.

40. Ibid., 188-209, esp. 208.

41. Chinua Achebe, *The Education of a British-Protected Child: Essays* (New York: Alfred A. Knopf, 2009), 161.

Part II

POVERTY IN THE HEBREW BIBLE

Chapter Two

Poverty in the Law Books

INTRODUCTION

This chapter examines the problem of poverty in the first section of the Hebrew Bible called the Law or the Pentateuch in Greek (Hebrew Torah).[1] I will explore the subject under three broad headings. The first part attempts to determine the structure and causes of poverty in the Law Codes. I will attempt to establish who the poor are, and why. The second part examines some of the coping mechanisms and social programs that were instituted in response to the state of the poor and their plight. Finally, I will try to determine the socio-ethical implications of my findings.

This chapter continues our investigation into why the poor continued to exist in ancient Israel. We will take a close look at the main legal codes where we find Israelite attempts to stem the continual presence of the poor and needy among them. The main emphasis in this chapter is placed on the Covenant Code, the Deuteronomic Code, and the Holiness Code, which are found in the books of Exodus, Deuteronomy, and Leviticus, respectively.[2]

STRUCTURE AND CAUSES OF POVERTY IN THE LAW CODES

A brief historical sketch is necessary in order to show the context out of which Israel, and the Law Codes, emerged. Scholars have noted that the term "Israel" is first mentioned outside the Bible on the Merneptah Stele (or Israel Stele) in the thirteenth century (1207) BCE. Although the context is that of Pharaoh Merneptah's victory over Libya and several Canaanite cities which bordered the Egyptian empire, Israel is the only entry referred to as a people and not as a city. According to Coote, this indicates that Israel was "a military force to be reckoned with" at that time.[3]

Current historical and biblical data indicate that the debate about the rise of Israel is far from over. There are areas of uncertainty, inconsistent or conflicting data, as well as unreliable sources. Thus, the precise history of Israel's emergence, the wilderness wanderings, and the occupation of the land of Canaan cannot be reconstructed with accuracy from the available data.

This has not, however, stopped scholars from drawing intelligent conclusions from scanty information, such as the single mention of the word "Israel" on the Merneptah Stele. John Bright suggests that one can claim that "the exodus group *was* Israel, in that without it Israel would never have been."[4] Baruch Halpern has made a different but similar-sounding statement which is at the heart of biblical studies today. He too makes this claim: "Historical Israel is not the Israel of the Hebrew Bible. Rather, historical Israel produced biblical Israel."[5] Although Bright's and Halpern's statements seem to be conflicting, they actually point in the same direction.

The historical and biblical accounts at our disposal indicate that Israel did not emerge out of slavery in Egypt as the nation it later became. The biblical narratives of Israel's wilderness wanderings portray Israel as traveling through the desert for a long period of time. The journey through the desert is a difficult and arduous one. It is filled with what sounds like "Deuteronomistic theology" features: problems arise when the people disobey Yahweh; the people complain to Moses and long for the fleshpots of Egypt; Moses intercedes with Yahweh; Yahweh delivers the people. And so the cycle continues.[6] Fretheim observes that "the journey from the Red Sea to the Promised Land is littered with freshly dug graves, and not a single birth is recorded."[7] The fact that no births are recorded does not mean that there were no children born during that time. The statement merely emphasizes the difficult nature of the journey through the desert. It also seems to support Bright's argument that the constitution of Israel on the verge of the Promised Land was indeed "a mixed group, by no means all descendants of Jacob."[8]

Once Israel settled in the land of Canaan, "a profound social transformation" occurred.[9] The small tribal units into which the people had been organized extended into the clan, the *mišpāḥâ* משפה, whose members settled in town-like villages. This clan-based form of organization endured the monarchy and still existed at the time of the return from Babylonian exile (Neh 4:7).[10]

During the early days of the settlement, de Vaux argues that all the Israelites enjoyed approximately the same standard of living. The land, which had been divided among families on a tribal basis, was the primary source of wealth (1 Kgs 21:1-3; Num 26:55-56, 33-54, 36:2).[11] This "free population" consisted of resident aliens (*gērîm* נרים), wage-earners, craftsmen, and merchants.[12] This egalitarian picture was to be shattered with the rise of the monarchy.

According to de Vaux, "a social revolution" took place between the tenth and eighth centuries BCE. Kingship created a class of officials who profited from their posts and the king's favors. Consequently, classes of "rich" and "poor" emerged as the weak and powerless suffered from the oppressive burdens of the monarchy. In this context prophecy arose to take up the cause of the poor and suffering.[13]

The laws of the Pentateuch therefore presuppose an agrarian and pastoral community. Whether these laws are original, borrowed, revised and/or (re) edited, like in any other society, they are meant to preserve the social order, provide a standard by which to judge actions or non-actions, preserve cultural practices, and ultimately protect citizens and their rights. In addition to addressing and deterring criminal activity, laws can be used to project a desirable state of affairs in society. Pentateuchal laws cover all these areas and even more, but my main concern is to demonstrate how these laws were intended to deal with the problem of poverty in Israelite society.[14] Ultimately, it was the disobedience to these laws that led to the continued existence of poverty in ancient Israel. We will proceed to analyze groups of people usually categorized as part of the poor.

SLAVERY

Introduction

The institution of slavery was a common phenomenon of the ancient Near East. Both Israel and its neighbors owned slaves as a matter of common practice. In fact, in the case of Israel, such ownership was divinely approved as the slave laws indicate (see for example, Exod 21:1-11). However, the major difference lay in Israel's treatment of its slave population. Scholars largely agree that Israel's treatment of its slaves was far more humanitarian than that of its neighbors. Perhaps this was the case because Israel itself had emerged out of a situation of slavery in Egypt.

Slaves in the Covenant Code

At least five categories of poor, powerless, or socially disadvantaged persons can be identified in the CC.[15] Before arriving at any definite conclusions, it is necessary to study the specific meanings, contexts, and usages of words for the poor and other socially disadvantaged people in the CC and other law codes, as well as the other sections of the Hebrew Bible. At each stage of my investigation I will be mindful of the following questions: Who are the poor? Why do they become poor? How are they treated? How do they cope? What are the ethical implications of the problem of poverty?

The beginning of the CC attests to the existence of the institution of slavery in ancient Israel (Exod 21:1-11; see Deut 15:12-18).[16] In this section, Exod 21: 1-11 states that Yahweh gives Moses the ordinances or laws (*mišpāṭîm* משפטים) which he is to set before Israel. These laws (called the slave laws) stipulate that when a male Hebrew slave is bought (*qānâ* קנה), he is to serve six years and be released in the seventh year, debt-free. The released slave is to depart single or married, depending on the status in which he arrived. If he married while in servitude, he is to leave his family behind, as the property of his owner. However, if he pledges allegiance to his owner, the owner will pierce his ear as a mark of his perpetual servitude.

Verses 7-11 (see Deut 15:12, 17) shift attention to a father's sale (*mākar* מכר) of his daughter as a slave and the conditions of her release, which are different from those of the male slave. If she does not please her master (sexually?), then he shall let her be redeemed and he must not sell her to a foreign people. If he gives her to his son, he is to treat her like a daughter. However, if he marries another wife, he is obligated to provide the first (slave) wife with food, clothing, and marital rights. If she is denied these rights, then she will be released debt-free and without any payment.

The rest of the slave laws in the CC pertain to many rights which were accorded to them. These range from compensation of an injured slave to resting on the prescribed seventh day of rest. Being a common phenomenon of the ancient Near East, both men and women (foreign or domestic) could become slaves.

Mendelsohn identifies five ways in which an individual became enslaved. These are: as prisoners of war, being of foreign birth, sold as minors due to economic distress, self-sold due to hunger or debt, and becoming insolvent due primarily to high interest rates on loans.[17]

In the "hierarchical ethos"[18] of the ancient Near East, slaves occupied the lowest position. Their legal status was that of chattel, a commodity to be bought, sold, leased, exchanged, or inherited. In essence, the slave had no individual identity other than the association with his or her owner.[19] In ancient Babylon, would-be runaway slaves were branded, tattooed, or marked with an *abbatum,* perhaps as an identifying mark.[20]

While slaves were regarded as property, they nevertheless had basic human rights. After six years of service, a male slave was to be released in the seventh year (Exod 21:2). That the slave was the owner's property is further evidenced by the fact that when an ox gored a slave, the slave owner, and not the slave him or herself, was compensated with thirty shekels of silver (Exod 21:32). The text does not say that the slave is gored to death, although that may be the assumption since part of it deals with an ox goring people to death.

Nevertheless, the slave had a right to compensation for injury by being set free (Exod 21:26-27). Wright sees this law as unparalleled in protecting the slave from arbitrary assault by the owner. He believes that "the basic humanity of the slave is given precedence over his property status."[21]

Mendelsohn detects a fundamental difference here between the slave laws of the ancient Near East and those of Israel. He notes that while both societies treat the slave in relation to a third party as a "thing," and while the slave's fate is at the owner's mercy in Mesopotamian law, the biblical legislator "recognizes the humanity of the slave by restricting the master's power over him."[22]

In addition to these slave rights was the right to be released or manumission. The Code of Hammurabi recognizes four ways in which a slave could be released.[23] In Hebrew law, just as there are five ways by which one could be enslaved, so are there five means by which a slave could be freed: (1) a Hebrew male or female slave was to be released in the seventh year, after six years of service (Exod 21:2-4; Deut 15:12); (2) a Hebrew girl sold by her father as the owner's wife or his son's wife is to be freed if the owner deprives her of food, clothing and marital rights (Exod 21:7-11); (3) a slave owner who maims a male or female slave shall free the slave as compensation for the injury (Exod 21:26-27); (4) fugitive slaves were not to be returned to their owners but instead be granted the right of asylum (Deut 23:15-16 [Heb 23:16-17]); and (5) a Hebrew who sold himself into voluntary slavery to a fellow Hebrew or resident alien was to be freed by purchase or redemption, or in the year of Jubilee (Lev 25:39-43, 47-55).

The most notable contrast between the release laws in Hammurabi's Code and the Israelite Code is the three-year release in the former and the six-year release in the latter. By limiting the period of forced labor to six years, "the Hebrew lawgivers sought to check the ruthless power of the creditors."[24]

There is a discrepancy in the slave release laws of Exod 21:1-6, Deut 15:12-18, and Lev 25:39-43. Scholarly discussion centers on the issue of their relationship. Roland de Vaux argues that these laws were simply not obeyed.[25] Lemche views "Jobel" as "manumission year" or the "year of release" in accordance with Exod 21:2-11 and Deut 15:12-18. Later, the redactor of Leviticus 25 placed "the Jobel Year as the seventh Sabbatical Year" for "practical and economic motives,"[26] giving rise to the discrepancy. The slave laws indicate the existence of poor and dependent people among the Israelites.

Mendelsohn comes closer to a solution by suggesting that these laws deal with different situations. He views the "subject" of the laws of Exod 21:2-4 and Deut 15:12 as "the Hebrew debtor-slave." The laws in these two texts are alike (six year release); the only difference is that in Deuteronomy women have now become debtor slaves to be released in the same way as male slaves. The difference is that the "subject" of Lev 25:39-43, 47-55 (manumission in Jubilee) is "the poor Hebrew who has sold himself voluntarily into slavery."[27] Since the majority of slaves were debt slaves, it means that these slaves would only serve six years and then be released. Such a situation would not likely have induced a creditor to lend to someone.

Christopher Wright adopts Mendelsohn's distinction but interprets it differently. The key to his approach lies in the meaning of the word "Hebrew" in the Exodus and Deuteronomy texts. He argues that the original law in Exodus deals with the "Hebrew" in the social, not ethnic sense. In this way he views the "Hebrews" as "a landless and rootless substratum of society who lived by selling their services to Israelites households."[28] On the other hand, Lev 25:39-43 describes a different situation. It is concerned with "Israelites who entered the service of another out of an increasing burden of poverty and debt but who in theory retain the legal ownership of their land and can 'return' to it" in Jubilee.[29] Wright calls the first distinction "'Hebrew' class slavery" and the second "Israelite debt slavery."[30]Wright goes on to clarify this distinction on the basis of the texts of the three codes. In the Jubilee text of Leviticus 25, the word "Hebrew" does not appear, indicating that the subject is the Israelite debt-slave. In Lev 25:39 "your brother" (*'āḥîkā* אחיך) is not qualified by a noun or adjective. He is selling himself because he has become poor. This qualification is lacking in the texts of Exod 21:2 and Deut 15:12. Wright explains that "it was sufficiently understood in those texts that a person described as a 'Hebrew' belonged to a landless class of people who sold themselves or were acquired as their way of life or means of livelihood—not as the result of a sudden reversal of fortune such as is implied by the *mûk* paragraphs."[31]

Another distinction is that the Exodus and Deuteronomy texts do not speak of any redemption rights by family since the "Hebrew" would not have had a wealthy family to redeem him. In fact the Exodus text indicates that a slave forfeited his family upon release if his owner had given him a wife. At that time, his wife and children remained the property of his owner. This is in agreement with verse 3 which states that if he comes in single, then he shall go out single. By contrast, the Jubilee text states that the bonded laborer is to be released unconditionally along with his family (Lev 25:41, 54). The text presupposes that those released would go back to their land and ancestral property and maintain family integrity. Wright sees the main purpose of the Jubilee as the restoration of family ownership of land and limiting the effects of debt-slavery and poverty to a single generation. Hence, this legislation would have been irrelevant to the "Hebrews" who had "no stake in the kinship-land structure of the nation."[32]

The "effects" of the release in the two cases present another significant difference. According to Exod 21:2 and Deut 15:12, the released "Hebrew" becomes a free person (*ḥopšî* חפשׁי).[33] Wright notes that *ḥopšî* חפשׁי is totally absent in Leviticus 25. Instead, the key word there (25:10) is *šûb* שׁוב ("return"). The Israelite debtor therefore "returns" to his ancestral property. The idea of return would thus be irrelevant to the "Hebrew." This explains why *šûb* שׁוב is absent from the Exodus and Deuteronomy texts as *šûb* שׁוב is in Leviticus. Therefore, Wright states:

> ✳ Thus, the primary concern of the "Hebrew" legislation was to prevent the indefinite exploitation of a member of that social class by any one owner, whereas that of the Jubilee was to preserve or restore the integrity, independence, and property of Israelite households—on theological grounds.[34]

It is notable that although both groups of people are released, it is only the *ḥopšî* חפשׁי who remains in a somewhat dependent social status because of lack of land and ancestral family. The freed bonded laborer of Leviticus stands at a higher social status with both land (to return to) and ancestral family.

In light of these differences, I agree with Wright's conclusion that the law of the Hebrew slave and the Jubilee legislation are concerned with essentially different phenomena.

Mendelsohn concludes that slaves did not play a great role in the economic development of the ancient Near East. Rather, their life and activities centered around the domestic sphere—as household servants of the rich.[35] This portrayal seems to agree with the picture and role of slaves in the Covenant Code. If so, it may be true that because slaves worked in close proximity to their owners, they were accorded significant rights in ancient Israel.

According to Iliffe's model, slaves were part of the "structural poor" whose poverty was due to social circumstances. They were able-bodied men and women who lacked access to land and perhaps family to provide for them. As a result, they depended on their own labor and the proceeds of that labor for survival. In this ancient economy, it is apparent that the institution of slavery was tolerated and not designed to be eliminated. Given the conditions of the time, and the reasons why some people ended up slaves, it is apparent that there would always be slavery as long as the system was designed to maintain it rather than dismantle it.

Slaves in the Deuteronomic Code

Slaves are treated in a more humanitarian way in the Deuteronomic Code than in the Covenant Code. This humanitarianism is evident in the way slaves are included in festivals, the conditions of their release, and the use of slavery as a "motive clause" for Israel's proper relationship with others.

Deuteronomy 12:12, 18 assert that when Israel enters the Promised Land, it is to include slaves in the celebration of family festivals. Here, slaves are mentioned alongside the Levites who have no inheritance.

The Exodus law of the Hebrew slave (Exod 21:2-11) is reflected in Deut 15:12-18, albeit in an expanded form.[36] Whereas the Exodus law simply refers to "a male Hebrew slave," Deuteronomy refers to "a member of your community, whether a Hebrew man or a Hebrew woman" (NRSV). The Exodus slave is bought but the Deuteronomic slave is sold, sometimes self-sold. Both laws agree that the slave serves for six years and is released in the seventh year, a free person. Whereas Exodus is silent about providing for the released slave, Deuteronomy specifies that the slave shall not be sent out empty-handed. Instead, the owner is to provide him or her liberally from his flock, grain, and vineyards. According to Driver, this provision "breathes the philanthropic spirit of the Deut. legislation."[37] The motivating factor is Israel's memory of its slavery in Egypt (v. 15). This law equally applies to the female slave (v. 17b).

It is therefore clear that this Deuteronomic legislation is more inclusive, humanitarian, and ethical than the Exodus law. Male and female slaves are put on an equal footing and treated alike. While there are separate requirements in Exodus, there is one and the same requirement in Deuteronomy.

In Deut 16:9-15 slaves are included in the festival of weeks and the festival of booths (tabernacles). They are mentioned alongside other disadvantaged members of the community such as Levites, widows, and the fatherless. They all stand to benefit from the harvest festivals. Again, Israel's memory of its slavery in Egypt is a motivating factor for its observance of these statutes (v. 12). It is also the reason why Israel must refrain from oppressing other disadvantaged members of the community (Deut 24:17-18, 22). While this injunction is desirable, it was not completely observed as we shall see later in prophetic literature. At that time the oppression of the poor increased so much so that prophets like Amos railed against this practice.

The next significant reference to slaves is a unique law in Deut 23:15-16. It provides asylum for a runaway slave, with freedom to settle anywhere and freedom from oppression. Patrick D. Miller notes that this law "is an important one for comprehending Israel's attitude toward slavery."[38] Miller, Driver, and von Rad all agree that the slave in question here is someone from a foreign country seeking refuge in Israel.[39]

This particular legislation extends the nature of Israelite slavery a step further. Miller captures the essence of this law by observing that previous regulations about slavery mostly concern indentured Hebrew slaves who could work off their debts. The new element here is the use of the word "escaped," which parallels Israel's own deliverance from Egyptian bondage. The escaped slave is a brother or sister in need of care and protection. In his view, this statute "helps to undercut slavery even in a setting where it was practiced."[40]

The uniqueness of this law in the rest of the ancient Near East is further evidenced by the fact that in Hammurabi's Code, the harboring of a fugitive slave was a capital offense. Moreover, a slave's mere denial of his or her owner cost that slave the loss of an ear.[41] While the release law in Hammurabi's Code was more progressive than in the Israelite Law Codes, it is apparent that most of Hammurabi's laws are quite harsh.

In general, the humanitarian nature of Deuteronomic laws concerning slaves cannot be denied. Although still properties of their owners, slaves are given a more human face in Deuteronomy. The released slave benefits from a community that extends its hand to him or her. The text, however, presupposes a cycle of slavery and release rather than an end to slavery or conditions contributing to its existence. In this cycle, there would have been no end to the institution of slavery.

Slaves in the Holiness Code

The Holiness Code makes very little reference to slaves, with the only comparable passage to the slave law in Exodus and Deuteronomy being Lev 25:39-46. The other references are minor. Leviticus 19:20 states that if a man seduces a betrothed slave woman, he need only pay a guilt offering for the forgiveness of his sins. In Deuteronomy, this is a capital offense (Deut 22:23-24; 22:25-27). Philip J. Budd argues that the absence of a death penalty shows that "the status of the woman as slave means that the offence is against property rather than life; in short it is not adultery."[42]

The law of the Sabbath of the land (Lev 25:2-7) reflects the fallow year of Exod 23:10-12. This Sabbath of the land provides sustenance for all members of the household, as well as domestic animals (vv. 6-7). Slaves too, as members of the household, are entitled to eat what grows in the fields during the Sabbath.

Leviticus 25:39-55 contains the major discussion about slavery in the Holiness Code. This section reflects slave laws in Exod 21:1-11 and Deut 15:1-18. In the Leviticus text, dependent Israelites who have become so impoverished (*yāmûk* יָמוּךְ)[43] as to sell themselves to fellow Israelites shall not be enslaved. Rather, such a person shall remain as a hired laborer (*śākîr* שָׂכִיר)[44] or a bound laborer (*tôšāb* תּוֹשָׁב)[45] until Jubilee. At that time, these people will return to their ancestral property. Slavery is forbidden because these impoverished Israelites whom Yahweh brought out of Egypt are Yahweh's servants. They are to be treated well (Lev 25:43, 46; see also vv. 53, 55).

While enslaving fellow Israelites is forbidden, the Israelites can acquire slaves (and treat them as such) from foreign nations or from the resident aliens among them. In the event that poor Israelites sell themselves to prosperous resident aliens (v. 47), they shall have the right of redemption—either by their families or by themselves. Barring this possibility, they shall be released in the Jubilee year (v. 54).

According to Driver, these provisions provide "a third law of slavery." The distinct features of this third law are that only foreigners are to be enslaved for life by the Israelites. Moreover, "Hebrew" slaves are to be freed, not in the seventh year as in Exodus and Deuteronomy, but in the year of Jubilee. The problem is harmonizing these three laws.[46] Driver's own explanation is that Leviticus has a provision for the mitigation of the servitude of Israelites, designed without reference to Exodus and Deuteronomy, and originating at a time when experience had shown (Jer 34:11, 14b-16) that the limit of service fixed by Exodus and Deuteronomy could not be enforced. Leviticus lengthens the legal period of service but compensates for it by insisting that the bonded Israelite is to be treated well.[47]

Leviticus therefore legislates the end of slavery for the Israelites from an ethical and theological perspective (25:55). Philip Budd puts it aptly as follows:

> The basic point is enforced by the fact that the exodus was a deliverance from service/slavery. There is therefore a recognition that there is something intrinsically incongruous about institutions such as slavery, and even hired service, as far as Israel is concerned. The laws formulated in this section constitute a concession to harsh economic realities. That concession does not, however, carry with it the assumption that such realities are acceptable or inevitable, still less desirable. The overall interests of Israel as a community demand that the effects of those realities be mitigated and the spirals of poverty be broken, and by force of law wherever that can be achieved.[48]

SUMMARY

The preceding discussion indicates that slavery was indeed part of ancient Israel's life. Slaves were among the poor, and dependent on the Israelite household for survival. Because of the possibility of abuse, the law legislates humane treatment of slaves. Exodus attempts to limit slavery, as does Deuteronomy with a more humanitarian approach. But there would always be slaves among the poor because Israel was somehow unwilling to end slavery as an institution. Leviticus therefore goes a step further than Exodus and Deuteronomy in attempting to end the slavery of the Israelites, but a step backward in maintaining the enslavement of foreigners and resident aliens.

RESIDENT ALIENS

Introduction

The next group of poor people in the Covenant Code are the resident aliens.[49] According to Max Weber, "The pre-Exilic metic (*ger*) was sharply differentiated from the total foreigner, *nokri*. The latter was without rights. The *ger* was of foreign stock, but was legally protected."[50] Pedersen describes resident aliens as defeated Canaanites, a view which van Houten disputes.[51] With much scholarly agreement, Spencer defines the *gēr* גר as "a foreigner who is traveling through a land or one who has taken up residence in that land. The key is that the sojourner has no familial or tribal affiliation with those among whom he or she is traveling or living."[52] Spina proposes to translate *gēr* גר, whether traveling or living in the land, as "immigrant" because it contains the nuances inherent in "resident alien" or "sojourner." In light of its socio-historical context, this translation also "calls attention to the original circumstances of social conflict which are inevitably responsible for large-scale withdrawal of people."[53]

The mass immigration of people is evident in the pages of the Hebrew Bible. The patriarchs were notably *gērîm* גרים constantly on the move. Abraham sojourned in Egypt (Gen 12:10) and Hebron (Gen 23:2-4); Moses was a *gēr* גר in Midian (Exod 2:22). Lot, Isaac, Esau, David, and Elijah were all sojourners.[54] The "wandering Aramean" (Jacob) of Gerhard von Rad's historical "Credo" was indeed a *gēr* גר (Deut 26:5-9).[55]

Spina observes that "*ger*-status" was obtained voluntarily or involuntarily, depending on the reasons for abandoning the original social setting. Hence, he concludes: "It was social and political upheaval due to war, famine, economic and social troubles, oppression, plague and other misfortunes that produced *gērîm*."[56]

While references to the resident alien are quite numerous in the Bible, van Houten notes that ancient Near Eastern laws hardly deal with this issue. According to her research, the Law Codes of Lipit-Ishtar (1868-1857 BCE), Eshnunna (1930 BCE), Hammurabi (1728-1686 BCE), and Mid-Assyrian laws (1112-1074 BCE) each have "only *one* law pertaining to the alien."[57]

Resident Aliens in the Covenant Code

In the legal texts under consideration, van Houten agrees with Weber that as Israel developed, so did the status of the *gēr* גר.[58]

As noted above, the Covenant Code has only three references to the resident alien (Exod 22:21; 23:9, 12). The NRSV renders these texts as follows:

> You shall not wrong or oppress a resident alien, for you were aliens in the land
> of Egypt (22:21).
>   You shall not oppress a resident alien, you know the heart of an alien, for you
> were aliens in the land of Egypt (23:9).
>   Six days you shall do your work, but on the seventh day you shall rest, so
> that your ox and your donkey may have relief, and your homeborn slave and the
> resident alien may be refreshed (23:12).

Evidently, the first two commands are similar. They both protest the ill-
treatment of a resident alien and they both have motivational clauses. These
commands are also written in apodictic style or prohibitive formula. Martin
Noth interprets the word "wrong" as primarily referring to exploitation at
work and "oppress" as deprivation of rights.[59] Van Houten points out that
the injunction not to oppress the alien may mean that there were oppressed
aliens in Israel.[60]

Scholars agree that one reason why resident aliens might be ill-treated is
because of their vulnerability due to lack of family or kin-group. Another
reason is their lack of full rights or protection as might be accorded to native
Israelites.[61]

In light of their social status, resident aliens in the Covenant Code are accorded divine protection. According to van Houten, they are members of the
household in a dependent position. They rely on the patriarch, who decides
when they can work or rest. Hence, treatment with kindness is called for.[62]

The law of the sabbath (seventh) day (v. 12) is another form of the sabbath
commandment (Exod 20:8-11; 23:10-12). Brueggemann comments that "the
rhythm of agrarian life requires such a day of rest. The rest is clearly egalitarian, applying to animals and resident aliens."[63] While this law is inclusive
enough, it also points to the position of the resident alien in the Israelite
household. The *gēr* גר is mentioned last, after the household head, the ox, the
donkey, and the home-born slave.

The question therefore arises as to whether resident aliens were necessarily poor or landless. The answer may only be partial until all the texts have
been analyzed. Both Pedersen and de Vaux matter of factly say: "As a rule
they were poor."[64] However, Lev 25:47 presumes that resident aliens could
be prosperous enough to buy a defaulting Israelite debtor.

As for the issue of land, de Vaux assumes that resident aliens did not own
land but Weber and Pedersen are more cautious. Weber writes that "landlessness was a normal though perhaps not universal criterion of the *ger*."[65] It has
been suggested that there is no evidence to suggest that resident aliens were

always landless. Though poverty and landlessness often go together, the wealthy resident alien of Lev 25:47 could possibly own land.[66]

From the preceding discussion of the resident alien in the Covenant Code, it is clear that the *gēr* גר was primarily someone in a subordinate and dependent position. He or she lacked full rights and protection, hence he or she was vulnerable to abuse by the wealthy and powerful. The Covenant Code attempts to protect these people's rights by appealing to Israel's historical conscience—an experience which should make the Israelites identify, and therefore sympathize, with the resident aliens among them.

Resident Aliens in the Deuteronomic Code

There are fourteen references to the resident alien in the Deuteronomic Code.[67] While the picture of the resident alien in the Covenant Code is that of someone who should not be oppressed and presumably a worker who is entitled to rest on the sabbath day, a more elaborate picture emerges in the Deuteronomic Code. The predominant picture in this Code is of the resident alien alongside the fatherless and the widow (and sometimes the Levite). In fact the formulaic expression "alien, orphan, and widow" is characteristic of Deuteronomy. Moreover, the alien is also depicted as someone in need of care by the larger society. He or she, along with the fatherless and widow, are entitled to this communal care. Briefly, Deuteronomy gives readers the impression of the resident alien as someone in such a precarious economic condition as to deserve the generosity of others.

In the Deuteronomic Code, resident aliens are overwhelmingly associated with festivals such as the tithe at the harvest festival and other farming or harvesting practices that are to benefit them.

After several intervening chapters, Deuteronomy returns to the subject of resident aliens towards the end of the Code. Chapter 24:14-15, 17, 19-21 contains "prime examples of Deuteronomy's famous humanitarian provisions for the poor and disadvantaged."[68] The wages of resident aliens and other hired labor are to be paid at the end of the day. Patrick surmises that employers withheld the wages of laborers in order to assure their return the following day and also to simplify accounting.[69] While this is a possibility, there is no textual basis for this argument. In any case, it is clear that the Deuteronomist views this practice as a matter of great injustice. Withholding wages would surely worsen the condition of the poor.

Such injustice is communicated in vv. 17-18. Patrick observes that these verses protect the legal rights of persons who cannot defend their rights in judicial proceedings.[70] Not only are the poor and weak protected, but also all members of the community are protected against acts that would jeopardize

their access to the basic needs of life. The result of these protections is evident in vv. 19-21. The forgotten sheaf is to be left behind, as are the remains
of beaten olives. Similarly, grapes are not to be over-harvested. All these
measures are intended to benefit resident aliens and other underprivileged
people. Yet they were not to take advantage of such provision by taking anything home to eat lest it be seen as theft (Deut 23:24-25). Therefore, Miller
comments that these laws "at one and the same time protect the goods of the
members of the community even as they open them up to help provide for
the needy persons."[71]

The Deuteronomic Code ends as it begins—with resident aliens and other
dependent persons at the harvest festival of weeks (26:1-19; see also 16:9-
12). After a recitation of Israel's historical "Credo" in which the people
themselves affirm being aliens in Egypt (26:5-9), all members of the community assemble to enjoy the tithe (14:28-29) of the produce (vv. 12-15)
in thanksgiving to the Lord. Miller maintains that these verses show the
importance of making available the goods of God's blessing to all members of the community: "No member of the community was ever free to
ignore those persons who lacked the necessities of life. All members were
expected to provide a portion of their income to provide for such sisters
and brothers."[72]

Deuteronomy therefore depicts resident aliens as dependent members of
the household, often mentioned after other members. This inclusion and
Deuteronomy's other humanitarian concerns for the marginalized prompts
van Houten to suspect "the existence of a well-to-do upper class and an often
impoverished lower class."[73]

While the Covenant Code has a few social justice laws, it is evident that
Deuteronomy consistently requires justice for the resident alien and other
marginalized groups. The sheer intensity of the laws speaks volumes about
Deuteronomy's concern for the welfare of the underprivileged. Hence, van
Houten concludes that these laws "created a permanent support system for
these groups which would prevent them from becoming poor. In this concern,
its [Deuteronomy's] character as a reform document is surely evident."[74]

In both the Covenant Code and the Deuteronomic Code, resident aliens are
identified as non-Israelites. They are foreigners who find themselves among
the Israelites. In the Deuteronomic Code, resident aliens are characterized as
needy and dependent members of the community. Their livelihood is dependent upon the charity and generosity expected of the more socio-economi-
cally privileged members of the community.

The fact that these protective measures are so widespread in Deuteronomy
and other legal codes is indicative of an ongoing social problem. Such legislation is needed as long as there are poor people in the community.

Resident Aliens in the Holiness Code

The Holiness Code has the greatest number of references to the resident alien.[75] In this document, the portrait of the resident alien is reinterpreted and expanded.

The Holiness Code is a block of material pertaining to regulations about holiness and proper conduct which was inserted into the priestly narrative. Indeed, scholars speak of a Holiness "school" in Leviticus 17 - 26.[76] Christiana de Groot van Houten argues that the priestly legislation and the Holiness Code are "a body of law which was revised by the priests in exile in response to the crisis that the Jews experienced."[77]

The first references to resident aliens in the Holiness Code occur in Lev 17:8-16. The general theme of this passage is that the Israelites, as well as the resident aliens among them, must not eat blood or an animal that dies of itself. Verse 8 depicts resident aliens in the holy sanctuary, presenting burnt offerings or sacrifices to Yahweh. This suggests their proximity to Israel's ritual life, in which they are allowed to participate. The prohibition from eating blood is because blood is the life force (*nepheš* נֶפֶשׁ) in the flesh. It belongs to God and must be poured out on the ground. It is sacrosanct and therefore unavailable for human use.[78]

In Lev 18:26, the resident alien, like the citizen, is exhorted to keep Yahweh's statutes and ordinances. Obviously, he or she is being treated like the Israelite.

According to Budd, Lev 19:9-10 has some "Deuteronomic elements."[79] This section is repeated in Lev 23:22 and is similar to Deut 24:19-22. The Leviticus passage prohibits gleaning or a thorough harvest of one's land. The edges (corners or borders) of the field, the gleanings, and the fallen grapes are to be left behind for the benefit of the resident alien (and the poor).[80]

In Lev 19:33-34, resident aliens are not to be oppressed or exploited (see also 25:14, 17; Exod 22:21; Deut 24:17; Jer 22:3). They are to be treated as native Israelites and the Israelites are to love them as they love themselves. This is punctuated by the motive clause that Israel itself was a resident alien in Egypt. The divine authoritativeness of this law is evident in the final phrase: "I am the Lord your God." Thus, the resident alien and the citizen have the same rights and obligations.

However, the injunction not to oppress the resident alien points to the possibility of somewhat dissimilar practices, or to the probability that some resident aliens were in fact being oppressed. Martin Noth seems to capture this understanding by remarking that these verses "forbid the 'oppression' of a guest, that is, making use of the economic advantage of a full land-owning citizen over a dispossessed Israelite or non-Israelite who looks to him for protection and the assurance of a livelihood."[81] Thus, it is suggestive that although equality is called for here, there is an apparent disparity.

The next reference to resident aliens appears in Lev 22:18-25. Like the citizen, the resident alien not only can sacrifice to Yahweh, but also is expected to give a pure offering. As a burnt offering wholly devoted to Yahweh, it is to be without blemish.

Leviticus 24:16, 22 contains a seminal teaching: when resident aliens or citizens blaspheme, they shall be put to death; there shall be one law for the resident alien and the citizen. There is therefore equality in both law and punishment. Any community member is expected to share its promises and burdens.

The status of resident aliens is used in Lev 25:23 to articulate priestly theology of the land. The land is not to be sold in perpetuity, for it belongs to Yahweh. The people of Israel are like resident aliens or tenants on the land. This description evokes the image of someone coming into a previously occupied land and settling there temporarily. Yahweh's ownership of the land points to a major theological construct that is often missed. While Israel is granted use of the land, it is not given exclusive claim to it. Indeed, Israel's "ownership" of the land is but a temporary measure since Yahweh is the true owner of the land. Israel is therefore entrusted to look after the land, but not to view it as its own possession. If the land ultimately belongs to Yahweh, then there should be no poor people if the stewards are using it appropriately.

The defaulting Israelite debtor[82] of Lev 25:35-55 is to be treated like a resident alien (25:35), and no interest shall be exacted upon him or her. He or she therefore has rights and privileges accorded to resident aliens, and even more.

While the Holiness Code has attempted to bring resident aliens as close to citizens as possible, a big difference emerges in Lev 25:45—resident aliens may be enslaved. This suggests second-class citizenship status for resident aliens. At the same time, native Israelite citizens may neither be enslaved nor treated harshly (25:39, 46, 53).

This double standard is even clearer in Lev 25:47. When an Israelite sells himself or herself to a prosperous resident alien, he or she is *not* to be treated like a slave. Moreover, this person has the right of personal or family redemption. If neither way frees such a person, then he or she is freed in Jubilee. Dale Patrick notes the singular "discrimination against the resident alien" in this passage, and the lawgiver's sensitivity to the rights of the Israelite.[83]

There is therefore a definite development in the status of the resident alien in the Holiness Code. Whereas Exodus has general prescriptions on social justice concerning the *gēr* גֵּר, and the Deuteronomic Code depicts the *gēr* גֵּר as someone in need of communal assistance, the Holiness Code encapsulates that understanding but also brings the *gēr* גֵּר closer to Israel's cultic life. The alien and the citizen are now subject to the same laws and punishments. Moreover, resident aliens can be prosperous enough to have Israelites under their employ.

In light of this development, I find van Houten's argument quite convincing. She theorizes that in the post-exilic period the term *gēr* גֵּר takes on new meaning. Resident aliens receive not only aid but also the rights of the members of the community. They have become part of the chosen people, an understanding which supersedes the original meaning of *gēr* גֵּר. It is now "the outsider who has become an insider in the cultic community."[84] Furthermore, she notes that in the Covenant Code and Deuteronomic Code, "The alien is precisely someone who has no power, who could not even compete, and is yet accorded fair, hospitable treatment."[85]

The development of the status of the resident alien in Israelite history is aptly summarized by van Houten:

> The legal status of the alien has changed dramatically over time. What began as legislation pertaining to a stranger needing hospitality and justice in the Covenant Code changed in Deuteronomy to legislation dealing with a class of vulnerable, landless people and created a system of support which gave them economic stability. It encouraged the Israelites to be just in their social dealings, but did not encourage them to allow the outsider to join the community. This was also the case for the first level of redaction in the Priestly laws. However, in the second level, in addition to the laws which treated aliens as outsiders and inferiors, there was also legislation allowed *[sic]* the outsider to join the community and be on equal terms with the Israelite.[86]

This analysis captures the changing status of the resident alien in the Israelite law codes. But we should not overlook the fact that the resident alien, though closer to the citizen in the Holiness Code, is still viewed as a second-class citizen.

SUMMARY

The picture of the resident alien from the three Law Codes is of someone who is poor, vulnerable to oppression, dependent, in need of communal caring, and finally, almost a full member of the community, but not quite. There is a progressive sense of inclusiveness, justice, and humanitarian concern regarding the resident alien in the Law Codes.

THE WIDOW AND THE FATHERLESS

Introduction

The widow and the fatherless minor child are often paired in the Bible as "widow and orphan." When the Bible speaks of "orphan," it is prudent to avoid reading modern meanings into this word. Oftentimes the so-called "orphan" had a mother but lacked a father, the more powerful and male member of the household. I suspect that because of the androcentric nature of the biblical text, a child without a father was automatically called an "orphan." It is not clear if a child without a mother was ever called an "orphan." Nor is it evident that both parents are dead. It is therefore more accurate to refer to the so-called "orphan" as a "fatherless child."[87] Siwo-Okundi argues that "someone defined as an orphan was the most vulnerable person in society, because she or he had lost *all* options for protection and support ordinarily provided by the family and extended family."[88]

The widow and the fatherless are frequently mentioned in the literature of the ancient Near East. According to Havice, concern for the underprivileged in Israel often appears in prohibition form in the Law Codes, in instructions, confessions of innocence, hymn-petitions, and prophetic indictments. In Egyptian literature it appears in instructions, biographical inscriptions, the declaration of innocence, and hymn-petitions. In Mesopotamia it appears in the law codes in casuistic stipulations, in instructions, in first person royal inscriptions, and in hymn-petitions. In Canaanite or Ugaritic texts it appears in epics, in a first person inscription, a petition, an indictment, and in a narrative description.[89]

Many Egyptian texts address the issue of the widow and the fatherless child along with other disadvantaged people. Oftentimes, it is the duty of the ideal king or ruler to protect these groups of people as part of the ruler's administration of justice.

Havice views ancient Near Eastern society as "hierarchical," with duties of a superior to an inferior, and vice versa. The two primary duties of this system are protection and beneficence to one's inferior and loyalty and obedience to one's superior.[90]

References to widow and fatherless in Egyptian literature date back to the Old Kingdom, but occur most frequently in the first intermediate period and the beginning of the Middle Kingdom. Fensham notes that with the rise of powerful kings in the eleventh and twelfth Dynasties (Middle Kingdom), the widow and fatherless were not mentioned until the twenty-first Dynasty (Late Period).[91]

Building inscriptions from the Old Kingdom attest to a ruler's good deeds as a mark of the ruler's reign. The Inscription of Harkhuf, during the sixth

Dynasty states: "I gave bread to the hungry, clothing to the naked, I ferried him who had no boat."[92] Furthermore, Kheti II's rule during the ninth and tenth Dynasties was also marked by wealth and generosity. The ruler declares:

> I was rich in grain. When the land was in need, I maintained the city with kha and with heket. I allowed the citizen to carry away for himself grain; and his wife, the widow and her son. I remitted all imposts which I found counted by my fathers (lines 9-11).[93]

It is obvious that these biographical inscriptions are written in a very self-laudatory and often bombastic style. Scholars agree that the aim was the writer's quest for immortality. Lichtheim views this "catalogue of virtues" as "a serious commitment to ethical values and a magical means for winning entry into the beyond."[94]

More teachings about the poor in general and the widow and fatherless in particular are contained in Egyptian Instructions. The Instruction is better understood as a form of teaching or didactic literature. It has literary resemblances to the wisdom literature of the Bible, especially the book of Proverbs. The instruction genre consists of brief teachings or maxims in the form of a father's teachings to his son.[95] It dates from the Old Kingdom to the Late Period in Egyptian history. Aside from the autobiography, it is "the second major literary genre created in the Old Kingdom."[96]

The Intermediate Period Instruction for King Merikare, which is very corrupt, was spoken by an anonymous old king for his son and successor, King Merikare. It is a royal instruction on the art of proper rule, with specific reference to the widow. King Merikare is instructed thus:

> Do justice, then you endure on earth;
> Calm the weeper, don't oppress the widow,
> Don't expel a man from his father's property,
> Don't reduce the nobles in their possessions.
> Beware of punishing wrongfully,
> Do not kill, it does not serve you.[97]

These prohibitions, written in the second person singular imperative, are not only intended as strong exhortations to do the right thing, but also as motivation to expect a greater reward. Simpson's translation best renders the reason and motive for King Merikare to follow this instruction: "Do justice, that you may live long upon earth." Regarding literary texts of this period, John A. Wilson remarks that "new values were increasingly expressed in spiritual and social terms."[98] Among other things, justice is demonstrated by refraining from oppressing the widow who does not have a male family member for protection and support. This conduct is expected of a good and successful ruler.

The Middle Kingdom Instruction of King Amen-em-het I (the first Pharaoh of the twelfth Dynasty) for his son Sesostris I (Sen-Usert I), is also a royal instruction but with a completely different intention. Scholars agree that it is most likely a posthumous speech written by a court scribe on the theme of regicide for a king assassinated during his reign. This unique Instruction against trusting any subjects contains a reference to the beggar, the fatherless, and the poor.

> I gave to the beggar, I raised the orphan,
> I gave success to the poor as to the wealthy;[99]

The brief reference to this group of underprivileged people accomplishes two tasks. First, it shows that it is the king's responsibility to care for the disadvantaged. Second, it heightens the threat that the king feels—despite his beneficent deeds, his subjects still turn against him. By these references perhaps the king not only intends to warn his son and successor, but also to instruct him on what is expected of the good king.

The Middle Kingdom wisdom text, "Protests of the Eloquent Peasant," is a masterpiece of Egyptian didactic literature. In this tale, the eloquent peasant who has been wronged and unjustly treated insists on his rights as he appeals for justice. In the first of nine petitions to chief steward Rensi, the poor man appeals his case by reminding the powerful man of his responsibilities.

> For you are father to the orphan,
> Husband to the widow,
> Brother to the rejected woman,
> Apron to the motherless.[100]

Fensham remarks that since a married woman had no legal status after the death of her husband, it was the duty of the king to protect her rights as her husband would have done.[101]

Most scholars agree that the New Kingdom Instruction of Amen-em-opet has a literary relationship to Prov 22:17 - 24:22. In the sixth chapter, Amen-em-opet urges the reader not to seize part of a widow's land. While this passage may indicate that a widow could own land, it also shows how vulnerable she was. Chapter twenty-eight also shows that the widow did have the right to glean from other people's fields: "Do not pounce on a widow when you find her in the fields; And then fail to be patient with her reply."[102]

The Late period Inscription of Wennofer carries through the same theme of care and protection for the disadvantaged:

> I was a good shelter for the needy,
> . . . .
> I was one who welcomed the stranger,
> . . . .
> I was one who protected the weak from the strong,
> So as to be a ferryboat for everyone.[103]

The concern for the widow and fatherless and other disadvantaged people is also found in Mesopotamian documents from early Sumerian times (2850-2360 BCE) and legal documents such as the reformatory measures of Urukagina, the last King of Lagash during the early dynastic period (2400 BCE). The god Ningirsu and King Urukagina make a treaty in which the powerful are not allowed to inflict injustice on the widow and fatherless.[104]

In the Law Code of Ur-Nammu, founding ruler of the Third Dynasty of Ur, it is stated that the ruler established equity in the land and banished violence and strife. In addition,

> The orphan was not delivered up to the rich man;
> the widow was not delivered up to the mighty man;
> the man of one shekel was not delivered up
> to the man of one mina.[105]

Clearly, it is the king's responsibility to establish justice by ensuring that the strong and powerful do not mistreat the weak and powerless.

The prologue and epilogue of the Code of Hammurabi echo the same sentiments. The gods commissioned Hammurabi:

> To cause justice to prevail in the land,
> . . . .
> In order that the strong might not oppress the weak,
> that justice might be dealt the orphan (and) the widow,
> . . . .
> to give justice to the oppressed.[106]

Again, justice seems to be at the core of Mesopotamian legal documents.

The goddess plays the same role as the god in Mesopotamian theology. A hymn singles out the goddess Nanshe for her ethical concern for the widow and fatherless. She is the one

> who knows the orphan, who knows the widow,
> knows the oppression of man over man, is the orphan's
> mother, Nanshe, who cares for the widow.[107]

Later in the hymn, the goddess Nanshe is described as the one "to comfort the orphan, to make disappear the widow."[108]

Mesopotamian laws show a great deal of concern for the widow after the death of her husband. There is lively scholarly debate about her legal status. Literature on this subject suggests that the widow (Akkadian *almattu*, Hebrew *'almānâ* אלמנה , Ugaritic *'lmnt*, Phoenician *'lmt*, Aramaic *'armalta*, Arabic *'armalat*)[109] not only had a dead husband but also lacked the financial support of her father-in-law or grown-up sons. Thus, the *almattu* is "a woman without males who are responsible for supporting her."[110] In any case, it is evident from the literature that she was well provided for, and in some cases even owned property. The bride price (*nudûnnû*) was given by the husband to his wife at their marriage and kept by him until his death. This would be her means of support as long as she lived in her husband's house. If she remarried, it went to her sons. If she died, it reverted back to the paternal estate. Dowry (*šeriktu*) was given by the bride's father at her marriage, as provision for her after her husband's death. If she remarried, she took it with her as her new dowry. If she died, it was divided among her sons. If there were no sons, it reverted back to her father's estate. Thus the *almattu* needed legal protection, or she could remain unmarried, remarry, or start a profession. Documents from Nuzi indicate that if there were no male children, daughters were sometimes appointed as sons to inherit both movable and immovable property.[111]

While this was generally the case, some scholars doubt if these provisions were enough to support a widow. In an excellent study, Paula S. Hiebert examines the nature and legal status of the ancient Near Eastern widow. She concludes:

> A woman's economic well-being was directly related to her link with some male. Though a married woman may have owned some property in the form of her dowry, she could not have supported herself on that alone, if at all, when her husband died. Ordinarily the widow's maintenance would have been the responsibility of either her sons or her father-in-law. When these male persons were nonexistent, then the widow's connection to the kinship structure was severed. She became an *'almānâ*.[112]

Two Ugaritic texts show that Canaanite kings were expected to care for the underprivileged. In the legend of King Keret, his son Yassib attempts to dethrone him by accusing him of neglecting his royal duties. KRT C reads:

> You do not judge the cases of widows,
> you do not preside over the hearings of the oppressed;
> you do not drive out those who plunder the poor,
> you do not feed the orphan before you,
> the widow behind your back.[113]

In the Tale of Aqhat, King Daniel (or Danel) is reported as sitting at the gate, judging cases:

> Danel, the Healer's man,
> the Hero, the man of the god of Harnam,
> got up and sat at the entrance to the gate,
> next to the granary on the threshing floor.
> He judged the cases of widows,
> presiding over orphans' hearings.[114]

Biblical scholars have long noted that the gate is the ancient Near Eastern seat of authority where justice was dispensed.

The preceding examples indicate that it was the duty of the gods or the rulers (the gods' representatives on earth) to provide justice by especially protecting the rights of disadvantaged members of society such as widows and fatherless children. Mafico argues that "failure to administer justice to the weak, such as the widows and the orphans, was a very grievous dereliction of duty that necessitated the king to vacate the throne."[115] Unfortunately given their lack of legal rights, the widow and fatherless child were continually precarious. Scholars agree that Israel's treatment of its vulnerable members grew out of this social and cultural milieu.[116] Hence, social concern was not a purely Israelite phenomenon, nor did it grow out of a vacuum.

Widow and Fatherless in the Covenant Code

There is only one reference to the widow and fatherless in the Covenant Code (Exod 22:22-24 [Heb 22:21-23]). These verses state in apodictic fashion that the widow and fatherless are not to be oppressed. There is a warning that if one abuses them, they will cry out to Yahweh who will bring talionic retribution upon the abuser by killing him, making his wife a widow and his children fatherless. Scholars agree that the widow and fatherless are vulnerable to abuse because they lack the husband and father to protect them. Like ancient Near Eastern rulers, gods, and goddesses, Yahweh assumes the role of judge, protector, and arbiter of justice.[117]

Widow and Fatherless in the Deuteronomic Code

Of the three Law Codes, the Deuteronomic Code has the most references to the widow and the fatherless (Deut 14:29; 16:11, 14; 24:17, 19-22; 26:1-13). In most of these references, the widow and the fatherless are the object of charity at the many communal harvest festivals.

The widow and the fatherless are paired in Deuteronomy and mentioned alongside other vulnerable people like slaves, resident aliens, and Levites. All of these groups need the care and protection of society. Using critical theory, Harold Bennett has argued the intriguing thesis that widows, strangers, and orphans, in the Deuteronomic Code were oppressed individuals such that the laws regarding them benefited the ruling elite rather than ameliorate the plight of the poor.[118]

The context of Deut 14:29 is that of the triennial tithe. This tithe was not to be brought to the central sanctuary but stored and consumed in local communities (v. 28). Driver notes that this tithe "was applied entirely, something in the manner of a poor-rate, to relieve the needs of the landless and destitute classes."[119] Widow and fatherless are among the benefactors of this third year tithe.

Deuteronomy 16:11, 14 deal with the feast of weeks marking the end of the corn harvest (cf. Exod 23:16 [feast of harvest or ingathering]; 34:22; Lev 23:15-20) and the feast of booths marking the end of the vintage harvest (Exod 23:16; 34:22; Lev 23:33-36, 39-44). Although the feast of booths was a most popular festival, Deuteronomy adopts the name without explanation. The reference is probably to the wilderness wanderings (see Lev 23:40-43).[120] Again, widow and fatherless are participants in, and benefactors of these feasts.

Deuteronomy 24:17 points to the kind of abuse to which a widow was vulnerable. This verse specifically forbids taking her garment as a pledge. According to Exod 22:26-27, a garment taken in pledge was to be returned by nightfall so it could be a source of warmth for the poor borrower. It is the breaking of this rule that Amos protests (2:8). This suggests that oppression of the widow continued through the times of the prophets.

Verses 19-22 contain some very ancient harvest rules which forbid gleaning when gathering corn, olives, or grapes from the fields. With regard to the festivals in Deuteronomy, Moshe Weinfeld observes that "all the festivals were altered and freed of their ties to the ancient sacral ceremonies."[121] Devoid of this ritualistic background, it is evident that Deuteronomy has appropriated these practices and transformed them for the benefit of socially disadvantaged people, including the widow and the fatherless.

Deuteronomy 26:12-13 returns to the issue of the third year tithe (see also 14:28-29) which, because of the centralization of worship, was to benefit the economically disadvantaged members of the community. Miller views this return as a stress on a fundamental Deuteronomic theme: "The importance of making available the goods of God's blessing to *all* members of the community."[122] The widow and fatherless, including other groups who did not own land or would not have otherwise benefited from its produce, are fully provided for in the Deuteronomic Code. Thus, the Deuteronomic Code stands out as a very socially-oriented and humanitarian document when it comes to care and provision for the widow and fatherless.

Widow and Fatherless in the Holiness Code

The Holiness Code has two references to the widow and none to the fatherless (Lev 21:14; 22:13). In any case, these references have nothing to do with the widow in the "Deuteronomic" sense. The first merely forbids an Aaronic priest from marrying a widow. The second allows a priest's widowed or divorced childless daughter to eat consecrated food if she returns to her father's house. It is surprising that Leviticus would overlook this group, since the Code mentions other disadvantaged groups and is aware of harvest practices. However, from these two references, two things are implicit about the status of the widow: (1) a widow could remarry (although not a priest); and (2) she could return to her father's house. One can therefore deduce that in both cases, the widow was cared for and protected by either her new husband or her own father.

SUMMARY

The widow and fatherless were objects of concern in both the ancient Near East and ancient Israel. Similar concern is evident in the Hebrew Bible in the form of care and protection accorded them. This is done because the widow lacked a male relative to care and provide for her, and the fatherless child was a minor child in need of adult care. In the Hebrew Bible, the widow and the fatherless are almost always paired. In the law codes of ancient Israel, this pair is grouped not only with the resident alien, but also with the poor.

From the foregoing research on the widow and fatherless, it is apparent that these depended and economically precarious individuals continued to exist in ancient Israel due to the social structure of the day and the fact that they lacked legal rights outside of male individuals in their lives. Despite provisions set for them, it is evident that these measures were simply designed to keep them in their place rather than to fundamentally alter their situation. Their fortunes would have changed if the widow remarried and the minor child grew up to be an adult man or woman.

THE POOR

Introduction

This section focuses on specific Hebrew words for "poor" and "poverty" in the three legal codes consideration above. First, I will discuss biblical terminology for "poor" and "poverty" in general. Second, I will briefly discuss the concept of the poor in the ancient Near East. Third, I will discuss the poor in the Law Codes and suggest reasons why they continued to exist in biblical times.[123]

Biblical Terminology

The Hebrew Bible uses a number of Hebrew words to refer to the poor. The most prominent ones are *'ebyôn* אביון, *dal* דל, *'ānî* עני, *'ănāwîm* עניים and *rāš* רש.[124] Only the first three words appear in the legal texts under investigation. From the distribution of these terms, it is obvious that *'ebyôn* אביון appears in Exodus and Deuteronomy only, but not in Leviticus. The word *dal* דל appears in Exodus and Leviticus only, but not in Deuteronomy. As for *'ānî* עני, it appears in all three with more occurrences in Deuteronomy. Thus *'ebyôn* אביון and *'ānî* עני are mostly concentrated in Deuteronomy where *dal* דל is missing.[125]

'ebyôn אביון

The word *'ebyôn* אביון appears sixty-one times in the Hebrew Bible.[126] It is used to refer to the poor in a material sense (Deut 15:7; Ps 109:16). Often these poor are reduced to the state of destitution or begging. Thus *'ebyôn* אביון refers to those who are "in want, needy, poor."[127] In the Hebrew Bible the term *'ebyôn* אביון is often used alongside *'ānî* עני, in the familiar expression "*'ānî we 'ebyôn*" (עני ו אביון, poor and needy [Deut 24:14; Amos 8:4; Isa 14:30-32; 32:7; 41:17; Jer 22:16; Ezek 16:49; 18:12; 22:29; Ps 35:10; 40:17; 70:5; 86:1; 109:22]). Pleins suggests that this usage "represents a somewhat stylized rhetorical device for speaking of poverty, and is the product of either prophetic or cultic influence, though which is difficult to determine."[128] While Pleins' suggestion is quite plausible, this expression also heightens the desperate nature of the person referred to as being both *'ānî* עני and *'ebyôn* אביון. It connotes the person who is not only poor and needy but also oppressed. This is likely the case since oppression is a major problem in the prophetic corpus. These distinctions may point to the specific nuances and usages of the various Hebrew words for poverty.

dal דל

The word *dal* דל appears forty-eight times in the Hebrew Bible.[129] It is an adjective derived from the root *dll* דלל, meaning to "hang, be low, languish." As an adjective, the basic meaning of *dal* דל is "low, weak, poor, thin." The word *dal* דל is thus used to refer to the poor who are powerless and of low social status. This term also refers to those who are physically weak or sick (Ps 41:1-3; 72:13; 113:7). Sometimes the *dal* דל are the opposite of the rich *'āšîr* אשיר; [Exod 23:3; 30:15; Lev 14:21; Prov 22:16]).[130] In 2 Kings and Jeremiah, the *dal* דל (referred to variously as *dallâ* דלה, *haddallîm* הדלים, *dallat* דלת, *dallôt* דלות) are connected to those who depend on the land. After the Babylonian exile, these poor are referred to as some of the poorest of the land (or of the people) who were either given land or left behind to work in the vineyards and fields (2 Kgs 24:14; 25:11-12; Jer 39:10; 40:7; 52:15-16).

'ānî עני

The term *'ānî* עני, the most frequently used word for poverty, occurs eighty times in the Hebrew Bible. It is derived from the root *'nh* ענה ("to be bowed down, afflicted"). The adjective *'ônî* עני therefore stands for "poor, afflicted, humble." The basic meaning of the word *'ānî* עני is poverty due to injustice and oppression. It is the poverty of the powerless caused by the oppression of the rich and powerful. This sense of injustice and oppression is highlighted by liberation theologians who view inequality and poverty as primarily caused by unjust and oppressive social structures.[131]

'ănāwîm עניים

Related to the word *'ānî* עני is the term *'ănāwîm* עניים (singular *'anaw* ענו) which occurs twenty-four times in the Hebrew Bible. Except for one case only (Num 12:3), *'anaw* ענו always occurs in its plural form *'ănāwîm* עניים. This plural usage may be an attempt to apply the word *'ănāwîm* עניים to a specific group of people. This term appears only in the prophetic and wisdom texts, as well as the book of Psalms. Previous scholarship has debated whether there is a connection between poverty and piety, or if *'ănāwîm* עניים points to a religious or political movement of the humble or pious poor. This has led, for example, to the identification of the *'ănāwîm* עניים as the meek who shall inherit the earth (Ps 37:11; Matt 5:5). However, recent scholarship has largely rejected this line of thinking. The word *'ănāwîm* עניים is now seen as a mere linguistic variant of *'ānî* עני, with the same connotation of impoverishment and oppression. Indeed there is a spiritual element in the Psalms, but the material or sociological sense is overriding. Pleins adds that "the relation between God and the poor is a matter of justice, not based on piety."[132]

rāš רש

The word *rāš* רש (participle of *rûš* רוש or *rîš* ריש) appears in the Hebrew Bible twenty-two times and mostly in the wisdom literature. Its basic meaning is economic: "To be poor, in want." The LXX translates it by *ptōchós* πτωχός (nine times), *pénēs* πε´νης (six times), and *tapeinós* ταπεινός (once). In the Deuteronomistic History, the word *rāš* רש is devoid of any economic flavor. Instead, it is used to refer to contrasting situations such as superiority versus inferiority (1 Sam 18:23). The wisdom literature has some very distinctive uses of the word *rāš* רש. For example, this term is notably used to refer to laziness as the cause of poverty (for example, Prov 10:4). This interpretation of poverty is also new and is not found in the prophetic corpus or the Law Codes of ancient Israel. This usage may reflect a different social setting for the wisdom writers, or at least to a very different perspective on poverty at the time the writings were compiled. Although part of wisdom literature, the book of Job avoids use of this term, which strengthens Pleins' theory that "the book of Job is more akin to the prophetic materials in terms of language and social analysis than it is to the wisdom tradition, at least insofar as Proverbs is a typical representative of this tradition."[133]

miskēn מסכן

The adjective *miskēn* מסכן ("poor, dependent, socially inferior") appears four times in the Hebrew Bible all in the book of Qoheleth (with two occurrences in the Hebrew of Ecclesiasticus). In Qoheleth, the LXX translates it by the word *pénēs* πε´νης. The word *miskēn* מסכן may also be related to the Akkadian term, *muškênu* ("beggar"). In Qoheleth's pessimistic attitude toward life, it is better to be poor and wise than mighty and foolish.[134]

maḥsôr מחסור

The word *maḥsôr* מחסור (n. m. s.) is derived from the verb *ḥsr* חסר ("to be needy, in want, lacking"). It occurs thirteen times in the Hebrew Bible. As a noun it refers to something needed, or a lack of something, hence poverty. Like the use of the word *rāš* רש in Proverbs, *maḥsôr* מחסור is also used to refer to laziness (Prov 6:11; 14:23; 21:5; 24:34). Due to the absence of this term in both Job and Qoheleth, and its frequency in Proverbs, Pleins remarks that it is "one line of argument for separating the social agenda of Job from that of Proverbs."[135]

This word study reveals how the poor continued to exist in ancient Israel. They were identified by their particular conditions as each word reveals. The study therefore demonstrates the different levels of poverty in which the poor found themselves. Ultimately, the word study discloses what citizens can become when society does not extend its hand to them. The fact that the majority of the poor in the Bible were oppressed individuals shows how far Israel had departed from its divine mandate.

The Poor in the Ancient Near East

Concern for the poor is also present in ancient Near Eastern literature. In the Egyptian tale of "The Eloquent Peasant," the peasant makes a fifth petition to the chief steward Rensi, reminding him of his duty to the poor:

> Rob not a poor man of his goods, a humble man whom you know! Breath to the poor are his belongings; he who takes them stops up his nose . . . . You were placed as a dam to the poor lest he drown, but you have become a swift current to him![136]

Since justice is not done to the peasant, he makes a seventh petition. He tries to remind Rensi of the necessity of law and order by arguing that if law is laid waste and order destroyed, no poor person can survive. Robbing a poor person like this peasant is true injustice.[137]

As the injustice continues, the peasant makes a penultimate plea, explaining what justice to the weak and poor such as himself means:

> Speak justice, do justice,
> For it is mighty;
> It is great, it endures,
> Its worth is tried,
> It leads one to reveredness.[138]

At the end of this tale, the peasant receives justice after the ninth petition and only after he has threatened to report Rensi to Anubis, the god of the dead. Not only is the peasant's property returned but he is also given Thutnakht's property.

The Instruction of Amen-em-opet includes some typical wisdom sayings that poverty is better than wealth. Chapter 6 states: "Better is poverty in the hand of the god, / Than wealth in the storehouse." Chapter 7 continues the same trend of thought with two characteristic statements; "Do not set your heart on wealth. . . . Do not rejoice in wealth from theft, / Nor complain of being poor."[139]

The emphasis on moderation continues in this Instruction. Chapter 11 states,

> Do not covet a poor man's goods,
> Nor hunger for his bread;
> A poor man's goods are a block in the throat,
> It makes the gullet vomit.[140]

The Instruction also exhorts one to reduce the debt of a poor person. According to chapter 13,

> If you find a large debt against a poor man,
> Make it into three parts;
> Forgive two, let one stand,
> You will find it a path of life.[141]

This instruction is squarely in agreement with the Mosaic Law which encouraged reduction of the debt of a poor person. In fact the Jubilee text of Leviticus 25 sets an even better example—that all debts should be forgiven in the year of Jubilee. Debt reduction and debt cancellation are ancient concepts that are still relevant in our contemporary world.

Jeffrey Sachs argues with reference to the global debt crisis that "rich countries should have given the poorest countries grants rather than loans, so that the poor countries would never have been indebted in the first place." He cites the Marshall Plan when the United States government rebuilt Europe after the devastation of World War II with grants rather than loans.[142] Poverty has thus continued to exist in the modern world because rich countries are unwilling to forgive the debts of poor counties. Essentially, they turn a deaf ear to the biblical mandate but with disastrous consequences. While they continue to profit from the debts of poor countries, those counties continue to decline further and further into poverty.

Chapter 29 of the Instruction of Amen-em-opet has one final advice with regard to the poor. While crossing a river, the writer advises the reader to take the fare of the wealthy person and let the poor person go free.[143] Thus, the poor are treated with consideration; and poverty is given as much attention as wealth is in this Instruction.

Mesopotamian documents also deal with the subject of the weak and powerless. The prologue and epilogue of Hammurabi's Code call for justice for such persons. In addition, a hymn to the goddess Nanshe describes her as the one "who seeks out (?) justice (?) for the poorest," and the one who "finds shelter for the weak."[144]

Babylonian wisdom literature presents the god Shamash (like the Israelite God Yahweh) as the protector of the poor, the weak, and suffering. In "The Babylonian Theodicy," a sufferer dialogues with a friend, cataloging the misery and injustice of the weak and powerless:

> They fill the [store house] of the oppressor with gold,
> But empty the larder of the beggar of its provisions.
> They support the powerful, whose . . . is *guilt,*
> But destroy the weak and drive away the powerless.[145]

The friend concurs, attributing such unjust behavior to Narru, the king of the gods.

Solemnly they speak in favour of a rich man,
"He is a king," they say, "riches go at his side."
But they harm a poor man like a thief,
because he has no *protection*.[146]

The sufferer ends by petitioning the god Shamash to redress these wrongs.

In a bilingual hymn to Ninurta, various things are forbidden including oppressing the poor or giving the weak into the power of the strong.[147] In another hymn to the sun-god Shamash, the poor and other disadvantaged people come before him in supplication:

The feeble man calls you from the hollow of his mouth,
The humble, the weak, the afflicted, the poor,
She whose son is captive constantly and unceasingly confronts you.[148]

The theme of caring for the poor is briefly encountered in Ugaritic literature. In the legend of King Keret, the king's son threatens to depose him with this charge: "You do not drive out those who plunder the poor."[149]

It is therefore clear that the poor were an object of concern for ancient Near Eastern rulers. Oftentimes it was the duty of the god, goddess, or the king, the divine representative on earth, to protect the poor and ensure that they received proper justice. The implications of this stance have contemporary relevance and are in line with the biblical mandate.

The Poor in the Covenant Code

The Covenant Code mentions the poor in a few but very important contexts. In this Code, the terms used for the poor are *'ānî* עני (Exod 22:25 [Heb 22:24]), *dal* דל (Exod 23:3), and *'ebyôn* אביון (Exod 23:6, 11).

Exodus 22:25 forbids the practice of usury or the charging of interest on loans to the poor (*'ānî* עני) [see Deut 23:19-20; Lev 25:36-38]. Charging interest on loans was a common practice in the ancient Near East. In fact interest on money loans was "very high," sometimes as much as fifty percent![150] In Exod 23:3, the lawgiver forbids one to show partiality to the poor (*dal* דל). Some scholars translate this verse with the Masoretic Text which suggests *gdl* גדל ("great") instead of *dal* דל. I am in favor of keeping the original translation, which forbids partiality to the poor as well.[151]

Exodus 23:6 seems to continue the issue addressed in v. 3. This time one is not to deprive the poor (*'ebyôn* אביון) of justice due to them. Cassuto understands this verse to mean "do not pervert the judgement against your enemy."[152] But the perversion of justice due to the poor is likely because of their powerlessness and vulnerability.

Exodus 23:11 gives us a sense of the nature of the poor in general. The poor and wild animals are to benefit from what grows in the field during the Fallow Year. The mention of the poor alongside wild animals shows their lowly social status. However, the same statement also points to the writer's concern for wild life—animals too are to be cared for. From this description we can deduce that the poor are landless and dependent on divine "charity." Therefore, the poor in the Covenant Code (whether *'ānî* עני, *dal* דל, or *'ebyôn* אביון), borrow to survive, may be taken to court, and are sometimes taken advantage of, or denied justice. Being landless, they depend on the charitable acts of society as directed by Yahweh.

The Poor in the Deuteronomic Code

The Deuteronomic Code refers to the poor as either the *'ebyôn* אביון or *'ānî* עני, and most of the occurrences are in chapter 15. The word *dal* דל is not used at all in this Code.[153]

In Deuteronomy 15, a central text in this book, the discussion about the poor appears in the context of the year of release (*šĕmiṭṭâ* שמטה). This release is a remission of debts every seventh year. Some scholars have argued that the *šĕmiṭṭâ* שמטה presupposes the fallow or sabbatical year of Exod 23:10-11 and the sabbatical year of Lev 25:1-7.[154]

The *šĕmiṭṭâ* שמטה law states that there should be no one in need (*'ebyôn* אביון) among the Israelites because Yahweh is sure to bless them. If Israel obeys the entire commandment, Yahweh will continue to bless it (vv. 1-6). However, should there be any poor people among them, Israel is to give ungrudgingly in order to continue to receive God's blessings (vv. 7-10). The poor continue to receive (interest-free) loans even as the *šĕmiṭṭâ* שמטה year approaches. The law ensures that such laws are in fact virtual gifts since they will soon be canceled in the *šĕmiṭṭâ* שמטה year. Verse 11, one of the most misunderstood verses in the Bible (partly because it is not read in full or in context), states that since the poor will never cease from the land, Israel is to give generously to the *'ānî* עני and *'ebyôn* אביון in its midst.

The thrust of this verse is that the poor do not cease from the land *because* Israel has disobeyed its divine mandate. This is why there were always poor people in biblical times. This is also why there are poor people today. As human beings, we have essentially disregarded our responsibility to each other in the pursuit of individual wealth and well-being.

Deuteronomy 15 is an important chapter on the subject of the poor and their treatment. It is one of the best examples of what it means to love one's God and one's neighbor. Scholars have interpreted the "release" as either suspension or cancellation of the debt of the poor.[155] In light of the slave release law (Deut 15:12-18), whose structure is similar to that of Deut 15:1-11, and the language of the text, I agree with the latter group of scholars that a full release is meant here.[156]

According to vv. 4-6, there should ideally be no poor (*'ebyôn* אביון) and therefore no need for a release as long as Israel fully obeys the law. After this qualification or hortatory reminder, the law of vv. 1-3 continues in vv. 7-11. Miller notes that because of the human reality that there might be some poor people, a series of prohibitive actions and commands are given, prescribing the proper way to act.[157] However, there will be poor people precisely because of Israel's disobedience to the divine mandate.

It is notable that the poor in this text are often described as members of the community or family. They are neighbors, "a member of your community" (NRSV), brothers, (or sisters) (15:2-3, 7, 9, 11-12). Should any of these be in need, the law instructs the people to give generously to them.

Verse 11, which is cited in the New Testament (Matt 26:11; Mark 14:7; John 12:8), is often understood to mean that "the poor will always be there." Rather, we should stress that this verse explains *why* the poor are always there when they are not supposed to. As Miller testifies, this is "exactly the opposite of what this text says."[158] Read correctly and in its proper context, Deut 15:11 urges members of the community to take care of those in need. In addition to calling for benevolence toward the poor, Deuteronomy is also:

> trying to eliminate the possibility of a debtor class in Israelite society by requiring that the cancellation of debts take place regularly. It is calling for charity and is trying to insure that Israelite society will not be divided *permanently* into two classes: the economically powerful and the economically dependent.[159]

According to Hamilton, the Sabbatical principle is: "Rest comes, sustenance comes, release comes, celebration comes regularly, periodically, and for the sake of the dependent."[160]

The final occurrences of *'ānî* עני and *'ebyôn* אביון are in Deut 24:12, 14-15. The subject matter concerns loans to the poor and the wages of the poor.

Deuteronomy 24:10-13 follows Exod 22:25-27 (see Lev 25:35-36) regarding loans given to the poor and the pledges they gave. Such loans are to be interest-free (Exod 22:26-27; Deut 23:19; Lev 25:35-38). Exodus 22:26-27 states that a pledge garment taken as collateral for the loan must be returned before the sun goes down (so Amos 2:8; Prov 20:16; 27:13; Job 22:6), since it is that person's only source of warmth at night. Deuteronomy expands upon this law forbidding the creditor from going into the poor person's house to take the pledge item. He or she must wait outside. If the borrower is poor (*'ānî* עני) Deuteronomy forbids the creditor from sleeping in the poor person's garment. The item must be returned by sunset. According to Hoppe, "Deuter-onomy's concern is to maintain the dignity of the poor in what was already a humiliating situation."[161]

Regarding wages, Deuteronomy (24:14-15) states that the wages of poor and needy (*'ānî we 'ebyôn* עני ו אביון) laborers, Israelite or resident alien, must not be withheld. They must be paid "daily before sunset," for this is their only livelihood (Lev 19:13). According to Hoppe, this law attempts to prevent "the kind of abuse that makes the cycle of poverty something that cannot be broken . . . . Withholding the wages of the poor makes it impos-sible to break the cycle of poverty and to heal the economic divisions of Israelite society."[162]

The picture of the poor (*'ānî we 'ebyôn* עני ו אביון) in the Deuteronomic Code is that of an economically deprived low social class, dependent on the generosity of the community at large, especially its well-to-do members. These poor could borrow for survival. They also benefited from the cancella-tion of their debt during the *šĕmiṭṭâ* שמטה year. Moreover, the poor in Deuter-onomy worked for their wages daily. They also depended on Yahweh, who promises to bless those who help the poor (Deut 15:4, 6, 10; 24:13). By the same token, and because of the possibility of oppression, Yahweh threatens those who abuse the poor by not lending them something as the *šĕmiṭṭâ* שמטה approaches (15:9), or withholding their wages (24:15). Overall, the Deutero-nomic Code shows a great deal of concern for the welfare of the poor, and it often expands previous legislation to the maximum benefit of the poor.

The Poor in the Holiness Code

The Holiness Code has a few references to the poor.[163] The context of Lev 19:10 is the harvest period. The law in vv. 9-10 forbids one to over-harvest a field, so that the poor and the resident alien might benefit from what is left behind (see also Deut 24:19-22). Commentators agree that this law is repeated in Lev 23:22, where the same word for the poor (*'ānî* עני) is used.[164] Thus, Leviticus depicts the poor as landless people who are dependent on the charitable acts of landed farmers.

Leviticus 19:15 calls for strict impartiality in the administration of justice (Exod 23:3). While the tendency might be to favor the poor because of their pitiful situation and the powerful for their influence, there are to be "no special favours" for the poor (*dal* דל) or the great and powerful (wealthy).[165] Leviticus therefore pictures the poor person at the gate, either pleading a case or as a defendant. Whatever the case may be, justice is to be rendered regard-less of a person's economic status, power, or influence. There is to be equality and one law for all (Lev 24:22).

SUMMARY

This survey has shown the poor in the Law Codes to be a diverse group of people. They include slaves, resident aliens, widows, the fatherless, bonded laborers, wage-earners, and day laborers, as well as those designated by specific Hebrew words. Whether able-bodied or lacking muscle power, they were all somewhat economically deprived and therefore dependent on the rich and powerful in society. According to Iliffe's model, these are the "structural poor" whose poverty is due to both personal and social circumstances. Realizing their vulnerability and dependent status, the Law Codes go a long way to make provisions for such people. The authoritativeness of these laws lies in the fact that they are mandated by Yahweh. The strong social concern in the Law Codes, especially in the Deuteronomic Code, may be a result of Deuteronomic reforms or the influence of the prophets who were very passionate about social justice in Israelite society. The provisions in these laws enable the poor to cope with their precarious economic situation. By and large, the spirit in these legal codes is still relevant today in explaining why poverty still exists in our world.[166]

COPING MECHANISMS AND SOCIAL PROGRAMS

The Law Codes present several coping mechanisms for the poor. These are evident in the institutions of the Fallow (or Sabbatical) Year, the Year of Jubilee, the nature of loans and wages, as well as the Israelite family. Essentially, these measures were instituted because the poor had continued to exist in ancient Israel.

The Fallow/Sabbatical Year

The oldest strata of the Hebrew Bible that mentions the Fallow Year is the Covenant Code. According to Exod 23:10-11, the land is to lie fallow in the seventh year, for the benefit of the poor and wild animals. This law is repeated, in modified form, in Lev 25:2-7, where the land is to observe a Sabbath for the Lord. Israel is to farm six years in a row but let the land rest or observe a Sabbath for the Lord in the seventh year. The people will eat what the land has yielded during its Sabbath (v. 6); moreover, Yahweh will bless the sixth-year harvest so that Israel can survive on it until after the Sabbath Year (25:18-22). This law is not found in the Deuteronomic Code but is evidently connected to the year of release (*šĕmiṭṭâ* שמטה) in Deut 15:1-18. The connecting element seems to be the release or cancellation of debts in the seventh year (15:1-3) and the release of slaves in the seventh year (15:12-18), which repeats the slave law of Exod 21:2-6 where release is also in the seventh year.

The origin and purpose of the Fallow/Sabbatical Year has been a subject of much scholarly debate.[167] Some believe that it originated in Israel's concept of time, which was tied to religious practices.[168] Others connect it to ancient Near Eastern practices.[169] A group of scholars also argues that the purpose of the Fallow/Sabbath Year was to appease the gods of the land, but Israel adapted this custom and gave it religious and social significance.[170]

Scholars also debate whether the Fallow Year was observed throughout the land or by individual farmers. In Exodus, one gets a sense of land rotation, but in Leviticus, this practice has become a single or universal Fallow Year for the whole land every seven years. Wright's suggestion is quite plausible. He argues that the poor and beasts would get little sustenance from a single fallow year every seven years. He thus favors individual observance of the Fallow Year in Exodus by explaining that "the continuous presence of some land lying fallow in every locality would obviously provide some relief."[171]

It is also greatly debated whether the Sabbatical Year was ever observed or if the Deuteronomic reforms were ever put into practice. Most scholars lean toward the negative. While drawing parallels with biblical and post-biblical times, other scholars see these parallels in the practice of ancient Near Eastern kings who would often cancel debts or offer freedom proclamations at the beginnings of their reigns through decrees.[172] The aim of these measures was often to ameliorate severe economic abuse which might threaten the state; to present the image of a good ruler who cared for his subjects; and to weaken the opposition.[173]

Despite these apparent problems, the meaning and function of the Fallow/Sabbatical Year is clear. It was an institution designed to assist the poor either by canceling their debts or by relieving them from debt obligations. It was another form of provision for their sustenance. The humanitarian aspect is evident in that it was "idealistic legislation proclaimed by the theologians of Israel to remedy the woes of the poor."[174]

The Jubilee Year

Scholars have argued that the word jubilee (Hebrew *yôbēl* יובל) has uncertain etymology. They largely agree that *yôbēl* יובל means "ram" because a ram's horn was used as a trumpet and Jubilee was preceded by the blowing of a trumpet.[175]

Jubilee legislation is the subject of Lev 25:8-55 (see also 27:16-24). Jubilee came at the end of the seventh Sabbatical Year (forty ninth year) or roughly

in the fiftieth year. It proclaimed liberty from debt and bondage and also prescribed the return of property to the original owners (vv. 8-12). Such property
could be redeemed either by a relative (*gō'ēl* גאל) or by the person who had
fallen into debt when he or she became prosperous. If neither method worked,
the property was returned in the Year of Jubilee (vv. 25-28). A dependent
fellow Israelite was to be treated like a resident alien and receive interest-free
loans (vv. 25-38). If this person sold himself or herself due to economic necessity, he or she was not to be enslaved but treated as a hired laborer. Such
a person's freedom would come in Jubilee (vv. 39-46). Finally, an Israelite
selling himself or herself to a resident alien was to be redeemed by a relative;
short of that, this person was to be freed in Jubilee (vv. 47-55).

There is much scholarly debate about the length, structure, meaning, and
intention of the Jubilee Year.[176] Like the Sabbatical Year, the origin of the
concept of Jubilee has sometimes been traced to ancient Near Eastern practices. Westbrook argues: "Cancellation of debts, release from slavery, and
restoration of land to its original owner, as the result of either a specific or
general enactment, were all regarded as common-place events in the ancient
Near Eastern sources."[177]

Scholars even question if the Jubilee was ever observed. Most of them feel
that it was merely a utopian vision of a better community. As de Vaux puts
it, "It was a Utopian law and it remained a dead letter."[178]

Despite this general view, Jubilee legislation was yet another institution
designed to help the poor. Scholars view its purpose differently.[179] However,
its importance cannot be underestimated. Since the poor had continued to exist, this legislation was intended to limit the period that one could be indebted
to another. Given the short lifespan of ancient peoples, most people would
have continued to be poor while waiting for the Jubilee Year.

The Family

Like the African family, the Israelite family was also an "extended family,"
comprising many members. It consisted of the tribe (*šēbeṭ* שבט / *maṭṭeh* מטה),
from the twelve tribes of Israel/Jacob. Next was the clan (*mišpāḥâ* משפה),
which comprised a significantly large number of families. Finally came the
house or father's house (*bêt 'āb* בית אב), comprising the head of the household
and those below him.[180]

The *mišpāḥâ* משפה was a socio-economic unit with important economic
responsibilities in the life of the family.[181] According to Lev 25:47-49, if a
kinsman (lit. "your brother" [*'āḥîkā* אחיך])[182] sells himself to a resident alien
because of economic necessity, he is to have the right of redemption. The
redeemer (*gō'ēl* גאל) is a member of the extended family, either a brother,

an uncle, a cousin, or any other blood relative. If the person prospers he may redeem himself.

Deuteronomy 25:5-10 outlines the law of the levirate (from the Latin *Levir,* brother-in-law). When a man died, his brother was supposed to marry his widow and raise children (especially sons) to carry on his deceased brother's name and to enjoy his brother's inheritance (see Genesis 38; Ruth 4).[183] This task also came with economic responsibilities, as evidenced by the *gō'ēl's* refusal to marry Ruth (4:6). When Boaz accepts this responsibility and fathers a child with Ruth, his actions are more praiseworthy. While the levirate law may be primarily concerned with raising male children for the deceased man (Deut 25:5-10), I think the economic part of it is equally important. Firstly, raising a child is an economic issue in itself. Secondly, instead of the widow returning to her father's house (Gen 38:11), she is now cared for and protected in her husband's family household. However, if she did return to her father's house, Clements argues that the extended family took responsibility for her needs. He notes that "the return of a widow to her parental family in order to find support among them illustrates the importance of the extended family as the chief support group for persons who were suddenly plunged into poverty."[184] According to Lev 25:23-28, a *gō'ēl* גאל also had the responsibility of redeeming land that had been temporarily sold by a relative experiencing economic difficulties. This land remained in the hands of the redeemer until Jubilee, when it reverted back to the original owner. Since land ultimately belonged to God,[185] it could not be sold permanently (Lev 25:23). Hence Jubilee was "an attempt to preserve, or periodically to restore, the economic viability and independence of the smaller family-plus-land units."[186]

The redeemer also had the responsibility of maintaining and supporting a kinsman in debt (Lev 25:35-55). Such support involved treating the kinsman as a resident alien and providing interest-free loans and food for no profit (vv. 35-37). It also included treating such persons as hired or bonded laborers (not slaves) free to go in Jubilee (vv. 39-43). As noted above, they were also to be redeemed by family members (vv. 47-55). Thus Wright points out that "the *mišpāḥâ* existed primarily for the good of the constituent families."[187]

This brief survey shows that the Israelite family was at the center of a household's economic well-being. Like the African family, the Israelite family was there for mutual support, caring, sharing, and ensuring the material well-being of other members of the extended family. As a global community we need to view each other as family members responsible for each other. In light of the biblical mandate, it is the responsibility of those family members who are in a position to help others to play their rightful role. If family members are not responsible for each other, then we can be guaranteed that there will always be some members who will be in need of assistance within the family.

Other Coping Mechanisms

In a myriad of ways the Law Codes have shown how the poor were cared for in ancient Israel.[188] I shall merely recount them here.

We have seen that the law prohibited taking interest on loans to fellow Israelites (see Exod 22:25; Deut 23:19-20; Lev 25:35-38; Neh 5:1-13; Ps 15:5; Prov 28:8; Ezek 18:5-8, 10-13; 22:12; 2 Kgs 4:1; Isa 50:1). While the Covenant Code merely prohibits charging interest to the poor who borrow, there is an increasing degree of protection in these three Law Codes.[189]

The law also protects the poor when they give pledges as collateral for loans (Exod 22:26; Deut 24:10-11, 17). In the Covenant Code, the pledge garment is to be returned by sunset to provide warmth for the poor person. Deuteronomy gives the poor person the choice to select a pledge item and keeps the creditor outside the door. While the poor person's garment may be taken as a pledge item, Deuteronomy protects the widow by making it a crime to take her garment as collateral (v. 17).

In addition, the law called for just measures of length, weight, and quantity in business transactions (Deut 25:13-15; Lev 19:35-36). In accordance with ancient Near Eastern laws, Israelite law forbade moving boundary markers (Deut 19:14, see 27:17). Malchow observes that "an unscrupulous person could move landmarks into the property of poor neighbors and thereby steal their land."[190]

We have already seen that the wages of the poor had to be paid promptly upon completion of work (Deut 24:14-15; Lev 19:13). This measure guaranteed their economic well-being. As for those who had become poor (*yāmûk* ימוך), they had to be treated with dignity and consideration (Lev 25:39-55).

The laws also called for justice in the law courts, justice for both rich and poor (or great and small); justice shown by refraining from taking bribes and by being impartial (Exod 23:3, 6-8; Deut 16:19-20; 24:17; 27:19; Lev 19:15). Justice is shown by avoiding false witnessing (Exod 23:1-2; Deut 19:15-21), an act that could potentially jeopardize the poor.

Other measures include the remission or cancellation of debt (Deut 15:1-6), support and provision for the poor through generous lending and charitable acts (Deut 15:7-11),[191] releasing slaves and providing for them liberally (Deut 15:12-18).

The various harvest festivals similarly provide another way of caring for the poor. The poor survived through the annual tithe (Deut 14:22-27), the triennial tithe (Deut 14:28-29, 26:12-15); the feast of weeks (Deut 16:9-12; Exod 23:16; Lev 23:15-16) and the feast of booths (Deut 16:13-15). Likewise, gleanings were to be left behind for the sustenance of the poor (Deut 24:19-22; Lev 19:9-10; 23:22).

Most importantly, the poor benefited from the provisions of the Fallow/
Sabbatical Year when the land lay fallow (Exod 23:10-12; Lev 25:1-7,
18-22), the *šĕmiṭṭâ* שמטה Year (Deut 15:1-11), and the Jubilee Year (Lev
25:8-55) which provided relief from debt, restoration, and rehabilitation of
families.

Finally, the prohibition against oppression and exploitation was designed
to protect the poor. Due to the continual existence of the poor in Israelite society, the legal codes attempt to relieve their precarious economic condition
in several ways. However, the multiplicity of the legislations is indicative of
a worsening economic situation. Bailey argues that social legislation in all the
legal codes was not designed to wipe out poverty but rather to preserve and
perpetuate it. Even the "perceived humanitarian" and "social consciousness"
of Deuteronomy was meant to buttress the system that benefits from the institutionalization of poverty.[192] In light of this argument, it is not surprising to see
why the poor continued to exist through different periods of Israelite history.

SOCIO-ETHICAL IMPLICATIONS

This survey clearly shows ancient Israel's pervasive concern for the well-
being of the poor and other disadvantaged members of the community. The
laws are legislated to protect these groups from abuse or exploitation. They
also have specific provisions that are meant to safeguard their economic well-
being. Behind these laws are situations of suffering on the part of the poor.
No wonder why the rabbis argued that the poor needed to exist so that the rich
could have an opportunity to give and thereby redeem themselves.

It is evident that the law-givers were aware of, and responded to, the
theological motivation behind many of the laws. Yahweh is presented as being concerned about such groups of people. This concern manifests itself in
Yahweh's deliverance of Israel from Egyptian bondage and oppression. Thus
Yahweh expects Israel to be mindful of this great deed in its dealings with the
poor. Failure to do so may provoke divine wrath. This is the primary motive
clause for Israel's social concern.

In the Law Codes themselves there is an increasing sense of concern for
the poor, from the general (CC) to the particular (DC) to the universal (HC).
Deuteronomy shows much humanitarian regard for the poor and expands
many of the laws in Exodus. As noted above, this concern may be due to the
Deuteronomic reforms under King Josiah, or to the influence of the prophets
and their passion for social justice. Indeed, the poor are at the center of the
Law Codes. I strongly agree with Wright, who points out that ancient Israel's
economic system "was geared to the needs of the lowest in society, with the

immediate goal of giving maximum assistance to the poor, and the ultimate ideal that there should be no poor."[193]

Regardless of the practicability of these laws, institutions, and social programs, it is evident that ancient Israel had very idealistic visions of social renewal. If all these measures had been put into effect and strictly followed (Deuteronomy 15), the plight of the poor and other dependent members of the community would have been greatly ameliorated if not eliminated. This research indicates that the sheer volume of social legislation regarding the poor in the law codes masks an economic crisis in ancient Israelite society. Despite massive legislation, the poor continued to exist because these laws were not being followed to the letter.

NOTES

1. On the composition of the Hebrew Bible, see Bernhard W. Anderson, *Understanding the Old Testament,* 4th ed. (Englewood Cliffs, NJ: Prentice-Hall, 1986), 2-5.

2. The relevant sections are Exodus 20:22 - 23:33, Deuteronomy 12 - 26, and Leviticus 17 - 26. Although this order is different from the order of the Hebrew Bible, it is based on the probable dates of these books. Scholars disagree on exact dates, but I have followed Dale Patrick who dates the Covenant Code (hereafter CC) in the period of the Judges (1200-1000 BCE) or the early monarchical period (1000-800 BCE). He dates the Deuteronomic Code (hereafter DC) between 700 and 621 BCE and the Holiness Code (hereafter HC) to the exile or after (580-450 BCE). See Dale Patrick, *Old Testament Law* (Atlanta: John Knox Press, 1985), 65, 146-47. It is clear that except for the CC, the Law Codes are preceded by the prophets and they may well have been influenced by the prophets, especially in their passion and zeal for justice.

3. See Robert B. Coote, *Early Israel: A New Horizon* (Minneapolis: Fortress Press, 1990), 72-73. See also Hershel Shanks, "Defining the Problem: Where We Are in the Debate," in *The Rise of Ancient Israel,* Symposium at the Smithsonian Institution 26 October 1991, Sponsored by the Resident Associate Program, by Hershel Shanks, William G. Dever, Baruch Halpern, and P. Kyle McCarter (Washington, DC: Biblical Archaeology Society, 1992), 17-19. Shanks states that for the Pharaoh to boast that he had defeated Israel, it means that Israel was a formidable power by 1212 BCE when Merneptah defeated it. The reference to Israel shows that "the most powerful man in the world, the pharaoh of Egypt, was aware of Israel. Not only was he aware of Israel—he boasts that one of the most important achievements of his reign was to defeat Israel" (p. 19).

4. John Bright, *A History of Israel,* Fourth Edition (Louisville, KY: Westminster John Knox Press, 2000), 134.

5. Halpern, *The Emergence of Israel in Canaan,* 239.

6. See Terence Fretheim, *Exodus,* Interpretation (Louisville: John Knox Press, 1991), 176. See also J. Philip Hyatt, *Commentary on Exodus,* New Century

Bible (London: Oliphants, 1971), 37-47; Brevard S. Childs, *Exodus: A Commentary, Old Testament Library* (London: SCM, 1974), 178-336.

7. Fretheim, *Exodus,* 171-72.

8. Bright, *A History of Israel,* 134. Halpern argues that the Exodus story is a national myth which explains Israel's xenophobia against the Canaanites and anyone else whose ancestors did not participate in the Exodus. This myth enables Israel to maintain a sense of separateness and independence. He writes: "We cannot know the precise relationship of the Exodus to the Israelite settlement in Canaan. What we *do* know is that the Exodus was certainly central to the ideology of the Israelites in Canaan already in Iron I. The victory at the sea in Exodus 15, the tradition that YHWH marched forth from Edom to conquer Canaan, the Egyptian reference to the land of the Shasu of Yahweh all point to the same conclusion. Sometimes, relatively early in Iron I, Israel began to subscribe to a national myth of escape from Egypt, mediated by a god residing in the south . . . with the purpose of establishing a nation in Canaan. That national myth—justifying Israelite land claims in Canaan—became a call to arms, a doctrine of Manifest Destiny, for a people newly arrived from the north and east" [Halpern's emphasis]. See "The Exodus from Egypt," 107-108. It should be noted that by calling the Exodus a "myth," Halpern does not deny the historicity of this event.

9. Roland de Vaux, *Ancient Israel: Its Life and Institutions,* trans. John McHugh (New York, Toronto, London: McGraw-Hill Book Company, 1961), 68. See also Johs Pedersen, *Israel: Its Life and Culture,* vols. I-II.

10. De Vaux, *Ancient Israel,* 68.

11. Ibid., 72; Herron, "The Land, the Law, and the Poor," 77. See also Eryl W. Davies, "Land: Its Rights and Privileges," in *The World of Ancient Israel: Sociological, Anthropological and Political Perspectives: Essays by Members of the Society for Old Testament Study,* ed. Ronald E. Clements (Cambridge, New York, New Rochelle, Melbourne, Sydney: Cambridge University Press, 1989), 349-69.

12. De Vaux, *Ancient Israel,* 74-79.

13. De Vaux, *Ancient Israel,* 72-74. Archaeology has confirmed the existence of different standards of living during the tenth and eighth centuries. Tenth century houses at Tell el-Farah were found to be of the same size and arrangement whereas those of the eighth century were bigger and better, indicating the wealth of the latter occupants (pp. 72-73). See also Lawrence E. Stager, "The Archaeology of the Family in Ancient Israel," *BASOR* 260 (November 1985): 1-35.

14. Robert K. Gnuse sees the laws of Israel as a "mandate for the poor." See Gnuse, *You Shall Not Steal,* 10. See also Bruce C. Birch and Larry Rasmussen, *The Predicament of the Prosperous* (Philadelphia: Westminster Press, 1978); and John D. Mason, "Biblical Teaching and Assisting the Poor," *Transformation* 4, no. 2 (1987): 1-14.

15. These are: slaves (Exod 21:2-11, 20-21, 26-27, 32; 23:12); resident aliens (Exod 22:21; 23:9, 12); widows (Exod 22:22-24 [Heb 22:21-23]); the fatherless (Exod 22:22-24 [Heb 22:21-23]); and the poor (Exod 22:25 [Heb 22:24] (*'ānî* עני); 23:3 (*dal* דל); 23:6, 11 (*'ebyôn* אביון). It is noteworthy that not all of these groups were necessarily poor. Instead, some of the groups are mentioned with reference to their low social status. For example, a widow may not have been poor as such but lacked a male member of the household to care and provide for her as well as to

protect her. Moreover, the different Hebrew words for "poor" encompass a variety of meanings including their physical condition, social standing, or existential situation. An in-depth study of these terms will appear below, but for now consult the following works: "The Vocabulary of Poverty" in Gildas Hamel's book, *Poverty and Charity in Roman Palestine, First Three Centuries C.E.* (Berkeley, Los Angeles, Oxford: University of California Press, 1990), chap. 5; Heinz-Josef Fabry, *"dal; dālal; dallāh; zālal,"* in *TDOT,* vol. III, ed. G. Johannes Botterweck and Helmer Ringgren, trans. John T. Willis, Geoffrey W. Bromiley, and David E. Green (Grand Rapids, MI: William B. Eerdmans Publishing Company, 1978), 208-30; G. Johannes Botterweck, *"'ebhyôn,"* in *TDOT,* III (1978): 27-41; Ernst Bammel, *"Ptōchós, Ptōcheia, Ptōchéuō,"* in *Theological Dictionary of the New Testament,* vol. VI, ed. Gerhard Friedrich, trans. and ed. Geoffrey W. Bromiley (Grand Rapids, MI: Wm. B. Eerdmans Publishing Company, 1968), 885-915.

16. See for example, Victor H. Matthews and Don C. Benjamin, *Social World of Ancient Israel, 1250-587 BCE* (Peabody, MA: Hendrickson Publishers, 1993), 199-210.

17. Mendelsohn, *Slavery in the Ancient Near East,* 1-14; idem, "Slavery in the OT," 384-85. Insolvency seems to have been the major reason for slavery because "insolvency inevitably led to the debtor's enslavement" (*Slavery in the Ancient Near East,* 23; idem, "Slavery in the OT," 385).

18. See Harriet Katherine Havice, "The Concern for the Widow and the Fatherless in the Ancient Near East."

19. Mendelsohn, "Slavery in the OT," 385; idem, *Slavery in the Ancient Near East,* 34.

20. Mendelsohn, *Slavery in the Ancient Near East,* 44; idem, "Slavery in the OT," 385. De Vaux notes that this branding was different from that of the slave who wished to stay with his or her owner (Exod 21:6; Deut 15:17). *Ancient Israel,* 84.

21. Ibid., 243.

22. Mendelsohn, "Slavery in the OT," 387. He adds that the slave owner did not have power over the slave's life and could not kill him or her with impunity (*Slavery in the Ancient Near East,* 66). Citing Exod 21:20-21, 26-27, 32, de Vaux adds that Israelite laws protected slaves even more explicitly than other ancient Near Eastern laws (*Ancient Israel,* 85).

23. (1) After three years of service, a defaulting debtor and his family are to be released in the fourth year (*ANET,* 163-180, par. 117); (2) after the death of their owner, a slave-concubine and her children are to be released, (par. 171); (3) the children of a free-woman and a slave remain free (par. 175); and (4) a native male or female slave bought in a foreign land and brought back to Babylon shall be freed (par. 280).

24. Mendelsohn, "Slavery in the OT," 388. Hammurabi's laws are obviously more liberal on this issue. See also Anthony Phillips, *Ancient Israel's Criminal Law: A New Approach to the Decalogue* (Oxford: Basil Blackwell, 1970).

25. R. de Vaux, *Ancient Israel,* 173-77.

26. N. P. Lemche, "The Manumission of Slaves—The Fallow Year—The Sabbatical Year—The Jobel Year," *Vetus Testamentum* 26, no. 1 (1976): 38-59, especially pp. 50-51.

27. Mendelsohn, "Slavery in the OT," 388. See also p. 389.

28. Wright, *God's People in God's Land,* 258.

29. Ibid.

30. Ibid., 253.

31. Wright, *God's People in God's Land,* 255. The *mûk* מוּךְ paragraphs are Lev 25:25, 35, 39, 47 (cf. Lev 27:8).

32. Ibid., 255-56. He also sees the occasion of release as very different in the two provisions. It was "a domestic affair" in the "Hebrew" case, in the seventh year, but Jubilee was "a festival of national scope and importance in a fixed year" (p. 256).

33. I.e., free from slavery, taxes, and obligations. *NBDB,* 344-45. See also J. Pedersen, "Note on Hebrew *hopšî,"* *Journal of Palestine Oriental Society* 6 (1926): 103-105.

34. Wright, *God's People in God's Land,* 257.

35. Mendelsohn, *Slavery in the Ancient Near East,* 120-23; idem, "Slavery in the OT," 390.

36. For theories on reconciling the slave laws of Exodus and Deuteronomy, See S. R. Driver, *A Critical and Exegetical Commentary on Deuteronomy.* International Critical Commentary (New York: Charles Scribner's Sons, 1895), 182. Driver surmises that "the law of Dt. springs from a more advanced stage of society than the law of Ex." It is a stage where a father no longer has absolute authority over a daughter, and the sexes are treated with equality (pp. 182-83). Gerhard von Rad argues that the setting assumes that "in the meantime the woman has become able to own landed property and thus to sell herself into slavery for debt also" (*Deuteronomy,* 107).

37. Driver, *Deuteronomy,* 183.

38. Patrick D. Miller, *Deuteronomy,* Interpretation (Louisville: John Knox Press, 1990), 171.

39. Ibid., 171; Driver, *Deuteronomy,* 264; Gerhard von Rad, *Deuteronomy: A Commentary,* OTL (Philadelphia: The Westminster Press, 1966), 147.

40. Miller, *Deuteronomy,* 172. Von Rad agrees and remarks that this rule "is intended above all to prevent anyone from exploiting the precarious position of the slave and from reducing him again to slavery" (*Deuteronomy,* 147).

41. *ANET,* 177, par. 282.

42. Philip J. Budd, *Leviticus,* New Century Bible Commentary (London: Marshall Pickering / Grand Rapids: William B. Eerdmans Publishing Company, 1996), 281.

43. From the verb *mûk* מוּךְ, to "be low, depressed, grow poor," used of all impoverished Israelites. See *NBDB,* 557; Holladay, *Concise Hebrew and Aramaic Lexicon,* 185.

44. "Hireling, hired labourer," *NBDB,* 969.

45. n. m. s. from the verb *yšb* יָשַׁב (to dwell). See "Sojourner" (*NBDB,* 444); "alien" (Holladay, *Concise Hebrew and Aramaic Lexicon*, 388).

46. Some explanations are that the law of Leviticus is intended to provide that if Jubilee arrives before the seventh year, the slave is to be released. The problem is the total lack of reference to the older laws of Exodus and Deuteronomy. Driver observes that Leviticus betrays as little consciousness of the law of Exodus or Deuteronomy as Deuteronomy betrays of Leviticus. See Driver, *Deuteronomy,* 185.

47. Ibid.

48. Budd, *Leviticus,* 359-60.

49. Hebrew *gēr* גר (pl. *gērîm* גרים, from the root גור). There are three references to resident aliens in the CC: Exod 22:21; 23:9, 12. This term has been variously translated as "stranger/alien" (RSV); "resident alien" (NRSV); "alien" (NIV, NEB, REB, NAB; NJB); "stranger" (AV, JB, KJV, *Tanakh,* The Dartmouth Bible, The Condensed Bible, The Bible Reader, The American Bible Society Edition); "foreigner" (GNB, CEV); "foreigner/alien" (The Berkeley Version). LXX *paraikos* παραικος, later *prosélútos* προσήλυτος ("stranger/foreigner"). See John Pickering, *A Comprehensive Lexicon of the Greek Language* (Boston: Wilkins, Carter, and Company, 1848), 1125.

50. Weber, *Ancient Judaism,* 32.

51. Pedersen, *Israel,* I-II, 40; van Houten, *The Alien,* 15, 62, 67.

52. Spencer, "Sojourner," 103. See also Matthews and Benjamin, *Social World of Ancient Israel,* 82-95.

53. Spina, "Israelites as *gērîm,"* 323. Spina thus attempts to incorporate the "outside Status" of the *gēr* גר as well as the reasons for becoming a *gēr* גר. Kellerman lists three reasons for becoming a *gēr* גר: (1) Famine (Ruth 1:1; 1 Kgs 17:20; 2 Kgs 8:1; Gen 26:3; 47:4); (2) military encounters (Isa 16:4; 2 Sam 4:3; Jer 35:7); and (3) individual distress or bloodguilt (Judg 17:7-9; 19:1, 16; Deut 16:11, 14) ["*gur,*" 443-44; Mauch, "Sojourner," 398].

54. Herron, "The Land, the Law, and the Poor," 79. Because the term *gērîm* גרים was first applied to non-Israelites and Israel as a nation is only referred to as *gērîm* גרים in the pre-settlement era, and because exilic literature is silent about the *gērîm* גרים, Spina argues that the tradition must therefore be pre-exilic and pre-settlement ("Israelites as *gerim,*" 329).

55. Gerhard von Rad, *Old Testament Theology,* vol. I, trans. D. M. G. Stalker (New York, Hagerstown, San Francisco, London: Harper & Row, 1962), 122.

56. Spina, "Israelites as *gērîm,*" 324.

57. Van Houten, *The Alien,* chap. 2, especially p. 34 [emphasis mine]. The lack of references to the resident alien in the ancient Near East does not mean that there were no sojourners in those societies. It is possible that Israel paid attention to the resident aliens in its midst because of its own historical experiences.

58. Weber, *Ancient Judaism,* 33-36; van Houten, *The Alien,* 42. I shall analyze this changing status of the resident alien after studying all the three biblical codes.

59. Noth, *Exodus: A Commentary.* OTL (Philadelphia: The Westminster Press, 1962), 186, 189; Childs, *Exodus,* 482.

60. Van Houten, *The Alien,* 52.

61. See Walter Brueggemann, "The Book of Exodus," in *NIB,* vol. 1, 868; Noth, *Exodus,* 186; Childs, *The Book of Exodus,* 478; de Vaux, *Ancient Israel,* 47; Spencer, "Sojourner," 104.

62. Van Houten, *The Alien,* 58.

63. Brueggemann, "Exodus," 871.

64. Pedersen, *Israel,* I-II, 41; de Vaux, *Ancient Israel,* 75. This is because resident aliens are often grouped with the poor, widows, and the fatherless, or the economically disadvantaged members of society.

65. Weber, *Ancient Judaism,* 33. Pedersen states: "Though as a rule they must have been deprived of fields, it does not necessarily follow that they always were so" (*Israel,* I-II, 42; see also de Vaux, *Ancient Israel,* 74-75).

66. Van Houten, *The Alien,* 41.

67. See Deut 14:21, 29; 16:11, 14; 23:7; 24:14, 17, 19-21; 26:5, 11-13.

68. Patrick, *OT Law,* 135. For Miller, these statutes are designed to protect persons from economic oppression that would keep them from securing the basic needs of life (*Deuteronomy,* 172).

69. Patrick, *OT Law,* 136.

70. Ibid.

71. Miller, *Deuteronomy,* 174.

72. Ibid., 184.

73. Van Houten, *The Alien,* 93. She argues that the monarchy brought a hierarchical social structure which drew wealth from the land and made lower classes more precarious. "It is to this new socioeconomic reality that the laws covering justice and charity are addressed" (p. 93).

74. Ibid., 107.

75. See Lev 17:8-16; 18:26; 19:10, 33-34; 20:2, 22:18; 23:22; 24:16, 22; 25:23, 35, 45, 47.

76. Budd, *Leviticus,* 240.

77. Van Houten, *The Alien,* 119; so Noth, *Leviticus,* 128; Patrick, *OT Law,* 146. These scholars have also noted some "Deuteronomic" features in the HC, as well as its similarity to Ezekiel 40 - 48 (see Budd, *Leviticus,* 37).

78. Budd, *Leviticus,* 247-48; see also Noth, *Leviticus,* 132; Patrick, *OT Law,* 156. Patrick adds that the blood must be allowed to "return" to its source and thus atone for human guilt (p. 156).

79. Budd, *Leviticus,* 271.

80. According to Noth, it is for "those who have no stake in the soil" (*Leviticus,* 141). It is also noteworthy that in Deuteronomy, it is the forgotten sheaf, not the crop on the edges of the field, which is for the benefit of the resident alien, the fatherless, and the widow. This is in addition to unbeaten olives and ungleaned grapes.

81. Ibid., 144.

82. See Wright, *God's People in God's Land,* 253.

83. Patrick, *OT Law,* 184-85.

84. Van Houten, *The Alien,* 123-56, especially p. 156.

85. Ibid., 177.

86. Ibid., 164.

87. For studies on the widow and the fatherless consult the following works: Paula S. Hiebert, "'Whence Shall Help Come to Me?' The Biblical Widow," in *Gender and Difference in Ancient Israel,* ed. Peggy L. Day (Minneapolis: Fortress Press, 1989), 125-41; Harriet K. Havice, "The Concern for the Widow and the Fatherless in the Ancient Near East"; Harry A. Hoffner, "*'almānāh;'almānûth,*" *TDOT,* vol. I, ed. G. Johannes Botterweck and Helmer Ringgren, trans. John T. Willis (Grand Rapids, MI: William B. Eerdmans Publishing Company, 1974, rev. ed, 1977), 287-91; Helmer Ringgren, "*yātôm,*" *TDOT,* vol. VI, ed. G. Johannes Botterweck and Helmer

Ringgren, trans. David E. Green (Grand Rapids, MI: William B. Eerdmans Publishing Company, 1990), 477-81; F. Charles Fensham, "Widow, Orphan, and the Poor in Ancient Near Eastern Legal and Wisdom Literature"; Richard D. Patterson, "The Widow, the Orphan, and the Poor in the Old Testament and the Extra-Biblical Literature," *Bibliotheca Sacra* 130 (July-September 1973): 223-34; Donald E. Gowan, "Wealth and Poverty in the Old Testament: The Case of the Widow, the Orphan, and the Sojourner," *Interpretation* 41 (October 1987): 341-53.

88. Elizabeth Siwo-Okundi, "Listening to the Small Voice," 37-38.

89. Havice, "Concern for the Widow and Fatherless," 11-12.

90. Havice, Ibid, 25, 94.

91. Fensham, "Widow, Orphan, and the Poor," 133; Havice, "Concern for the Widow and Fatherless," 30-31. Scholars do not fully agree on the exact chronology of Egyptian history. I will mostly follow the chronology of Miriam Lichtheim's *Ancient Egyptian Literature: A Book of Readings,* vols. I-III (Berkeley, Los Angeles, London: University of California Press, 1973-1980).

92. See James Henry Breasted, *Ancient Records of Egypt: Historical Documents from the Earliest Times to the Persian Conquest,* 5 vols. (Chicago, IL: The University of Chicago Press, 1927), especially vol. 1, p. 152.

93. Ibid., vol. 1, 189.

94. Lichtheim, *AEL,* I, 4.

95. Carol A. Newsom refers to the practice whereby the reader of Proverbs 1 - 9 "is called upon to take up the subject position of son in relation to an authoritative father" as "interpellation." She further states that "what is important for Proverbs 1 - 9 is the issue of interpellation and the need for continual reinterpellation." See Newsom, "Woman and the Discourse of Patriarchal Wisdom: A Study of Proverbs 1 - 9," in *Gender and Difference in Ancient Israel,* 143-44.

96. Lichtheim, *AEL,* I, 5. See also Steindorff and Seele, *When Egypt Ruled the East,* 274-75; William Kelly Simpson, ed., *The Literature of Ancient Egypt: An Anthology of Stories, Instructions, and Poetry,* new ed. (New Haven and London: Yale University Press, 1973), 159-265; and *ANET,* 412-35.

97. Lichtheim, *AEL,* I, 100; *ANET,* 415; and Simpson, *The Literature of Ancient Egypt,* 180.

98. See *ANET,* 414.

99. Lichtheim, *AEL,* I, 136; *ANET,* 418; and Simpson, *The Literature of Ancient Egypt,* 194.

100. Lichtheim, *AEL,* I, 172; *ANET,* 408; Simpson, *The Literature of Ancient Egypt,* 35. Hanson notes that this is a rare text which gives the view-point of the lowly and oppressed since most Egyptian materials "are always viewed from the perspective of those in positions of wealth and power." See "The Ancient Near Eastern Roots of Social Welfare," 15.

101. Fensham, "Widow, Orphan, and the Poor," 132.

102. Lichtheim, *AEL,* II, 161; *ANET,* 424; Simpson, *The Literature of Ancient Egypt,* 264. This unique right is evident in other translations—*ANET*: "Do not *recognize* [lit. find] a widow if thou catchest her in the fields."

103. Lichtheim, *AEL,* III, 55.

104. Cited in Fensham, "Widow, Orphan, and the Poor," 130. See also Bruce V. Malchow, *Social Justice in the Hebrew Bible: What is New and What is Old* (Collegeville, Minnesota: The Liturgical Press, 1996), 1-7.

105. *ANET,* 524.

106. Ibid., 164, 178.

107. Cited in Havice, "Concern for the Widow and Fatherless," 153.

108. Ibid. Ninurta, son of Enlil, a fertility god, is also described as helping "the orphan boy and the orphan girl. You take the hand of the weak, raise the one without strength" (p. 155).

109. Hiebert, "The Biblical Widow," 127.

110. Ibid., 128. See also Harry A. Hoffner, *"'almānāh; 'almānûth,"* 288.

111. Havice, "Concern for the Widow and Fatherless," 130-34; Katarzyna Grosz, "Some Aspects of the Position of Women in Nuzi," in *Women's Earliest Records: From Ancient Egypt and Western Asia,* ed. Barbara S. Lesko (Atlanta, GA: Scholars Press, 1989), 167-89. See also the following essays in Lesko's book: Rivkah Harris, "Independent Women in Ancient Mesopotamia?" 145-65; Amelie Kuhrt, "Non-Royal Women in the Late Babylonian Period: A Survey," 215-43; Martha T. Roth, "Marriage and Matrimonial Prestations in First Millennium B.C. Babylonia," 245-60; and Carol Meyers, "Women and the Domestic Economy of Early Israel," 265-81.

112. Hiebert, "The Biblical Widow," 137. Thus Hiebert deduces that in Israel, Yahweh takes the place of the missing male family member who would have been concerned about her economic well-being (p. 137).

113. Translation of Michael David Coogan, ed., and trans. *Stories from Ancient Canaan* (Louisville: The Westminster Press, 1978), 74; see also *ANET,* 149. Simon B. Parker comments that "Keret is now under attack, being charged with incompetence and neglect, and threatened with displacement. As *Krt* A introduced Keret's loss of family and *Krt* B his loss of health, this new section also introduces a new threat: loss of throne." See *The Pre-Biblical Narrative Tradition: Essays on the Ugaritic Poems Keret and Aqhat,* Society of Biblical Literature Resources for Biblical Study 24 (Atlanta, GA: Scholars Press, 1989), 198.

114. Coogan, *Stories from Ancient Canaan,* 35, 40-41; see also *ANET,* 151, 153.

115. Temba L. J. Mafico, *Yahweh's Emergence as "Judge" among the Gods: A Study of the Hebrew Root Špṭ* (Lewiston, Queenston, Lampeter: The Edwin Mellen Press, 2006), 82. See also Absalom's revolt in 2 Samuel 15.

116. Malchow, *Social Justice in the Hebrew Bible;* idem, "Social Justice in the Israelite Law Codes," *WW* 4 (Summer 1984): 299-306; H. Eberhard von Waldow, "Social Responsibility in Early Israel"; Stephen A. Kaufman, "A Reconstruction of the Social Welfare System of Ancient Israel," in *In the Shelter of Elyon: Essays on Ancient Palestinian Life and Literature in Honor of G. W. Ahlström,* ed. W. Boyd Barrick and John R. Spencer (Sheffield, England: JSOT Press, 1984), 277-86; Paul D. Hanson, "The Ancient Near Eastern Roots of Social Welfare," 7-28.

117. Noth, *Exodus,* 186; Childs, *The Book of Exodus,* 478. In the Bible, a widow's status could be improved (1) by remarrying, (2) by returning to her father's house, and (3) by entering into levirate marriage. See Hoffner, *"'almānāh; 'almānûth,"* 290-91;

Baab, "Widow," 842-43; von Waldow, "Social Responsibility," 187; and Gowan, "The Case of the Widow, Orphan, and Sojourner," 344-45.

118. See Harold V. Bennett, *Injustice Made Legal: Deuteronomic Law and the Plight of Widows, Strangers, and Orphans in Ancient Israel* (Grand Rapids, MI. / Cambridge, UK: William B. Eerdmans Publishing Company, 2002).

119. Driver, *Deuteronomy,* 168.

120. Ibid., 195-97; von Rad, *Deuteronomy,* 113.

121. Moshe Weinfeld, *Deuteronomy and the Deuteronomic School* (Oxford: The Clarendon Press, 1972), 217. Gerhard von Rad essentially agrees with him when he states that "the memory of the originally sacral background . . . has certainly disappeared here" (*Deuteronomy,* 152).

122. Miller, *Deuteronomy,* 184 [Miller's emphasis]; von Rad, *Deuteronomy,* 159-60.

123. For general works on poverty, see the following references: Craig L. Nessan, "Poverty: The Biblical Witness and Contemporary Reality," *Currents in Theology and Mission* 13 (August 1986): 236-38; James W. Skillen, ed., *The Problem of Poverty* (Washington, DC: The Center for Public Justice / Grand Rapids, MI: Baker Book House, 1991); Wolfgang Stegemann, *The Gospel and the Poor,* trans. Dietlinde Elliott (Philadelphia: Fortress Press, 1984); William R. Domeris, "Biblical Perspectives on the Poor," *JTSA* 57 (December 1986): 57-61.

124. The others like *maḥsôr* מחסור and *miskēn* מסכן are used mostly in wisdom literature. For a detailed study of the etymology and meanings of these words, see the following works: Botterweck, *"'ebhyôn," TDOT* I (1974): 27-41; Fabry, *"dal; dālal dallāh; zālal," TDOT* III (1978): 208-30; Bammel, *"Ptōchós, Ptōcheia, Ptōchéuō," TDNT* VI (1968): 885-915; Wolf, "Poor," *IDB* 3 (1990): 843-44; idem, "Poverty," *IDB* 3, (1990): 853-54; Keck, "Poor," *IDBSup* (1990): 672-75; *The International Standard Bible Encyclopedia,* 1986 ed., s.v. "Poor," by David E. Holwerda; *ISBE,* 1986 ed., s.v. "Poverty," by Allen D. Verhey; Pleins, "Poor, Poverty (Old Testament)," *ABD* 5 (1992): 402-414; Paul Humbert, *"Le mot biblique 'ebyōn," Revue d'histoire et de philosophie religieuses* 32 (1952): 1-6; Miscall, "The Concept of the Poor in the Old Testament"; Hamel, *Poverty and Charity in Roman Palestine;* Conrad Boerma, *The Rich, the Poor—and the Bible* (Philadelphia: The Westminster Press, 1979), 7-10; Phil Skote, "The Problem of Poverty in the Old Testament," *The Bible Today* 26 (1988): 87-93; and George V. Pixley and Clodovis Boff, *The Bible, the Church, and the Poor,* trans. Paul Burns (Maryknoll, NY: Orbis Books, 1989).

125. The distribution is as follows: *'ebyôn* אביון: Exod 23:6, 11; Deut 15:4, 7, 9, 11; 24:14; *dal* דל: Exod 23:3; Lev 19:15 *'ānî* עני: Exod 22:25 [Heb 22:24]; Deut 15:11; 24:12, 14, 15; Lev 19:10; 23:22.

126. The distribution is as follows: 17 times: Prophets; 23 times: Psalms; 4 times: Proverbs; 6 times: Job; 9 times: legal materials; 1 time: Deuteronomistic History (historical narratives); 1 time: Esther. Wolf, "Poor," 843; Botterweck, *"'ebhyôn,"* 29; Pleins, "Poor, Poverty," 403-404; and Hamel, *Poverty and Charity,* 167; KB, vol. I, 4-5; Koehler-Baumgartner, *HALOT,* vol. I, 5; idem, *HALAT,* vol. I, 5.

127. *NBDB,* 2; Wolf, "Poor," 843; Jenni and Westermann, *THAT,* vol. I, 23-25; Harris et al, eds., *TWOT,* vol. 1, 4-5. Pleins translates *'ebyôn* אביון as "the beggarly poor" (see "Poor, Poverty," 403). This sense of begging is also explored by Botter-

weck ("*'ebhyôn,*" 28). Hamel interprets *'ebyôn* אביון as the needy poor "in the most extreme of circumstances, for instance lacking in water and bread." The *'ebyôn* אביון "needed to be helped at once if he was to survive" (*Poverty and Charity,* 167). Hamel equates *'ebyôn* אביון with the LXX equivalent, *ptōchós* πτωχός. A *ptōchós* πτωχός was considered poor and destitute or a beggar, someone "on the margins and recognized by everyone as such." He or she had lost ties to family or society (pp. 170, 167). Bammel defines *ptōchós* πτωχός as "destitute," "mendicant" (see *"Ptōchós,"* 886). The other word used by the LXX is *pénēs* πέ'νης, referring to "anyone having a paid menial occupation. He was a person making a living, though often with difficulty" (Hamel, *Poverty and Charity,* 167). In today's terminology, the *ptōchós* πτωχός would be equivalent to poor beggars and the *pénēs* πε΄νης to "the working poor."

128. Pleins, "Poor, Poverty," 408. See also Botterweck, "*'ebhyôn,"* 29. While *'ebyôn* אביון means "severe economic deprivation" (Pleins, "Poor, Poverty," 404), an exploration of the various ways or contexts in which these words are used will follow.

129. 12 times: Prophets (13 times: George); 5 times: Pentateuch; 5 times: Psalms (6 times: George); 21 times: wisdom literature (20 times: George); *dallâ* דלה: 2 times: 2 Kings; 3 times: Jeremiah (See Pleins, "Poor, Poverty," 405-407; George, "Poverty in the OT," 5-6). See also Koehler-Baumgartner, *HALAT,* vol. I, 212-13.

130. Etymologically, the root *dll* דלל is to be distinguished from the root *dlh* דלה. The distinctions are as follows: *dll* דלל I ("door"); *dll* דלל II ("low, poor, helpless, powerless, insignificant, unimportant"); *dlh* דלה I ("to draw water"); *dlh* דלה II ("to dangle"). In Middle Hebrew, the distinctions are as follows: *dll* דלל I ("to become little, tiny"); *dll* דלל II ("to hang down, dangle"); and *dll* דלל III ("to glorify, praise"). See KB, vol. I, 210; Koehler-Baumgartner, *HALOT,* I, 221-23. Pleins interprets *dal* דל as "the poor peasant farmer" (See "Poor, Poverty," 405-407). He adds that "in the prophetic texts . . . the term *dal* depicts the politically and economically marginalized elements of society" (p. 405) and in the narrative texts, the word *dal* דל does not refer to poverty per se but rather political weakness (Judg 6:15 and 2 Sam 3:1).

131. The distribution of the *'ānî* עני in the Hebrew Bible is as follows: 25 times: Prophets; 31 times: Psalms (30 Kethib and 1 Qere) [32 times: George]; 16 times: wisdom literature (8 times: Proverbs; 7 times: Job, and 1 time: Qoheleth); 7 times: Pentateuch. (Augustine George wrongly says 70 times in the Law Codes!). The root *'nh* ענה has four distinct meanings in the Hebrew Bible: *'nh* ענה I ("to reply, answer"); *'nh* ענה II ("to be wretched, emaciated, cringe, be crouched, hunched up, suffering"); *'nh* ענה III ("to be troubled"); and *'nh* ענה IV ("to sing"). *'ānî* עני and *'ănāwîm* ענוים are therefore derived from the second meaning of the root *'ánh* ענה. See Koehler-Baumgartner, *HALOT,* vol. II, rev. Walter Baumgartner and Johann Jakob Stamm, trans. M. E. J. Richardson (Leiden, New York, Cologne: E. J. Brill, 1995), 851-57; idem, *HALAT,* vol. III (Leiden: E. J. Brill, 1983), 810; KB, vol. II, (Leiden: E. J. Brill / Grand Rapids, MI: William B. Eerdmans Publishing Company, 1953), 718-21.

132. The distribution is as follows: 13 times: Psalms; 7 times: Prophets; 3 times: Proverbs; 1 time: Job. See also George, "Poverty in the OT," 4-5; *NBDB,* 776; Pleins, "Poor, Poverty," 411-13; Miscall, "The Concept of the Poor in the Old Testament," 267; and Malchow, *Social Justice in the Hebrew Bible,* 12-13. According to Pleins,

the statistics show that *'ānî* עני / *'ānāwîm* עניים is "the predominant word for poverty in the Hebrew Bible" ("Poor, Poverty," 413).

133. Pleins, "Poor, Poverty," 408. He defines *rāš* רש as "political and economic inferiority" (p. 407). The distribution of the word *rāš* רש is as follows: 12 times: Proverbs; 1 time: Psalms; 4 times: Deuteronomic History; 2 times: Ecclesiastes (Qoheleth). See also the following works: *NBDB,* 930; KB, vol. II, 883; Koehler-Baumgartner, *HALAT,* vol. IV (Leiden, New York, Kopenhagen, Cologne: E. J. Brill, 1990), 1128; Harris et al, eds., *TWOT,* vol. 2, 840; Benjamin Davidson, *The Analytical Hebrew and Chaldee Lexicon,* 3d printing (Peabody, MA: Hendrickson Publishers, 1984), 680; and Pleins, "Poor, Poverty," 407-408.

134. See Ecclesiastes 4:13; 9:14-16. Consult also the following works: *NBDB,* 587; George, "Poverty in the OT," 6; Holwerda, "Poor," 905; Pleins, "Poor, Poverty," 407; KB, vol. II, 542; Koehler-Baumgartner, *HALOT,* II, 605-606; and Harris et al, eds., *TWOT,* vol. 1, 517.

135. Pleins, "Poor, Poverty," 407. He adds that "since the ethic of Proverbs is the ethic of the bureaucratic elite . . . the text tends to stress hard work and moderation. As a result, the wise are terribly concerned about the dangers of laziness" (p. 407). The distribution of *maḥsôr* מחסור is as follows: 8 times: Proverbs; 1 time: Pentateuch; 1 time: Psalms; 3 times: Judges. See also Pleins, "Poor, Poverty," 407; *NBDB,* 341; Holladay, *A Concise Hebrew and Aramaic Lexicon of the Old Testament,* 191; KB, vol. II, 514; Koehler-Baumgartner, *HALOT,* vol. II, 571; Harris et al, eds., *TWOT,* vol. 1, 309. Miscall concentrates his study on only four words: *'ebyôn* אביון, *dal* דל, *'ānî* עני, and *rāš* רש. From his study, the typical Israelite concept of the poor has social, economic, and religious connotations. The poor are landless, disinherited, and dispossessed social outcasts. He writes: "The most important Israelite characteristic of the concept of the poor is the fact that Yahweh is the ultimate defender of the needy and the weak;" See "The Concept of the Poor in the Old Testament," 34.

136. Lichtheim, *AEL,* I, 178.

137. Ibid., 180.

138. Ibid., 181.

139. Lichtheim, *AEL,* II, 152-53; see also p. 156.

140. Ibid., 154-55. Chapter 12 continues:

> Do not desire a noble's wealth,
> Nor make free with a big mouthful of bread;
> If he sets you to manage his property,
> Shun his, and yours will prosper" (p. 155).

141. Ibid., 155-56.

142. Jeffrey Sachs, *The End of Poverty,* 280.

143. Ibid., 162.

144. Cited in Havice, "Concern for the Widow and Fatherless," 153.

145. Lambert, *Babylonian Wisdom Literature* (Oxford: The Clarendon Press, 1960), 87.

146. Ibid., 89 [author's emphasis].

147. Ibid., 119.

148. Ibid., 135; *ANET,* 389. Fensham notes that "the assistance of the poor was regarded as a virtue. Very important is the fact that kings were called on to carry through this policy." See "Widow, Orphan, and the Poor," 132.

149. Coogan, *Stories From Ancient Canaan,* 74.

150. See Roland de Vaux, *Ancient Israel,* 170-71. In Hebrew, interest is called *néšek* נשך (lit. "a bite") and *tarbît* תרבית ("increase, extra charge").

151. See the textual apparatus, in *Biblia Hebraica Stuttgartensia,* ed. R. Kittel (Stuttgart: Deutsche Bibelgesellschaft, 1984), 123. See also Dale Patrick, *OT Law,* 89; Cassuto, *A Commentary on the Book of Exodus* (Jerusalem: The Magnes Press / The Hebrew University of Jerusalem, 1967), 297.

152. Cassuto, *A Commentary on the Book of Exodus,* 298. His emendation of *'ebyônĕka* אביוניך to *'oyēbĕka* איבך has no textual basis and must be rejected.

153. The distribution is as follows: *'ebyôn* אביון: Deut 15:4, 7, 9, 11a, c; 24:14; *'ānî* עני: Deut 15:11; 24:12, 14, 15.

154. See Wright, *God's People in God's Land,* 143-51; Leslie J. Hoppe, "Deuteronomy and the Poor," *TBT* 24 (June 1986): 371-75, especially p. 372; Gnuse, *You Shall Not Steal,* 32-36; Driver, *Deuteronomy,* 176-78; Patrick, *OT Law,* 111-12; Pleins, "Poor, Poverty," 410; Miller, *Deuteromomy,* 134-35; von Rad, *Deuteronomy,* 105. The *šĕmiṭṭâ* שמטה is a remission (or a release from) debt (note the parallel release from slavery in Deut 15:12-18). The fallow year in Exodus is explicitly for the benefit of the poor and wild animals; the sabbatical year in Leviticus is presented as primarily "a sabbath of complete rest for the land, a sabbath for the Lord" (v. 4). It secondarily benefits the landowner, other members of the household, as well as both domestic and wild animals (vv. 6-7). More discussion will follow below.

155. The scholars who favor a suspension are: Driver (*Deuteronomy,* 179); North (*Sociology of the Biblical Jubilee,* 186); and Wright (*God's People in God's Land,* 148). Those who favor a full release or cancellation are: Miller (*Deuteronomy,* 135); Gnuse (*You Shall Not Steal,* 34); Patrick (*OT Law,* 112); von Rad (*Deuteronomy,* 106); Lemche ("The Manumission of Slaves" 45); and Leslie J. Hoppe (*Being Poor: A Biblical Study* [Wilmington, DE: Michael Glazier, 1987]), 17.

156. See also Jeffries M. Hamilton, "Ha'areṣ in the Shemiṭṭâ Law," *VT* 42 (April 1992): 214-222; idem, *Social Justice and Deuteronomy: The Case of Deuteronomy 15,* Society of Biblical Literature Dissertation Series 136 (Atlanta, GA: Scholars Press, 1992).

157. Miller, *Deuteronomy,* 136. He focuses on prominent "body language" used here (vv. 1-2, 7-11, 18). "Such language indicates to the hearer that both attitude and action, disposition and conduct, are involved in relating to those who are poor" (p. 136). Hamilton also focuses on negative and positive commands, as well as "act and attitude" in this passage (*"*Ha'areṣ in the Shemiṭṭâ Law," 219-20; idem, *Social Justice and Deuteronomy,* 13-19).

158. Miller, *Deuteronomy,* 137. He translates v. 11a thus: "For the poor will never cease *off the earth"* (p. 137) [Miller's emphasis]. This verse makes sense when read fully, in context, and in conjunction with v. 4. A classic example of eisegesis is the editorial in the *Chicago Tribune* of July 6, 1966. In its attempt to discredit Sargent Shriver's "War on Poverty," it quoted Deut 15:11a wholly out of context: "We have

it on the authority of Deuteronomy that 'the poor shall never cease out of the land,' but Mr. Shriver is more optimistic and feels that the Great Society can attend to that with efficiency and dispatch, and at only a modest outlay." See "*'Chicago Tribune'* Eisegesis," *The Christian Century* 83 (July 1966): 856. See also R. S. Sugirtharajah, "'For You Always Have the Poor with You': An Example of Hermeneutics of Suspicion," *Asia Journal of Theology* 4, no. 1 (1990): 102-107; Paul Ewing Davies, "Poor You Have with You Always: The Biblical View of Poverty," *McCormick Quarterly* 18 (January 1965): 37-48.

159. Hoppe, "Deuteronomy and the Poor," 372 [author's emphasis]; idem, *Being Poor,* 17. He also views poverty as caused by human beings who disobey God's laws of equality ("Deuteronomy and the Poor," 371). According to Sugirtharajah, the intention of the Deuteronomist is "a vision of hope for humanity which seeks to create a society without want and with equal opportunities. The programmatic vision provides an inspiration to transform the society" (see "For You Always Have the Poor with You," 106).

160. Hamilton, *Social Justice and Deuteronomy,* 136.

161. Hoppe, "Deuteronomy and the Poor," 373. He adds that "to allow creditors inside the homes of their debtors in order to rummage about for a suitable item to take as collateral was demeaning to the families that found themselves in severe economic need. Keeping creditors outside the home of their debtors preserves at least a modicum of dignity and self-respect for the poor" (p. 373).

162. Hoppe, "Deuteronomy and the Poor," 375.

163. Here the poor are referred to as *'ānî* עני or *dal* דל. The word *'ebyôn* אביון does not appear in this Code. The references are as follows: *'ānî* עני: Lev 19:10; 23:22; *dal* דל: Lev 19:15.

164. Noth, *Leviticus,* 172. Budd, *Leviticus,* 324.

165. Budd, *Leviticus,* 276.

166. See also Robert Wafawanaka, "African Perspectives on Poverty in the Hebrew Law Codes," in *The Bible in Africa: Transactions, Trajectories, and Trends.* Edited by Gerald O. West and Musa W. Dube, 490-497, (Leiden, The Netherlands, Boston, Koln: Brill Publishers, 2000).

167. On this topic see the following works: Roland de Vaux, *Ancient Israel,* 173-75; Pedersen, *Israel,* I-II, 479-80; León Epsztein, *Social Justice in the Ancient Near East and the People of the Bible* (London: SCM, 1986), 128-33; Gnuse, *You Shall Not Steal,* 32-36; Lemche, "The Manumission of Slaves," 38-59; Julian Morgenstern, "Sabbatical Year," *IDB* 4 (1962): 141-44; Ben Zion Wacholder, "Sabbatical Year," *IDBSup* (1990): 762-63; Wright, *God's People in God's Land,* 143-151; idem, "Sabbatical Year," *ABD* 5 (1992): 857-61.

168. Epsztein, *Social Justice in the ANE,* 129; Morgenstern, "Sabbatical Year," 141-42; Wacholder, "Sabbatical Year," 762.

169. Epsztein, *Social Justice in the ANE,* 129.

170. Noth, *Exodus,* 189; Childs, *Exodus,* 482; Wacholder, "Sabbatical Year," 762; Boecker, *Law and the Administration of Justice,* 91-92.

171. Wright, *God's People in God's Land,* 145. Wright argues that there are three major aspects of the Sabbatical Year—legislation concerning land, debt, and slaves.

He therefore maintains that the Sabbatical Year was "clearly a primarily socioeconomic institution" (see "Sabbatical Year," 857).

172. Gnuse, *You Shall Not Steal,* 34-35. For detailed study of this issue, see Moshe Weinfeld, "Freedom Proclamations in Egypt and the Ancient Near East," in *Pharaonic Egypt: The Bible and Christianity,* ed. Sarah Israelit-Groll (Jerusalem: The Magnes Press / The Hebrew University, 1985), 317-27; idem, *Social Justice in Ancient Israel and the Ancient Near East* (Jerusalem: The Magnes Press / The Hebrew University, 1995), especially chaps. 1 and 8; and Marvin L. Chaney, "Debt Easement in Israelite History and Tradition," in *The Bible and the Politics of Exegesis,* 127-39, especially p. 131.

173. Hanson agrees that these measures were "a means of winning the popular support necessary for a peaceful reign, and of maintaining social and economic stability in the land." See "The Ancient Near Eastern Roots of Social Welfare," in *Through the Eye of a Needle,* eds. Hanawalt and Lindberg, 13.

174. Gnuse, *You Shall Not Steal,* 36. According to Wright, "the sabbatical year, therefore, was one among many dimensions of a total economic system that was intended to reflect not only the sovereignty of Yahweh, but also his moral demands" (see "Sabbatical Year," 860).

175. See Wright, "Jubilee, Year of," 1025. He add that the more common *šôpar* שׁופֿר is used in Lev 25:9. Other expressions for trumpets are found in Exod 19:13; and Josh 6:4-8, 13 (p. 1025).

176. See Gnuse, *You Shall Not Steal,* 36-47; idem, "Jubilee Legislation in Leviticus: Israel's Vision of Social Reform," *BTB* 15, no. 2 (1985): 43-48; A. van Selms, "Jubilee, Year Of," *IDBSup* (1990): 496-98; Epsztein, *Social Justice in the ANE,* 133-34; North, *Sociology of the Biblical Jubilee;* Jeffrey A. Fager, "Land Tenure in the Biblical Jubilee: A Moral World View," *Hebrew Annual Review* 11 (1987): 59-68; idem, *Land Tenure and the Biblical Jubilee;* Wright, "Jubilee, Year of," *ABD* 3 (1992): 1025-30; Lemche, "The Manumission of Slaves," 38-59; Weinfeld, *Social Justice in Ancient Israel,* 152-78.

177. Westbrook, *Property and the Family in Biblical Law,* 48; The *misharum*-acts were measures designed to restore equilibrium in the economic life of society (p. 49).

178. De Vaux, *Ancient Israel,* 177. Epsztein agrees with him (*Social Justice in the ANE,* 134). Wright argues that "the Jubilee was an attempt periodically to halt the relentless economic forces in society whereby the rich get richer and the poor get poorer" *(God's People in God's Land,* 178-79). Miscall thinks it "highly doubtful" that the *šĕmiṭṭâ* and Jubilee were ever enforced, however he cautions against just dismissing these programs as "utopian schemes" (see "The Concept of the Poor in the Old Testament," 107). Dale Patrick however argues that the eradication of poverty was not the intention of ancient Israelite society or the biblical text, but rather managing the resources it had. Private communication, 2009 SBL Meeting.

179. Gnuse calls it "an idealistic and unhistorical creation of exilic theologians," hence a mere vision of social reform ("Jubilee Legislation," 47).

180. On the nature of the Israelite family, see the following works: Otto J. Baab, "Family," *IDB* 2 (1962): 238-41; Joshua Roy Porter, *The Extended Family in the Old Testament,* 1-21; Christopher J. H. Wright, *An Eye for an Eye,* chap. 8; idem,

God's People in God's Land, chaps. 1-3; idem, "Family," *ABD* 2 (1992): 761-769; and Norman K. Gottwald, *The Tribes of Yahweh,* part 6. Porter has reconstructed the Israelite extended family as follows: "The head of the family and his wife, his father and mother, step mothers, sisters (and sometimes their husbands), sons and daughters and their spouses, grandsons and grand-daughters (and sometimes perhaps their husbands), the father's sisters (and perhaps their husbands), the mother's sisters (and perhaps their husbands), the father's brothers and their wives, the head's brothers and their wives, and his mother-in-law or mothers-in-law" (*The Extended Family in the Old Testament,* 21).

181. Wright, "Family," 763.

182. Gabriel Barkay notes that *'aḥ* אח ("brother") is used in Pentateuchal laws relating to justice. It was used in the ancient Near East to refer to someone of equal rank or status and is "most commonly used in the Bible as an epithet for 'fellow Israelite.'" See "Your Poor Brother: A Note on an Inscribed Bowl from Beth Shemesh," *Israel Exploration Journal* 41 (1991): 239-41, especially p. 241. Barkay argues that the bowl was probably meant to contain food for the poor who were referred to as *'āḥîkā* אחיך ("your brother"). That it was found in a burial cave probably reflects its secondary use as a container for burial gifts (p. 241).

183. See Gerald Larue, *Sex and the Bible* (Buffalo, NY: Prometheus Books, 1983), [chap. 3: "The Levirate"] 35-37.

184. Ronald E. Clements, "Poverty and the Kingdom of God—An Old Testament View," in *The Kingdom of God and Human Society: Essays by Members of the Scripture, Theology, and Society Group,* ed. R. S. Barbour (Edinburgh: T. & T. Clark, 1993), 13-27, especially p. 20.

185. Habel, *The Land is Mine;* Walter Brueggemann, *The Land: Place as Gift, Promise, and Challenge in Biblical Faith,* OBT (Philadelphia: Fortress Press, 1977); and Lee, "The Theological Concept of Divine Ownership of the Land."

186. Wright, *God's People in God's Land,* 124. He notes that "the only legal method by which land in the Old Testament changed hands was by inheritance within the family" (See "Family," 764).

187. Wright, "Family," 763.

188. Malchow, *Social Justice in the Hebrew Bible,* 22-26. Poverty could ideally have been eliminated from Israelite society had Israel followed Yahweh's commandments strictly. There is also a possibility that that reality could have been compromised given other considerations. Iliffe has pointed to climatic changes and political insecurity as the chief causes of "conjunctural poverty" (*The African Poor,* 6). It is evident that a sudden and drastic change of circumstances could irreversibly worsen the status of the poor. However, the biblical material presupposes a situation whereby the condition of the poor could have been reversed. To state it differently, the Bible presupposes the existence of "structural poverty" due to both personal and social circumstances, but circumstances which could have been overcome by responding appropriately to the needs of the poor. Occurrences of conjunctural poverty would have worsened the condition of citizens.

189. Malchow, *Social Justice in the Hebrew Bible,* 23. For further studies on interest law see the following works: Hillel Gamoran, "The Biblical Law Against Loans

on Interest," *JNES* 30 (April 1971): 127-34; John Sutherland, "Usury: God's Forgotten Doctrine," *Crux* 18, no. 1 (1982): 9-14; Bruce Ballard, "On the Sin of Usury: A Biblical Economic Ethic," *Christian Scholar's Review* 24 (December 1994): 210-28; William J. Larkin, "The Ethics of Inflation: A Biblical Critique of the Causes and Consequences," *Grace Theological Journal* 3, no. 1 (1982): 89-105; and Paul A. Wee, "Biblical Ethics and Lending to the Poor," *EcR* 38 (October 1986): 416-30. Sutherland remarks that borrowing was an indication of serious financial trouble. Consequently, debt was seen in the Old Testament as a form of slavery ("Usury," 11).

190. Malchow, *Social Justice in the Hebrew Bible,* 23; Chapter 16 of the Instruction of Amen-em-opet teaches:

> Do not move the scales nor alter the weights,
> Nor diminish the fractions of the measure;
> Do not desire a measure of the fields,
> Nor neglect those at the treasury.
>
> . . . .
> Do not make for yourself deficient weights,
> They are rich in grief through the might of god. (Lichtheim, *AEL,* 2, 156-57).

191. See Charles C. West, "The Sharing of Resources: A Biblical Reflection," *EcR* 38 (1986): 357-69. According to Maimonides, the best charity is that which helps the poor dispense with [the need for] charity (Sacks, *Wealth and Poverty: A Jewish Analysis,* 5).

192. Bailey, private communication, January 6, 2010. He adds that the poor are hardly the main concern of these laws which deal with issues of power, powerlessness, and control.

193. Wright, "Sabbatical Year," 860.

Chapter Three

Poverty and the Prophets

INTRODUCTION

In this chapter we turn our attention to select groups of prophets among the Former Prophets, as well as the Minor and Major Prophets. Here in the prophetic corpus it becomes clearer that Israel had indeed continued to depart from its divine mandate. The prophetic rhetoric and critique of social injustice and oppression is indicative of the people's failure to fulfill the divine mandate. By and large, the prophetic literature attributes the existence of poverty to the exploitation and oppression of the poor and powerless by the rich and powerful landowners of the time. The continued existence of poverty in both biblical and modern societies has other explanations which we will address in this book. One general explanation is that the poor have continued to exist because someone else is profiting from their condition. The prophetic critique of social injustice opens a window into the oppressive social world of ancient Israel. In this context, the responsibility for reducing poverty lay primarily with the rich and powerful and secondarily with the poor themselves.

The problem of poverty is a major subject in the prophetic tradition. It appears in limited form with the inception of the prophetic office but flowers with the rise of the classical prophets, especially in the eighth century BCE. In general, the prophets view poverty as a social evil resulting from human beings who have disobeyed the divine mandate. They call for justice and criticize those who profit from, and hence perpetuate poverty. It is apparent that in all of biblical literature, the prophets are the most ardent critics of the existence of poverty in Israelite society.

In light of the biblical mandate especially as formulated in the book of Deuteronomy, it can be argued that the prophets are troubled by the continual existence of the poor in Israelite society. It is they who remind Israel of the demands of the Torah and its mandate regarding the poor. The prophets are disturbed by the nation's disregard of the law such that the rich and the poor exist in the same community when in fact the poor should not ideally exist.

This chapter explores the problem of poverty in the prophets, both Former and Latter.[1] Scholars refer to the historical narratives in the Former Prophets as the "Deuteronomistic History," with the book of Deuteronomy serving as an introduction.[2] Since there is not much reference to poverty in the Former Prophets, I will treat them together as a unit. The second part of this chapter examines two representative prophets from each of the Minor and Major Prophets, namely, Amos and Micah, and Isaiah and Jeremiah, respectively.

STRUCTURE AND CAUSES OF POVERTY IN THE PROPHETS

According to Frank Moore Cross, "the institution of prophecy appeared simultaneously with kingship in Israel and fell with kingship."[3] As such, this period spans more than four centuries of prophetic activity in Israel. It is also noteworthy that the phenomenon of prophecy is present in other ancient Near Eastern societies as well as in modern societies.[4]

Wilson has gone beyond traditional scholars who view the prophets as mere messengers of God. He proposes to call them "intermediaries" and their activity "intermediation." As intermediaries the prophets function between both the divine and the human worlds and their performance is integrally tied to their societies for guidance and support.[5]

The history recounted in the books of Joshua and Judges took place during the pre-monarchic or tribal league period. As such, these books are primarily concerned with the conquest of the land of Canaan, a subject of much debate among biblical scholars. The manner of the settlement in Canaan has been attributed to one of four dominant models: the conquest or invasion model; the immigration or peaceful infiltration model; the revolt or social revolution model; or the endogenous model.[6] The third model has great relevance to the subject under consideration. Leslie Hoppe puts it succinctly:

> The value of this model for an understanding of poverty in the Bible is that it shows how ancient Israelite society was formed in the midst of a social revolution against economic and political oppression. The biblical tradition is the memory of a people who emerged out of a conscious and deliberate rejection of an oppressive economic situation. In other words, ancient Israel grew out of a revolt against poverty enforced by a ruling elite upon peasants. It was a revolt against the elite of the Canaanite city states and their determination to control the peasant farmers. This control did not benefit the peasants but the ruling elite.[7]

This theory of social revolution due to oppression is a very credible one and it resurfaces at other stages of Israel's history. Indeed, oppression ignites the ire of the Latter Prophets in their criticism of social injustice.

The rise of the monarchy was another major cause of poverty in ancient Israel. The monarchy, which was modeled on Canaanite kingship patterns, proved to be an oppressive institution, especially under Solomon, who often made alliances with foreign kings to protect his rule. Solomon also introduced heavy forced labor (corvée) in order to fund his court and many of his building projects (1 Kgs 4:7-19; 9:15-22). Israel's demand for a king in order to be "like other nations" (1 Sam 8:1-22) caused Samuel to warn them of the oppressive nature of the king who would rule over them (vv. 11-18). Procuring a king was not so much a rejection of Yahweh as an acceptance of Canaanite overlordship. According to Bennett's research, the burden of supporting state bureaucracy would have fallen on the common people or the majority peasants.[8]

Gnuse views kingship as a contributing factor to "the decline of the Israelite ethos." Israel's syncretistic religion led to an erosion of values such as morality and justice, resulting in the oppression of the poor. Kingship also introduced class structures and oriental despotism. As a result, "a great gap widened between rich and poor in the following two centuries, and the rural poor were victimized again and again by the urban rich."[9]

During the United Kingdom of David and Solomon, oppression and suffering reached great heights under King Solomon. It was precisely the oppressive policies of Solomon and his son Rehoboam (1 Kgs 11:26-43; 12:1-33; 13:25-33) that led to the revolution of Jeroboam I and the division of the Kingdom into two (922 BCE). Through a quick succession of kings and coups, the kingdom of Israel would survive until 722/21 BCE. The more stable kingdom of Judah survived until 587/86 BCE.

While the two kingdoms experienced periods of intermittent peace and security and the constant threat of war (as a buffer state), the poor continued to suffer even in peaceful times. The time of Jeroboam II (786-746 BCE) was an especially successful period in Israel's history, but it was also the height of the suffering of the poor. The poor were losing their land and being sold into slavery because of debt and high interest rates; the courts were taking bribes from rich landowners and the influence of Canaanite culture was at its highest.[10] Gnuse describes this period succinctly:

> At that time Israel was at its pinnacle of power and prosperity, and Samaria was the center of tremendous affluence. But by then the gap between rich and poor was at its widest, and the Yahwistic religion had been subtly transformed into a syncretistic Baal cult under the royal patronage of shrines at Bethel and Dan.[11]

It was at this time that the classical prophets arose, beginning with Amos'
biting critique of the oppression of the poor (750 BCE).

The classical prophets under consideration burst upon the scene during
the middle to late eighth century BCE (Amos, Isaiah, Micah) and the late
seventh to the early sixth century BCE (Jeremiah). This period encompasses
a time of great prosperity culminating in the fall of Jerusalem (587/6 BCE).
It is notable that these prophets viewed poverty as a result of Israel's many
sins such as oppression, exploitation, injustice, greed, and a rejection of the
traditional/Mosaic values of justice, compassion, and righteousness.[12] All
these offenses are contrary to the letter of the law which called for advocacy
on behalf of the poor.

While the prophets primarily delivered messages of hope and salvation
from Yahweh to the people, they also had messages of doom and destruction
as a result of disobedience.[13] The latter message is tied in part to their strong
criticism of social injustice and the oppression of the poor. This has caused
the prophets to be viewed as social reformers, ardent social critics, and cham-
pions or advocates of the poor. Gnuse summarizes it well:

> Though prophets saw themselves as messengers of Yahweh rather than as
> spokesmen of oppressed classes in a struggle of rural poor against rich urban
> oppressors and a despotic king, their message is as virulent as any marshaled by
> modern social critics, and it has been the inspiration of modern reformers and
> social critics. The rich, powerful classes of Samaria and Jerusalem were accused
> of oppression, which defied the will of Yahweh. Prophets were advocates of the
> dispossessed and exploited against the injustices perpetrated and perpetuated by
> the wealthy. The prophets argued passionately for the benefit of the weak and
> hurled wrathful curses against the great and rich.[14]

It is evident at this point that oppression is a major cause of poverty in the
Hebrew Bible.[15] While the Former Prophets deal with the oppression of the
Canaanites and the early Israelite monarchy, the Latter Prophets are con-
fronted with the oppression of the later monarchy. While the voice of the
poor themselves remains largely silent in these texts, the Latter Prophets give
voice to these silent poor.

The Former Prophets

Joshua, Judges, 1 & 2 Samuel, 1 & 2 Kings

None of the traditional words for poverty are present in the book of Joshua. A
few scattered references appear in Judges and the books of Samuel and Kings.[16]

The first reference to a word connoting poverty occurs in Judg 6:6. The
tribe of Midian is said to have so much impoverished (*dal* דל) Israel that it

cried out to the Lord for help. The context is typical of Deuteronomic theology in which there are blessings for obedience, and curses and punishment for apostasy and disobedience (Deuteronomy 28). Thus, Israel's story in the Deuteronomistic history is a cycle of sin/apostasy, punishment, obedience, salvation, and back to sin again.[17] Because Israel has done evil before the Lord, the Lord sends Midian to punish it for seven years. The word *dal* דל here is used to refer to material lack or want due to oppression or an external force. It also has the connotation of being physically weak or less strong than the other. The story continues with the Lord's appointment of Gideon to save Israel from Midian (Judg 6:7-40). In the classic style of people called to a divine task[18] (see Exod 3:7 - 4:16; Isa 6:5-8; Jer 1:4-10), Gideon shows his reluctance by claiming that his clan is the poorest (or weakest [*dal* דל]) in Manasseh and he is the youngest one in his family (6:15). The Lord reassures him, and he goes on to defeat Midian. In light of the context, *dal* דל is used to refer to physical weakness or powerlessness, as opposed to the strength of the Midianites.

The book of Judges has a brief reference to the language of poverty. In Judg 18:10, the Sidonians are said to lack nothing (*maḥsôr* מחסור) because they are prosperous (see v. 7).[19] Thus, although *maḥsôr* מחסור usually denotes poverty or lack of something, it is used in this context to refer to the lack of poverty (or abundance of provisions) among the Sidonians. The same application of the word *maḥsôr* מחסור is used in Judg 19:19-20. In this story, the Levite tells the old man that he does not need anything; and the old man replies that he will supply whatever he needs. As in the situation above, the Levite is stressing the fact that he is not poor or needy.

The word *'ônî* עני appears in the text of 1 Sam 1:11 on the lips of Hannah, who is asking Yahweh to look upon her affliction and give her a male offspring. Judging from the context, *'ônî* עני here does not strictly refer to poverty but to the misery and suffering of a childless woman.

After the birth of Samuel, Hannah composes a song of praise for the Lord. In 1 Sam 2:7-8, three words for poverty appear, namely, *rāš* רש, *dal* דל, and *'ebyôn* אביון. These words are used in this poetic text to show contrasting situations. In v. 7 Hannah states that Yahweh sends poverty (*rāš* רש) and wealth (*'āšîr* אשיר) in as much as Yahweh humbles and exalts. In v. 8, Yahweh raises the poor (*dal* דל) from the dust and lifts the needy (*'ebyôn* אביון) from the ash heap (Ps 113:7), in order to seat them in a seat of honor with princes. These contrasting situations reflect Hannah's own situation from being childless and miserable to being fruitful and happy.

Two words for oppression, *'āšaq* עשק and *rāṣaṣ* רצץ,[20] are used in Samuel's farewell speech (1 Sam 12:3-4). In these verses, Samuel asks the people if he has oppressed (*'āšaq* עשק) or ill-treated (*rāṣaṣ* רצץ) anyone, and they reply that he has done neither of these things. Samuel is therefore an upright judge who has not done anything to impoverish anyone.

The word *rāš* רש is used in 1 Sam 18:23 with reference to David's description of himself when offered the opportunity to marry King Saul's daughter. He is reluctant to become the king's son-in-law because he is a poor man (*rāš* רש)[21] and little known. While Hertzberg remarks that David is not in a position to offer the bride-price for the king's daughter, I agree with Pleins who notes that *rāš* רש is used here to specify "political inferiority."[22] Once again, the Deuteronomistic historian uses a traditional word for poverty to describe contrasting situations. David, the warrior, is definitely not of equal status with Saul, the king.

This same sense of weakness and inferiority is communicated by the use of the word *dal* דל in 2 Sam 3:1. The conflict between David and Saul is contrasted. While David grows stronger and stronger (*ḥazaq* חזק), Saul becomes weaker and weaker (*dal* דל).

Similar usage is evident in Nathan's parable in 2 Sam 12:1-25. This text immediately follows the story of David's adultery with Bathsheba and her husband Uriah's subsequent death. In this parable, which is intended to rebuke David for his abuse of power, Nathan tells the contrasting story of two men—one rich (*'āšîr* אשיר) and one poor (*rāš* רש). The rich man takes the poor man's only lamb in order to feed his guest while refraining from slaughtering one of his many animals. In this context *'āšîr* אשיר and *rāš* רש are not so much used to describe poverty and wealth as to denote power and powerlessness. Pleins remarks that while *rāš* רש has a strong economic flavor to it here, "the purpose of the text is not to critique economic relations in the manner of the prophetic texts or the book of Job . . . rather, the text seeks to make explicit the political miscalculations of King David."[23] Again, two situations are contrasted. David is the powerful king who takes advantage of Bathsheba, just as the fictitious rich man takes advantage of the poor man.

2 Samuel 13:14 (so vv. 12, 22, 32) uses the verb root *'anh* ענה[24] to describe a contrasting situation. The context is the rape of Tamar by Amnon. Since Amnon is stronger than Tamar (*wayyeḥĕzaq mimmenāh* ויחזק ממנה), he overpowers her (*wayĕ'annehā* ויענה) and rapes her (*wayyiškab 'otāh* וישכב אתה). In this context, *'anh* ענה simply refers to Amnon's strength as compared to Tamar's vulnerability.

At the end of the Deuteronomistic history, the historian writes that after the Babylonian conquest of Jerusalem in 587/6 BCE, all of the Israelites were exiled to Babylon except the poorest of the land. These are referred to as the *dallat 'am-hā'āreṣ* דלת עם הערץ (2 Kgs 24:14) or the *dallat hā'āreṣ* דלת הערץ (2 Kgs 25:12). Chapter 25 specifies that they are left behind to work in the vineyards and fields (see Jer 40:7; 52:15, 16). This gives credence to Pleins' translation of *dal* דל as "the poor peasant farmer."[25]

It is therefore evident that in most of the usages of Hebrew words for "poverty" in the Deuteronomistic history, the writer is not primarily interested in the question of poverty per se. Instead, the writer uses these words to describe contrasting situations such as the contrast between being rich and poor, or being powerful and/or powerless. I agree with Pleins who suggests that in the Deuteronomistic history, *rāš* רש and *dal* דל "are used to stress political weakness and are not drawn on to analyze or critique the situation of the poor in their society."[26] I think this characterization is true of other usages of the words for poverty in the same literary block.

This background discussion sheds light on a few pertinent texts that shed some light on the sociological conditions of the poor in the Deuteronomistic history. I have already discussed the theory that Israel settled in Canaan by means of a social revolution against Canaanite landlords. Hoppe argues that Israel rejected Canaanite social systems which were oppressive to peasants. Moreover, Canaan waged wars which were supported by taxes levied from the peasants. The Israelites were the catalysts for the oppressed peasants to rebel against their overlords.[27] This perhaps explains why there is hardly any discussion about poverty in the books of Joshua and Judges.

Since Israel had emerged out of Egypt as a band of runaway slaves, it was familiar with a God who took the side of the weak and the oppressed. The song of Hannah (1 Sam 2:1-10) seems to reflect this understanding. Yahweh is portrayed as making some poor and others rich; moreover, Yahweh reverses the situation of the poor. According to Hoppe, "The God of Israel is the One who takes the side of the poor so that they can enjoy the full benefits of God's creative work."[28]

Once Israel settled in Canaan, perhaps its largest miscalculation was to demand a king in order to be like the surrounding nations (1 Sam 8:1-22). If Israel had revolted against Canaanite rule, then kingship would have been a step backward or an adoption of Canaanite lifestyle. This may explain Samuel's reluctance to yield to this demand and Yahweh's luke-warm approval of it. Samuel accordingly warns Israel of the oppressive nature of the kings who will rule over it (1 Sam 8:10-18; so Deut 17:14-20). As we shall see later, Samuel's warnings were realized in some of Israel's kings.

The abuses that Samuel warns about were not long in coming. The story of David and Bathsheba (2 Sam 11:1-27) illustrates how kings could easily abuse their power and privileges at the expense of their subjects. The ensuing parable of Nathan (2 Sam 12:1-25) is a strong protest against royal absolutism.[29] It clearly illustrates some of the oppressive tendencies of the monarchy.

Perhaps the most revealing incident about the oppression and injustice done to the poor is the story of Naboth's vineyard (1 Kgs 21:1-29). King Ahab desires to secure for himself Naboth's adjoining vineyard, but Naboth swears by God and refuses to sell his ancestral land (*naḥălâ* נחלה:) because Israelite law specified that land shall not be sold in perpetuity (1 Kgs 21:3; Lev 25:10, 13-17, 23-24, 34). The reason for this was "to avoid creating a permanent poor caste within Israel."[30] However, through the scheming machinations of his Phoenician wife, Queen Jezebel, the king illegally secures Naboth's land by having him falsely accused and publicly stoned to death (v. 13). The prophet Elijah appears upon the scene to pronounce judgment upon the faltering king. Ahab will die a violent death; so will his wife. Moreover, his household will face disaster.

This narrative typifies the oppressive nature of kingship and it has fueled the passions of many a critic. Bruce Malchow calls this story "a good example of social injustice in the monarchic period," and Nelson calls it "royal tyranny."[31]Norman Habel, who has identified six land ideologies in the Bible, views the story of Naboth as a case of conflicting ideologies of land, namely, royal and peasant (ancestral household).[32] Closely related to Habel's view is Ferdinand Deist's analysis of the Naboth story and its parallels to the South African situation. Deist maintains that this narrative has "*two perceptions of land ownership*: Naboth sees land as an inalienable gift from God; to Ahab it is a commercial article that can change hands."[33]

As we have seen in some of the cases noted above, poverty at this stage in Israel's history had more to do with power and oppression than lack of material goods. Commenting on the Naboth situation, Gous brings out this point clearly:

> Since the king (actually the queen) was more powerful than he [Naboth], he could use his power to dispose of Naboth in an underhand way. Hence the point at issue in this passage is political rather than economic poverty. Naboth and his followers did not suffer want because they did not have possessions; they lacked the *power* to resist the actions of the king. In addition Naboth had no right of appeal.[34]

This is very likely the case since Naboth did have an ancestral piece of land from which he could subsist. In both the story of Naboth's vineyard and David and Bathsheba, Karen Lebacqz sees what she terms "abuse of kingly power" through "deceit and violence" because the king desires something he cannot have without violating a law.[35]

A number of legends about the prophets Elijah and Elisha shed some light on the nature of poverty during the first half of the monarchical period. In 1 Kgs 17:1-7 Elijah is fed by ravens because there is a drought during the reign of King Ahab. This drought is in the context of the great "showdown" between Yahwism and Baalism in 1 Kings 17-19.

1 Kings 17:8-16, tells the story of Elijah and the widow ('iššâ 'almānâ הׇ־ אׁשׇה אלמ) of Zarephath for whom he performs a feeding miracle. When Elijah asks this woman for a little water and a morsel of bread, her reply is quite telling. It exposes her dire situation: because of the drought, she has no bread but only a little flour and a little oil for one final meal for herself and her son to eat and before starving to death.[36] When she does what Elijah requests, she is miraculously provided with enough flour and oil to last throughout the drought period. It is interesting to note that according to Iliffe's distinctions, this is one of the few instances in which structural and conjunctural poverty coincide. The fact that the widow (structural poor person) is experiencing a drought (conjunctural poverty) doubtlessly aggravates her situation. Although Elijah reverses her circumstances, he does it only for her but the prevailing conjunctural poverty atmosphere seems unabated.

A related story is told in 2 Kgs 4:1-7 concerning the prophet Elisha and a widow whom he rescues from bankruptcy. This widow, the wife of one of the members of the prophetic guild, is identified as having a dead husband and two sons. Her situation is worse than that of the widow of Zarepath: she is in debt, and a creditor is about to seize her children as debt slaves; moreover, she has *nothing* except a little oil. As we saw in the Book of the Covenant, debt slavery was practiced in ancient Israel (Exod 21:1-11; Deut 15:12-18; Lev 25:39-46; see also Jer 34:8-22; Isa 50:1; Neh 5:5; and the Code of Hammurabi, #117). When the widow obeys Elisha's instructions, she is also miraculously provided with enough oil to sell and pay off her debts, as well as to live on.

This chapter also describes a famine (another conjunctural poverty situation) in Gilgal during which Elisha makes food wholesome for a prophetic guild (2 Kgs 4:38-41). Another story describes how a hundred people are miraculously fed from only twenty loaves of barley, even leaving leftovers. These stories are connected by the theme of "life rescued from death, hope from hopelessness."[37]

The suffering of the poor does not seem to have abated even in more prosperous times. A century later, from the time of Ahab and Elijah (850 BCE) to the time of Jeroboam II and Amos (750 BCE), the poor are still suffering. We are left wondering about the effectiveness of the divine mandate.

As noted above, the time of Jeroboam II was an era of great contrasts: Israel was at the height of its success, peace, and security, yet the poor were at their nadir of poverty. In its false sense of security, Israel looked forward to the eschatological Day of the Lord[38] as a day of salvation, but the prophets reversed this expectation and proclaimed it as a day of doom and disaster. The prophets of the eighth century appear on the scene at this time and criticize the rampant oppression of the poor. This suggests that Israel had strayed far from its responsibility toward the poor.

The Latter Prophets

Although the prophetic books are arranged in the Hebrew Bible starting with the Major Prophets, that is not necessarily their chronological order. While Isaiah begins the series, the minor prophet Amos is in fact chronologically first. My analysis does not follow the exact order of the prophets but begins with the Minor Prophets.

The Minor Prophets

Of the twelve Minor Prophets (regarded as one book in the Hebrew Bible), I will focus on two representative prophets of the eighth century BCE, namely Amos and Micah. The choice of these two prophets is rather obvious—they have more to say about the situation of the poor than the rest of the Minor Prophets.

Amos

The prophet Amos[39] came from the small rural town of Tekoa, a few miles south of Jerusalem in Judah. He uttered his prophetic oracles in Israel in the north. Amos prophesied in the middle of the eighth century BCE.[40] He was a sheep breeder (*bôqēr* בוקר) and a dresser of sycamore trees (*bôlēs* בולס [7:14]). As such, he was "a man of some reputation and substance."[41] Wilson argues that Amos was "a government employee" or "a member of the Judean upper classes, if he was not actually a part of the political or religious establishments in Jerusalem."[42] However, Victor Matthews argues that Amos had "no 'establishment' credentials."[43] Judging from his oracles and their impact on his audience, Amos seems to have been "a gifted" and passionate speaker.[44]

Amos was "a very angry prophet"[45] and has often been called the prophet of doom because of his devastating and relentless attacks on Israel's socio-economic sins.[46] For his message to achieve maximum effect, Amos begins his oracles by attacking Israel's surrounding nations for their oppressive misdeeds—Damascus, Gaza, Tyre, Edom, Ammon, and Moab. With shocking effect, Amos unexpectedly criticizes Israel for *its* sins. The rest of his oracles are directed against Israel. It is therefore no coincidence that the prophet who is prophesying in Israel ends the attack by criticizing Israel itself. Thus, he gets into conflict with Amaziah, the priest of Bethel, and is expelled (7:10-17).

Of the various Hebrew words for poverty, Amos uses three significant ones, namely, *'ebyôn* אביון, *dal* דל, and *'ănāwîm* ענוים.[47] From the distribution of these words, it is clear that Amos uses them nearly in the same context and place. In fact, all three words are used in 2:6-7 in the context of economic injustice. Bennett has argued that the *'ebyôn* was the "victim of crimes in the economic sphere," the *dal* was the "target of fraud" and "extortion" while the *'ănāwîm* was "a peasant who experienced some type of injustice in the North."[48]

Amos begins his oracles with the words, "Thus says Yahweh," the so-called messenger formula.[49] In his oracles against Israel, Amos criticizes the people "because they sell the righteous (*ṣaddîq* צדיק) for silver, and the needy (*'ebyôn* אביון) for a pair of sandals" (2:6; NRSV). In this verse *ṣaddîq* צדיק and *'ebyôn* אביון are used as parallel expressions, but they are not synonymous. Rather, they are used in a complimentary sense.[50] Scholars have shown that the *'ebyôn* אביון are not necessarily righteous but rather "innocent." Wolff argues that the above expression refers to the sale of the innocent into debt-slavery on account of the silver owed to the creditor (see Exod 21:7-8; Lev 25:39; Deut 14:12). The *ṣaddîq* צדיק are "guiltless" before the law. The reference to sandals suggests a paltry or insignificant debt for which people were being enslaved. This is likely the case, and it strengthens the problem referred to here.[51] Andersen and Freedman are not sure if the reference to sandals was a proverbial bribe or merely a symbol of a paltry sum. So they provide four possible explanations of this verse. The expression may mean the sale of the righteous poor for a paltry sum such as the value of sandals; there is a possible relationship between the sale of a person and the price for the sale; the pair of sandals may be seen as a bribe (though meager) paid to the judge for a favorable verdict; or the reference is a description of debt-slavery which Amos criticizes. For a trivial debt, harsh leaders and rapacious creditors are forcing the innocent poor into debt slavery. Amos does not criticize the principle but the practice of debt-slavery.[52]

A different interpretation of this verse has been proposed by Shalom Paul. He finds the above interpretations problematic because of the use of the expression *nā'ălāyim* נעלים ("a pair of sandals"). He argues that this expression is not used anywhere else in the Bible to symbolize a paltry sum. Its use here in Amos makes it a *hapax legomenon* whose singular noun *(n'lm* נעלם *)*, derived from the root *'lm* עלם ("to hide"), was confused with the dual or plural form *nā'ălāyim* נעלים ("sandals"), and was repointed with "the final *mem* being mistakenly understood as the masculine plural suffix rather than the third radical of the stem."[53] He therefore translates the verse thus: "Because they have sold for silver the innocent, and the needy for a hidden gain." While Paul's interpretation is thought-provoking, I agree with the view of the majority of scholars given the overall context of Amos' criticisms. It makes sense that Israel's creditors are so heartless that even for the smallest of debts, they are willing further to impoverish a helpless debtor.

Verse 7 focuses on the oppression and abuse of the poor (*dal* דל). Here scholars agree that the expression to "trample the head of the poor into the dust of the earth," refers to the rights of the poor which are trampled upon and crushed as if they were dust upon the ground.[54] The parallel expression, to "push the afflicted (*'ănāwîm* ענוים) out of the way," also refers to justice denied to the poor in the law courts. Mays correctly points out that "the courts are being used to oppress the poor instead of to maintain *mišpāṭ*."[55]

Some scholars have interpreted 2:7c to mean the immorality of cultic prostitution. Others see it as a reference to a father and son having sexual relations with the same slave girl (Exod 21:8). In any case, Amos is attacking immoral behavior possibly involving women sold for a debt.[56]

Verse 8 denounces behavior that is inconsistent with the letter of the law. While most commentators believe that this verse refers to "garments taken in pledge" (see Deut 24:12-13, 17), Shalom Paul argues that the reference is to "the confiscation of clothing as distraint for an unpaid debt."[57] According to Exod 22:26-27 (see also Deut 24:12-13, 17), a garment taken in pledge was to be returned by nightfall, as a source of warmth. In fact, a widow's garment was not supposed to be taken at all (Deut 24:17). For Matthews, the poor were not to be "reduced to the indignity of naked slaves."[58] Scholars generally agree that the reference to wine means payment of a debt in kind.[59] While laws regarding debt were designed to protect the poor, their violation only served further to victimize those who were already in distressful situations. Thus, Paul concludes that "Amos deplores and denounces actions that go beyond the actual prescriptions of the law."[60]

The rest of chapter 2 (vv. 9-16) states how Yahweh destroyed the Amorites despite their strength. These verses warn Israel of the fate awaiting it because of its disobedience.

Destruction shall be the fate not only of the people but also of their acquisitions. Amos shows the level of injustice and inequality by referring to the summer and winter houses—symbols of luxury at the expense of the poor—which shall be destroyed. Some scholars think they were separate houses in different places because of the extreme temperatures during the two seasons. Others believe these were two dwellings within one house, or a two-storied house (see 1 Kgs 21:1, 18; 22:39; Jer 36:22; Ps 45:8). Another symbol of the indulgence and decadence of the rich were the "houses of ivory," or "luxury manor houses whose walls and furniture were adorned and decorated with ivory."[61]

The oracle in Amos 4:1-3 continues the theme of the oppression and exploitation of the poor. Amos refers to his audience as "you cows of Bashan." Their crime is that they oppress (*'āšaq* עשק) the poor (*dallîm* דלים) and crush (*rāṣaṣ* רצץ) the needy (*'ebyôn* אביון).[62] The concentration of the vocabulary of oppression and the language of poverty in the same verse heightens the sense of injustice experienced by the poor and powerless.

Scholars are torn about who exactly is addressed in these verses. The Hebrew does not help because the grammar in this passage is too convoluted. Both masculine and feminine forms are mixed:

> Hear (2d. m. pl.) this word
> You cows (f. pl.) of Bashan
> . . . .
> Saying (f. pl.) to their (m. pl.) lord(s)
> "Bring (m. s.) that we may drink!"
> . . . .
> When they will take you (m. pl.) away with grappling hooks,
> And your (f. pl.) rear guard with fishhooks.[63]

Most commentators believe that the upper-class women of Samaria are being referred to here. Bashan, to the east of the Sea of Galilee, was known for its rich pastures, timber, and fine cattle (Deut 32:14; Ps 22:12; Ezek 39:18). Because Bashan was "a hallmark of quality," Mays argues that the imagery of women as cows "was not in itself an insult."[64] Limburg thinks this figure of speech was hardly a compliment.[65] Wolff sees it as "a shocking term of abuse" and Paul sees it as introducing "an element of surprise."[66] In the same way, some scholars have assigned responsibility for the crimes to women while others have assigned it to both sexes. Even though the Hebrew in this passage is not perfect, I agree with the latter group of scholars. Although the image of women seems to stand out prominently in this passage, a closer reading shows that the men are equally to blame for actions that further impoverish the poor.[67] Thus Amos proclaims that the perpetrators of such injustices shall be removed from their comfortable positions with fishhooks.

Amos continues to explore the theme of the exploitation of the poor in 5:10-12. The people's iniquities continue to mount, and justice and righteousness are perverted (5:7). Verse 10 notes that the one who sits at the gate or who speaks the truth is hated. Traditionally, the gate of the city "was the spot where public legal hearings took place and where justice was administered."[68] Not only is the judicial process undermined, the poor (*dal* דל) are further exploited by the rich who take away the meager food that they have. This is done in the form of a tax, rent, or interest on a loan.[69] The punishment for such behavior is that those who have built magnificent houses shall not dwell in them, neither shall they enjoy their cultivated wine.

The intensity of Israel's sins is heightened in v. 12. The judicial system, which is supposed to protect the poor, stands accused. The judges themselves afflict (*ṣārar* צרר) the righteous and accept bribes (*kōper* כֹּפֶר); the needy (*'ebyôn* אביון) are denied justice in the gate of justice.[70] The only way that Israel can save itself is by seeking good rather than evil and establishing justice in the gate (5:14-15).

Amos attempts to give Israel a sense of reality by shattering the people's expectation of the Day of the Lord. Israel had perceived this day as a day of salvation, but Amos reverses this expectation by stressing that it is a day of darkness and gloom. None can escape from it (5:18-20). Even fervent religious practices will be to no avail unless the people do justice (v. 21). This theme of doing what is right appears in the most central verse in the book of Amos:

> But let justice [*mišpāṭ* מֹשׁפֹּט] roll down like
> waters,
> and righteousness [*ṣĕdāqâ* צדקה] like an
> everflowing stream (5:24; NRSV).

According to Temba L. J. Mafico, the call for justice "does not solely refer to moral norm, but also refers to basic human rights."[71] The poor and powerless were being denied their God-given rights. Again, Mafico states, "True worship of Yahweh was not to consist solely of acts of ritualistic practices, but was to be manifested in *mišpāṭ*, that is, a state of harmonious relationship among people."[72] Paul puts it succinctly: "The proper divine-human relationship is based upon a correct human-human relationship."[73]

Such a relationship, however, was lacking in the Israel of Amos' time. The difference between the rich and the poor was a glaring picture of inequality. While the destitute peasants could not even afford to pay a small debt, the rich were wallowing in luxury and comfortable lifestyles. Amos paints such a picture in 6:4-6. It is what Paul refers to as a "marvelous satire of their comfortable, indulgent life style."[74] The rich lie on ivory-inlaid beds, recline on comfortable couches, and eat choice meats; moreover, they enjoy cultivated music and drink the finest of wines.

This merry scene shall not last, for the revelers shall go into exile (6:7). Their crime: they have turned justice into poison and the fruit of righteousness into wormwood (a poisonous and bitter fruit [6:12; see also Deut 29:17; 32:24]). Such a perversion of justice shall not go unpunished: Yahweh will let the self-confident nation taste the fruit of its own oppression (6:13-14).

Chapter 7 begins the book of visions of judgment upon a disobedient people. In his criticism of Israel, Amos spares no one. Even the King (Jeroboam II) is indicted and given such a devastating sentence that Amos is banned from prophesying in Israel ever again. Yet Amos stands his ground and continues to prophesy doom upon the King and the nation. For example, the vision of a basket of summer fruit (*qayiṣ* קָיִץ) forebodes the end (*qeṣ* קֵץ) of Israel, a marvelous pun in the Hebrew (8:1-2).[75]

Amos ends his accusations against Israel as he began (8:4-6; see 2:6-7). This inclusio recounts the basic themes of the book and thus brings it to its logical conclusion. Amos continues his attack upon Israel, this time focusing on its corrupt business practices which are detrimental to the survival of the poor.

The final indictment of Israel is delivered in very familiar vocabulary. Amos targets those who trample (*haššō'ăpîm* הַשֹּׁאֲפִים [8:4; cf. 2:6; 5:11]) upon the needy ('*ebyôn* אֶבְיוֹן [2:7—*dal* דַּל]) and ruin the poor of the land ('*ăniwwê-'āreṣ* עֲנָוֵי אֶרֶץ [cf. 2:7—'*ănāwîm* עֲנָוִים]). He also includes those who buy (*qānâ* קָנָה) the poor (*dallîm* דַּלִּים) for silver (*késep* כֶּסֶף) and the needy ('*ebyôn* אֶבְיוֹן) for a pair of sandals (8:6). This expression is reversed in 2:6. There Amos indicts those who sell (*mākar* מָכַר) the righteous (*ṣaddîq* צַדִּיק) for silver (*késep* כֶּסֶף), and the needy ('*ebyôn* אֶבְיוֹן) for a pair of sandals.[76]

As in Amos 2:6, the context of 8:6 is that of debt-slavery. Andersen and Freedman argue that Amos is not criticizing the price of the slave (which would have been higher) but "the amount of money for which the righteous poor are being sold to satisfy the debt."[77] In their haste to engage in unethical business practices, the people wish for festivals like the Sabbath (see Exod 23:12; 34:21; 20:8) to be over soon. They plot to use false measures and balances for their own gain. Because they rig the scales, "The unwitting customer pays more than he should for his goods."[78]

Such corrupt business dealings were rampant in eighth-century Israel and Bennett sees it as a symbol of the exploitation and impoverishment of the masses of peasants. Thus Amos denounces the injustices suffered by this lower socio-economic subgroup.[79] Mays argues that the situation portrayed by Amos is relatively new in Israel. In the older peasant society, people owned land and were fairly autonomous. As a result, buying and selling or the exchange of money played a minor role. The monarchy changed things:

> The rise of urban culture under the monarchy led to the development of commerce and an economic upper class. As more and more small farmers were pressed off their land and forced to shift to service and labour, their dependence upon the market became acute. The urban merchants appear to have monopolized the market; they were able to sell to landless peasants at a high price. They had the resources for stockpiling grain, and in a time of poor crops were in a position to control the economy completely . . . Amos applies to this new situation the old norms of the covenant. What appeared to be progress and good business to the merchants was in his eyes disobedience to Yahweh.[80]

Dishonesty in buying and selling was also criticized by other eighth-century prophets. Hosea (12:7) and Micah (6:9-11) both denounced the practice. In fact,

Israelite law called for just weights and measures by forbidding one to own different sets of scales (Deut 25:13-16; Lev 19:35-37). Wisdom literature also focuses on the same issue (Prov 11:1; 16:11; 20:10, 23).

This concern for fairness in business dealings was also a concern of the ancient Near East in general. Chapter 16 of the Instruction of Amen-em-opet reads as follows:

> Do not *lean on* the scales nor falsify the weights,
> Nor damage the fractions of the measure.
> Do not wish for a (common) country measure,
> And neglect those of the treasury.
> The ape [Thoth, god of just measure] sits beside the balance,
> And his heart is the plummet.
> . . . .
> Make not for thyself weights which are deficient;
> They *abound in grief* through the will of god.[81]

Thus, Amos merely echoes a long-standing tradition of early Israel which has its roots in the cultural milieu of the ancient Near East. Amos' clamor for justice is therefore a call for "a fair deal from the merchants."[82]

Yahweh vows to punish Israel because of its misdeeds (8:7-14). Amos 9:8b, widely viewed as a secondary redaction or a later interpolation,[83] is regarded by others as an original clause that expresses the quality of Yahweh's mercy.[84] Despite this shift, it is clear that the book of Amos severely criticizes the oppression and abuse of the poor. Limburg eloquently expresses the double-standard in Israel's life that Amos' prophetic word rejects:

> Religion, it [Amos' word] says, has to do with the whole of life, holy day and holy place, but also every day and every place. It also compels its hearers to examine their attitude toward possessions and wealth, with a reminder that in the ancient church one of the seven deadly sins was greed.[85]

The foregoing discussion leaves no doubt as to why Amos is often called the champion of the poor. His prophecy is "an uncompromising attack on the social evils of the 8th century in Israel."[86] His God is a God of justice. According to Schottroff,

> The God of Amos is not the defender of the political and social system, as the Israel of that age thought him to be, or of its questionable "achievements." Rather he refuses it any permanence and even any right to permanence. The God of Amos is the God of the lowly, the victims who were crushed without pity in the economic machinery of the Israel of that age.[87]

Amos therefore seems to be aware of Israel's ancient covenantal traditions. He reveals the plight of the poor who are also mentioned in Israel's legal texts. For him, poverty is something caused and perpetuated by human actions. In his vision of social justice, such actions shall not go unpunished.

Micah

The prophet Micah[88] was an exact contemporary of First Isaiah or Isaiah of Jerusalem. He was from Moresheth-Gath (1:1, 14), a rural town about twenty-five miles southwest of Jerusalem. He prophesied during the days of Jotham (750-735 BCE), Ahaz (735-715 BCE) and Hezekiah (715-687 BCE), kings of Judah. A precise date is difficult to determine but scholars generally date Micah's prophetic activity from before 722 to about 701 BCE.[89]

Micah may have begun prophesying in his home town but probably ended up in Jerusalem where he did most of his speaking.[90] Micah spoke with the passion of Amos, but his language (for example, see 3:1-3) is said to be coarser than that of any other prophet.[91] Unlike Amos, Micah does not use any of the traditional words for "poor" or "poverty," but his rhetoric indicates that he has them in mind. Micah has been called "a revolutionary."[92]

Micah begins his prophecy by directing threatening indictments against Israel and Judah because of their transgressions. These transgressions become more specific as Micah continues to deliver his oracles.

Chapter 2 spells doom for those who devise evil deeds. The theme of covetousness dominates the text. According to the Ten Commandments (Exod 20:17; see also 34:24; Deut 28:32; Josh 7:21), coveting someone else's property was forbidden. Yet here the people are accused of coveting (*ḥāmad* חמד) fields and houses and seizing (*gāzal* גזל) them. In addition, they oppress (*'āšaq* עשק) the householder and deprive people of their inheritance (*naḥălâ* נחלה , [Micah 2:1-2; see Lev 5:21; 19:3; Deut 24:14]). The language used here betrays acts performed by force and violence. Mays correctly points out that:

> The powerful are expropriating the property of small landowners through oppression. The engine which drives the enterprise is covetousness, breaking the instruction of YHWH to his people: 'You shall not covet your neighbour's house(hold).'[93]

By acting in this selfish manner, those accused violate some of the fundamental laws of ancient Israel which protected the poor and powerless.

In 2:8-9 Micah apparently directs his oracles to the rich who oppress the poor. From the reference to stripping the robe (2:8), Hillers suggests that perhaps "the rich had seized garments taken in pledge (Amos 2:6), and robbed widows' houses."[94] Indeed an unpleasant picture is painted. The women are driven out of their pleasant houses, which leaves children without support. Mays argues that these children are left in poverty with no future but slavery and servitude.[95]

In chapter 3 Micah directs his oracles to the "heads of Jacob" and rulers of the house of Israel. These are public officials who are indicted for their injustice. He describes their actions and conduct "with a metaphor that is both coarse and shocking."[96] They hate good and love evil. Their deeds are shown to be violently cannibalistic acts. They tear (*gāzal* גזל) the skin off the bones of their victims and eat it; they break their bones and boil them up (3:1-3). By using such repulsive language, Micah intends to heighten the utterly helpless situation of those who are victimized by the powerful officials in Jerusalem.

The same addressees (as in 3:1) are envisioned by Micah in 3:9. The theme is justice, of which the prophet himself is the greatest example (3:8). The rulers of Jerusalem are accused of perverting justice (3:9) when in fact they are expected to uphold and enforce it. Under them, Jerusalem knows no equity, for the city is built with blood and wrongdoing. Everyone seeks after profit. Judges, priests, and prophets all perform their services for financial gain. Mays refers to them as "the triad of greed."[97] Justice is perverted when the goal is money rather than services. Their complacency and ignorance are evident in their mistaken belief that Yahweh is with them and no harm shall come to them (v. 11). Because of their perversion of justice, Micah prophesies that "Jerusalem shall become a heap of ruins" (3:12).

Micah presents a different picture in chapter 4—it is a vision of hope, peace, and restoration. In fact 4:1-3 is so similar to Isa 2:2-4 that scholars have suggested some form of literary dependence.[98]

In this vision of hope, God is at the center as judge of the nations (4:1, 3).[99] In this role Yahweh will assemble the lame and preserve them as a remnant. Those driven away and afflicted will be made into a strong nation. This eschatological passage recalls the reversal of the fate of those victims Micah spoke about in his earlier oracles. Micah uses the imagery of a woman in labor (4:9-10, 5:3) to illustrate the pain and suffering Israel must first undergo before its restoration.

The heart of Micah's teaching about justice is contained in 6:6-8. The worshipper asks, "With what shall I come before the Lord?" (6:6). He or she recites possible answers to this question, in what Limburg refers to as a "step-by-step escalation."[100] It is clear that Yahweh does not want burnt offerings of any kind, either animal or human (see Lev 22:27; 1 Chron 29:21; 1 Kgs 3:4; Exod 29:40; Gen 22). The answer comes in verse 8, in the third person:

> He has told you, O mortal, what
> is good;

and what does the Lord require
of you
but to do justice, and to love
kindness,
and to walk humbly with your
God (NRSV).

This famous passage is the crown of Micah's teaching. Like Amos 5:24, Micah calls for the worshipper to *do* justice. In previous oracles, Micah reported on the lack of justice because of oppression and exploitation of the poor and powerless (2:1-2, 8-9; 3:1-3, 9-11). Limburg notes: "To do justice means to work for the establishment of equity for all, especially for the powerless."[101]

Micah also exhorts the hearer to love kindness. Loving kindness (*hésed* חסד) is a theme of the prophet Hosea. It has been variously translated as "steadfast love" or "loyalty" (see Hos 6:4, 6). According to Mays, *hésed* חסד is "based on the kindness and mutuality which recognizes the needy and responds in brotherly identification."[102]

The final element God requires is walking humbly with one's God. The image of walking together implies proximity, communion, and association. Doing justice, loving kindness, and walking with one's God are *actions* that require a proper relationship between one and one's fellow beings, as well as one and one's God. Micah may well have been thinking of the divine mandate about how to treat the vulnerable members of his society in order to establish a proper relationship with God.

The prophet returns to the theme of justice by pointing out unethical business practices (6:10-12). As we saw in Amos, merchants are using false measures and weights to defraud buyers (6:11; Amos 8:5; Hos 12:7-9), a practice specifically prohibited by Israelite law and ancient Near Eastern laws in general. The wealthy acquire their wealth through violence and other dishonest means (6:12). Clearly, such practices only serve to worsen the condition of the poor or those without power or economic clout. Yahweh promises stern action against the offenders (6:13-16) by reversing their fortunes and reducing them to poverty.

Micah ends his prophecy by recounting a familiar theme. He bemoans the perversion of justice and the ubiquity of sin (7:2-6). The faithful have disappeared from the land and no one left is upright. He specifies the evils that exist: thirst for blood; the corruption of the judicial system; and the misuse of authority by the powerful. In all these actions, justice is perverted. No one can be trusted, not even a loved one or family member. Micah uses the image of gleaning to show his frustration (7:1). Like a poor gleaner, he cannot find any gleanings, although the law dictated that something had to be left behind for him (Lev 19:9-10; 23:22; Deut 24:19-21, Ruth 2 - 3). Hillers correctly observes: "Implicit in the picture of a frustrated, hungry gleaner is an accusation of injustice and lack of pity."[103] Despite Israel's sins of injustice, Micah ends his oracles by portraying a compassionate God who will save Jacob-Israel.

It is therefore clear that Micah, like Amos, is passionate about social justice. His criticism of Israel's sins is unrestrained, and he lodges it in very graphic language. Although he does not use the traditional words for poverty like Amos and other prophets, it can hardly be doubted that he has the poor in mind. These poor persons are exemplified by victims of injustice: those who had their fields and houses seized; those who lost family members and inheritances; those who were literally dismembered by the system; victims of the legal system; and those who were victimized by greedy merchants. In very precise terms, Micah (and Amos) spells out paradigms that constitute God-pleasing behavior.[104]

The Major Prophets

This section discusses two representative major prophetic books, namely, Isaiah[105] and Jeremiah. The authors of these two books follow closely in the footsteps of Amos and Micah.

Isaiah

Traditional Isaian scholarship in the form of form-criticism and the historical-critical method has tended to dissect the book of Isaiah into two or three parts.[106] While moving away from single authorship for Isaiah 1 - 66, such scholarship has tended to do so without much regard for unifying elements within these respective parts of Isaiah. The common divisions of the book, based on historical epochs (the dominance of Assyria, Babylon, and Persia) and certain theological motifs are: First Isaiah (or Isaiah of Jerusalem [1 - 39]); Second Isaiah (or Deutero-Isaiah [40 - 55]); and Third-Isaiah (or Trito-Isaiah [56 - 66]).[107] Conrad explains that the problem with focusing on the "three Isaiahs" is that "the Book of Isaiah was understood to be a collection having no coherence of thought and no unity giving shape to the whole."[108]

Recent Isaiah scholarship has, however, tended to move in new directions.[109] Scholars are increasingly treating the book of Isaiah as a redactional and literary unity. They contend that although multiple authorship underlies the entire scroll of Isaiah, "Isaian unity does not require sole authorship by the prophet Isaiah."[110] Instead, scholars are seeking and finding "unity and coherence" in what Rolf Rendtorff calls the "reciprocal relationships" between the literary blocks of First, Second, and Third Isaiah.[111] Such unity and coherence

are evident in the following characteristics of the book: there is only one superscription (Isa 1:1), "the vision of Isaiah," for the entire book; there is only
one clear commissioning of First Isaiah (Isa 6:1-13, cf. 40:1-11 and 61:1-11);
the literary boundaries between the three parts of Isaiah are not marked in
any special way; and there are recurring literary and theological themes and
motifs, such as references to "former and latter things," the "servant," and
"Zion/Jerusalem."[112]

This sense of Isaian unity and the continuity of themes and motifs is most
evident when Isaiah is read in a "sequential" manner rather than on a "pericope by pericope basis."[113] Darr has unrolled the scroll of Isaiah by means
of "diachronic and synchronic approaches," informed by "a reader-oriented
method." Through this methodology, she explores child and female imagery
and the "rhetoric of rebellion," and shows how these are interconnected in
the entire scroll of Isaiah. These devices contribute to the reader's "sequential
construal of Isaiah as a coherent literary work."[114] In light of these arguments,
I now proceed to discuss the subject of poverty in Isaiah as if I were unrolling
the entire scroll of Isaiah.

First Isaiah (or Isaiah of Jerusalem) was a contemporary of Micah and
Hosea, and he prophesied under the following Judean kings: Uzziah, Jotham,
Ahaz, and Hezekiah (Isa 1:1; 6:1). Scholars believe he prophesied intermit-
tently from 742-701 BCE or even later.[115] Wilson believes that First Isaiah was
"an upper-class Jerusalemite who was part of the city's central social structure
but not necessarily a part of its religious establishment."[116] While Isaian oracles
were largely directed to Judah and Jerusalem, scholars believe that Second and
Third Isaiah prophesied at the time of the Babylonian exile and return. No biographical information is known about Second or Third Isaiah.

Like Amos and Micah, the book of Isaiah is also concerned with social
justice. This concern is evident in the criticism of social injustice, usage of
the traditional words for the poor, references to vulnerable people, and the use
of the language of oppression.

The words *'ebyôn* אביון, *dal* דל, and *'ānî* עני appear in the oracles in Isaiah
with *'ānî* עני / *'ănāwîm* ענוים appearing most prominently.[117] The book also
makes references to the widow and fatherless.[118] Moreover, it uses words that
indicate oppression or exploitation.[119] I will proceed to analyze the context and
usage of these words in order to determine their meaning in the book of Isaiah.

Isaiah begins with oracles which call for Judah to seek justice, do what is
good, and shun evil (1:17-18). The book also calls for the protection of the
widow and fatherless, groups that were traditionally vulnerable.[120] In Isaiah,
criticism is directed at the corrupt princes who accept bribes and illegal gifts
instead of defending the widow and fatherless (v. 23). Yahweh is portrayed
as the judge of the elders and princes (3:14-15) who brings a case (*rîb* ריב)

against them. They are charged with oppressing (*nāgaš* נגש) the poor (*'ānî* עני). Isaiah condemns:

> Their exploitation of their own people, probably through excessive interest, land foreclosures, debt slavery, and the use of the apparatus of government to fill their own coffers.[121]

Thus, the enforcers of the law are charged with being the worst offenders. The poor in this context are those who depend on the land for their survival.

In Isa 5:1-7, the parable of the vineyard is used to illustrate how the people of Israel and Judah have failed to meet Yahweh's expectations. This is clearly illustrated by a play on words in verse 7:

> He expected justice [*mišpāṭ* משפט],
> but saw bloodshed [*miśpāh* משפה];
> righteousness [*ṣĕdāqâ* צדקה],
> but heard a cry [*ṣĕ'āqâ* צעקה]! (NRSV)

Obviously, the nation as a whole has yielded bitter fruit.

Isaiah 5:8-10 attacks those who join "house to house" and "field to field." This refers to the practice of latifundia or land accumulation in the hands of a few rich landowners at the expense of the peasantry. This obviously worsens the situation of those who depend on the land. D. N. Premnath writes:

> The opulence of the rich is achieved at the expense of the poor. The consequence of all the aspects of latifundialization is the steady deprivation and impoverishment of the peasantry.[122]

The problem of latifundia also appears in other eighth-century prophets: Amos, Hosea, and Micah.

Chapter 5 continues with more "woes" attacking those who, because of strong drink, acquit the guilty for a bribe and deprive the innocent of their rights (5:22-23). Isaiah foresees the coming of a messianic prince of Davidic descent who will establish justice and righteousness and uphold the rights of the poor (*dal* דל and *'ānî* עני [9:6-7; 11:1-9]).

Isaiah also brings an interesting perspective: none is exempt from judgment, not even the poor. Yahweh refuses to show compassion to widows and the fatherless who are evil-doers (9:17). In fact, those who love pleasure shall be made widows and childless (47:8-9).

The poor (*dal* דל and *'ānî* עני), the widow, and the fatherless are the subjects of Isa 10:1-4. They are presented in a vulnerable position in which their rights are abused. The accused exploit their economic power and social standing to the disadvantage of the insignificant and peripheral members of society.[123] As a result, Yahweh will punish Israel and Judah through the agency of a foreign nation like Assyria (10:5-6).

Isaiah 14 envisions a period of restoration for Israel, possibly after the Babylonian exile. Yahweh will have compassion on the people. A sign of their prosperity will be the resident aliens and slaves residing among them (14:1-2; see Lev 25:44, 47). The former oppressors will be the new oppressed. Here Isaiah uses the term *nāgaš* נגש in a "song of derision" to mock the fate of Babylon.[124] Isaiah makes reference to the *'ānî* עני, *dallîm* דלים, and *'ebyôn* אביון in 14:30-32. The context is the death of the Assyrian King, Tiglath-pileser III. The oracle itself is a warning against Philistine cities, instructing them not to rejoice at the death of a former oppressor. The reason for mentioning these groups of the poor is not entirely clear but the implication is a change of fortune for the formerly poor, oppressed, and landless people.[125] These people shall be prosperous and safe while the Philistines shall die of famine.

In a hymn of thanksgiving, the words *dal* דל and *'ebyôn* אביון are paired, but the context and usage indicate that these words do not refer to economic poverty as such (25:4-5). In fact, the reference is to those who have been oppressed, dominated, or simply those without power. The key word is *ṣārar* צרר, which means to "bind, tie up, be restricted, narrow, scant, cramped."[126] Yahweh has been a fortress for those in distress or simply the oppressed. The same situation is envisioned in Isa 26:6, where a city is defeated and trampled upon (*rāmas* רמס) by the feet of the *'ānî* עני and the *dallîm* דלים. Again, the context shows that these words for "poor" are really used to refer to formerly oppressed or liberated subjects who are now rejoicing.

The *'ănāwîm* ענוים and *'ebyônê 'adam* אביוני אדם are paired in Isa 29:19. Both shall rejoice and exult in the Lord. The preceding and succeeding verses deal with the issue of reversal of fortune (29:18, 20-21). While the meek and neediest rejoice, the perpetrators of injustice shall be cut off. The word *'ānî* עני seems to have a religious connotation in 66:2. According to Edward J. Young, *'ănāwîm* ענוים and *'ebyônê 'adam* אביוני אדם in Isa 29:19 bear "a secondary connotation of piety."[127]

The *'ănāwîm* ענוים and *'ebyôn* אביון are also shown to be victims of those who devise evil deeds (32:7). In a chapter that focuses on justice and righteousness (vv. 1, 16-17), evil-doers are portrayed as heartless people who victimize those who are in the right. The poor plead in vain because of lies devised by those who are evil.

A new context for *'ănāwîm* ענוים and *'ebyôn* אביון is evident in Isa 41:17. Here the reference is simply to those who are thirsty and in search of water. In their calamity, Yahweh will answer them.[128] In fact vv. 18-20 proceed to explain how Yahweh makes water plentiful so that Israel may see the magnitude of this divine act.

Toward its end, the book of Isaiah tends to focus more on Israel's oppression at the hands of its neighbors (48:9-10; 49:17, 26; 51:13-14, 22-25; 52:4). Yahweh is shown as the liberator from such oppression (*nigaš* נגשׂ [53:7]) and injustice (53:8). Part of Israel's restoration shall be the lack of oppression *'ōšeq* עשׁק [54:14]).

In order to establish the right relationship with God, Israel needs to perform "action directed towards human beings," rather than paying attention to ritual.[129] This can be done by loosening the bonds of injustice, freeing the oppressed (*rĕṣûṣîm* רצוצים), sharing food with the hungry (*'ănāwîm* ענוים), and housing the homeless (58:6-8). The salvation of the nation is, however, delayed. McKenzie claims that in chapter 59, the author "returns to the classic answer of prophecy. Neither weakness nor hostility in Yahweh is responsible for present conditions; it is sin and only sin which delays the arrival of salvation."[130] God, the God of justice (61:8), will see to it that justice is done to all the victims of injustice.

The preceding discussion highlights Isaiah's concern for the fate of the poor and oppressed through his use of words for the poor and poverty in a variety of ways. Like other eighth-century prophets Isaiah has a strong focus on the social and economic dimensions of poverty. Isaiah's basic message repeats "the familiar themes of social justice, the obligation to aid and not oppress the weak" because this is "what the covenant had stipulated as the basic requirement for life with God."[131] The book of Isaiah also expands its concept of poverty to include victims of the political and chaotic period during which this book was composed.

Jeremiah

The prophet Jeremiah[132] came from the village of Anathoth, about four miles northeast of Jerusalem. He was descended from a priestly family (Jer 1:1). Jeremiah directed his oracles to Judah and Jerusalem. His prophetic activity covered the years of Josiah, Jehoiakim, Jehoiachin, and Zedekiah, kings of Judah. Some scholars believe that he began prophesying in 627/6 BCE, but others think this was the year of his birth.[133] In any case, his recorded activity lasted beyond the fall of Jerusalem in 587/6 BCE, which makes him one of the longest serving Israelite prophets. After the Babylonian deportation, Jeremiah is said to have fled to Egypt (Jeremiah 42 - 43) where he presumably died.

According to Wilson, Jeremiah functioned as a peripheral prophet with respect to the people and the Jerusalemite establishment.[134] Jeremiah was probably a person of means, since he managed to purchase his own piece of land (chap. 32). Moreover, he was "independent enough financially to be able to afford his own scribe, from 609 onwards."[135]

Like Amos, Micah, and Isaiah, Jeremiah's oracles indicate that he was also concerned about the divine mandate for Israel. This concern is evident in his use of words traditionally indicating poverty, his advocacy for vulnerable persons, and the language of oppression.[136]

Jeremiah first refers to the poor (*'ebyônîm* אביונים) in an oracle that criticizes Israel for its sins (2:34). Scholars generally agree that *'ebyônîm* אביונים, which does not appear in the Septuagint, is a gloss that otherwise overloads a phrase about the murder of the innocent.[137] However, it is important to note that this crime does not go unpunished by Yahweh, the defender of such victims (2:35).

The next reference to the *'ebyônîm* אביונים occurs in Jer 5:28. The chapter generally details the sins of a nation for which it shall be punished. Jeremiah accuses the Judeans of a range of evils. Their households are full of treachery (v. 27), making them great (*gādôl* גדול) and rich (*'āšîr* אשיר). Part of their misdeeds is not defending the rights of the needy (*'ebyônîm* אביונים). Thus, the poor are not only contrasted with the rich, they are also victims of the injustice perpetrated by the rich.

Jeremiah 20:13 refers to the needy as the *'ebyôn* אביון. Although this verse is regarded as a secondary addition,[138] it nevertheless portrays them as victims of evildoers. In addition, Yahweh is shown as the savior and deliverer of such victims.

The last reference to the *'ebyôn* אביון occurs in 22:16. This chapter contains oracles against the kings of Judah: Shallum (Jehoahaz) son of Josiah (22:10-12); Jehoiakim son of Josiah (22:13-19); and Coniah (Jehoiachin) son of Jehoiakim (22:24-30). This chapter might well be titled, "The evils that kings do." The acts of King Josiah (the beloved king of Judah) are contrasted with those of his son Jehoiakim. Josiah judged the cause of the *'ānî* עני and *'ebyôn* אביון, and it was reckoned as a good deed. In other words, he fulfilled the ancient Near Eastern and traditional Israelite duty of the king—to ensure that proper justice was given to the poor and vulnerable members of the community.

The *'ebyôn* אביון here are those who are powerless and have become victims of oppression and exploitation by the powerful. The context especially suggests this interpretation. The evils of Jehoiakim involve refusing to pay workers their wages (22:13; see 1 Kgs 5:27-28; 11:28; Deut 24:14-15) and unjust building projects such as apparently trying to enlarge Solomon's palace.[139] For these offenses, the king shall receive the ignoble burial of a donkey (22:19; 36:30; 2 Kgs 24:1-7). Jerusalem itself is doomed (22:20-23).

The word *'ānî* עני is used once only in Jeremiah (22:16). As we saw above, the *'ānî* עני (and *'ebyôn* אביון) are those who were being exploited but whom Josiah protected. William L. Holladay argues that in this verse the word *'ānî* עני "forms a hendiadys" with *'ebyôn* אביון and they are indistinguishable.[140] A note of interest is that in Jeremiah 22, the words *'ānî* עני and *'ebyôn* אביון are used in the same context that the widow, fatherless, and resident alien are used (22:3). As noted above, these groups were often mentioned together as a class of vulnerable persons.

Jeremiah refers to the poor as *dallîm* דלים on two occasions (5:4; 39:10). In chapter 5, which is reminiscent of Abraham's conversation with Yahweh (Gen 18:23-33), Yahweh orders Jeremiah to run through the streets of Jerusalem looking for one just person in order for Yahweh to pardon the city.[141] Jeremiah finds only equally sinful poor and rich people. He refers to the former as only the *dallîm* דלים with no sense and no knowledge of God's ways. These are "simply the powerless and insignificant, as opposed to those with power and influence."[142] It is also clear that in this text Jeremiah views the *dallîm* דלים as the opposite of the *haggĕdōlîm* הגדלים. While the *dallîm* דלים lack sense and knowledge, the *gĕdōlîm* גדולים know the way and law of God.

Jeremiah refers to the victims of 39:10 as *haddallîm* הדלים (the poor ones). This chapter recounts the second fall of Jerusalem (587 BCE) under Nebuchadrezzar, king of Babylon (see also Jer 52:4-16; 2 Kgs 25:1-12; 2 Chron 36:11-21). When Nebuzaradan, the captain of the guard, exiled the nation to Babylon, he is said to have left behind only some of the poorest people who owned nothing. To these he gave vineyards and fields.[143] Jones notes that although Jer 39:10 varies slightly from 2 Kgs 25:12, the meaning is the same and its effect is "to emphasise the complete poverty of those left in the land."[144] Therefore Jer 39:10 uses *haddallîm* הדלים to refer to the poorest, landless, and propertyless people left behind after the exile. They are the objects of charity yet still subjects of a despotic benefactor.

It is this same group of people, now under the governorship of Gedaliah, who are referred to in Jer 40:7 (see also 39:10; 2 Kgs 25:12). However, Jeremiah uses a different expression this time. He calls them the *umiddallat hā-'āreṣ* ומדלת הארץ (some of the poorest of the land—from those who had not been exiled to Babylon). Bright makes the good point that this expression "is best taken as in apposition to 'men, women, and children.'"[145]

Finally, Jeremiah mentions those persons left behind during the second exile in 52:15-16. This chapter is chronicled from 2 Kgs 24:18 - 25:30 and is regarded as "a historical appendix."[146] Jeremiah 52:15 reports that Nebuzaradan exiled some of the poorest of the people (*umiddallôt hā-'ām* העם ומדלות) to Babylon. He left behind some of the poorest of the land (*umiddallôt hā-'āreṣ* ומדלות הארץ [v. 16]) to be vine dressers and tillers of soil (see also Jer 39:10). It is notable that v. 15 appears neither in 2 Kings (24:14; 25:11-12) nor in the Septuagint, possibly due to haplography.[147] While its authenticity is questionable, it is not unlikely that some of the poor may well have been deported to Babylon. A note of interest is that some of the poorest of the *people* are deported along with other groups of *people* while some of the poorest of the *land* are left behind to work on the *land.* Perhaps the association of one group of people with people and another with land is intentional, but it may also point to some minute degree of difference between these groups of people. While the very poor (*haddallîm* הדלים) of Jer 39:10 are given land, those of Jer 52:16 (*umiddallôt* ומדלות) are not described as such but certainly have access to land. Although referred to by different expressions, it seems that the two groups are basically the same in constitution, but perhaps with the possibility of a slight variation.

It is therefore clear that in Jeremiah, the *haddallîm* הדלים, *umiddallôt* לות־ ומד, *umiddallôt hā-'ām* ומדלות העם, and *umiddallôt hā-'āreṣ* ומדלות הארץ are the poorest people who survived the Babylonian exile of 587 BCE. Due to the context and usage of these expressions, Pleins correctly views them as "poor farm laborers."[148]

Several references to the widow and fatherless appear in Jeremiah. The first occurs in 5:28, where the rich inhabitants of Jerusalem are perverting justice. Because of their wickedness, they are accused of not defending the rights of the fatherless. Their rights are violated because they lack a male member to defend them.[149]

In Jeremiah's famous temple sermon (7:1-15), the widow and fatherless are mentioned alongside the *gēr* גר. The reference to these three groups of persons is familiar from other texts (Exod 22:20-21; Deut 10:18; 16:11, 14; 24:19-21; Isa 1:17; 10:2; Zech 7:10; Ps 68:6; and Jer 7:6; 15:8; 18:21; 22:3; 49:11). Jeremiah states that it is both deceptive and hypocritical to say "this is the temple of the Lord" when the widow, the fatherless, and the resident alien are being oppressed. Matthews states it poignantly, "Jeremiah decries rote ritual behavior that does not contain the desire to obey Yahweh's covenant."[150]

In a lament, Jeremiah bemoans the fate of a disobedient people. Such disobedience has caused Yahweh to make widows "more numerous than the sand of the seas" (cf. Gen 22:17; 32:13). Yahweh has also destroyed "the mothers of youths" (Jer 15:8). The implication is that Yahweh has killed the husbands, thus making women "widows," and Yahweh has also killed mothers, making the children not only "fatherless" but also motherless.

Jeremiah's fourth lament advocates violence against children, women, and men (18:21). The prophet has obviously created some enemies who are after his life (vv. 19-20). Perhaps in search of retribution, Jeremiah asks Yahweh to let children die by famine and the sword; the youth in battle; and the men by disease. In so doing, the women not only become childless but also widows. This is a terrible curse to pronounce upon anyone because a woman was vulnerable without a man in her life and childlessness was a source of great sorrow for women.[151] Jeremiah's wish is therefore of the worst kind. By lacking a husband and sons, a woman had no protection or security.

The widow, fatherless, and resident alien are again mentioned together in an oracle to the royal house of Judah (Jer 22:3). Jeremiah exhorts the Judean kings to administer justice by refraining from doing any wrong or violence to this triad of vulnerable persons. This echoes the ancient Near Eastern and ancient Israelite view of the king as the protector and defender of the powerless. Just as Yahweh cared for Israel, a weak and dominated nation, so was Israel expected to care for its own weak members.[152]

The final reference to the widow and fatherless occurs in an oracle against Edom (Jer 49:11). After killing the men of Edom, Yahweh rather surprisingly states that he will care for the Edomite widows and orphans.[153] Although this may seem "strange," I think it indicates that Yahweh is a compassionate and generous God. Moreover, Yahweh is the judge of all the earth (Gen 18:25), and consequently, the judge of all nations (Amos 1:1 - 2:16). Clearly, Yahweh's actions and deeds cannot be limited by human expectations. Finally, I think Yahweh would also show compassion for Edomite widows because the Edomites and Israelites were blood relatives.[154]

Jeremiah also uses the vocabulary of oppression or exploitation. In 6:6 Jerusalem is to be besieged and punished (Heb. "cut down") for its oppression ('āšaq עשׁק). Chapter 5 chronicles some of the ways Jerusalem was oppressing its inhabitants (5:1-6, 26-29). In the temple sermon (Jer 7:6), Jeremiah uses 'āšaq עשׁק with reference to the exploitation of the widow, orphan, and resident alien. In the oracle to the Judean royalty (22:3), Jeremiah instructs the kings to rescue a victim from an oppressor ('āšôq עשׁק) who is also a robber. Finally, in Jer 50:33, the prophet refers to the national oppression ('ăšûqîm עשׁוקים) of Israel and Judah by the Babylonians. The general meaning of 'āšaq עשׁק in Jeremiah is therefore the exploitation of the poor by the rich. It also means the oppression of the powerless by the powerful, just as Israel is being oppressed by Babylon. Jeremiah refers to the agent of oppression as the hayyônâ היונה (25:38; 46:16; 50:16).

In one instance, Jeremiah uses the verb laḥaṣ לחץ to describe oppression. An oracle of consolation for Israel states that Yahweh will restore the fortunes of his people and punish (pāqad פקד) those who oppress them (30:20). Again, this oppression is at a national level and it is perpetrated by an outside force.

Lastly, Jeremiah describes a mostly distressful situation using the verb ṣārâ צרה (14:8). During a drought (an incident of conjunctural poverty), the people of Judah call upon Yahweh as their savior. Such appeals to Yahweh are typical of the history of Israel (see Ps 22:4-5; Hos 13:4; Isa 43:11).

From this survey, I disagree with Carroll's statement that the oppression of the poor is not a main theme of Jeremiah.[155] I contend that it is more correct to say that it is a significant theme of Jeremiah. The only obvious fact is that its presentation in Jeremiah does not have the prophetic passion and verve of Amos or Micah.

Summary and Conclusions

There is much truth in the claim that the prophets are major advocates for the poor and oppressed. Their oracles call for justice and appear to have shaped the social consciousness in some of the Law Codes. Amos, Micah, Isaiah, and Jeremiah all have concern for the poor and other victims of the injustice of oppression and exploitation. This concern is much more pronounced in the books of Amos and Micah than in the books of Isaiah and Jeremiah. I agree with Hoppe's assertion that, "For the prophets, poverty is an evil created by the wealthy who engage in immoral practices to enrich themselves in land and property."[156] As such, the responsibility to ameliorate the situation of the poor lies with human beings. If only Israel had followed the divine mandate (Deut 15:4-5), there would have been no poor persons in ancient Israel. This is the essence of the prophetic call for justice and righteousness (Amos 5:24; Micah 6:8).

Applying Iliffe's model to a study of the prophets reveals that the vast majority of the poor that the prophets advocate for are the "structural poor." These are poor persons whose poverty is caused by unjust social, political, and economic structures. Since land was more readily available during the pre-monarchic era, we can argue that there were very few structurally poor people at that time. Their poverty would be mostly due to "personal circumstances," such as being young, elderly, or incapacitated. The rise of the monarchy and latifundialization in general created the vast majority of the structural poor whose poverty is due to "social circumstances." These are the able-bodied men and women who own the labor but lack the resources to exploit, or who are "unable to sell their labour power at a price sufficient to meet their minimum needs."[157] Such poor persons are the subjects of the prophetic critique of social injustice.

COPING MECHANISMS

This study of the prophets of ancient Israel presents some interesting perspectives for our consideration.

The discussion of the Former Prophets indicates that the problem of poverty arose during that era and continued to worsen in Israel's later history. Because kingship was a contributory factor to the problem, the ancient role of the king as protector of the poor is seriously violated. Thus the poor have to rely on their own resources as well as the assistance of others such as the prophets.

The foregoing discussion shows that the poor were subjected to the worst forms of injustice during the monarchic era. They coped with their situation through various means such as trading, buying and selling, working for wages, or working on their meager lands. Even then they were liable to be victimized at the marketplace and their places of labor. With the erosion of some of the ancient social structures designed to protect them, they needed other forms of support. It seems that the classical prophets appeared on the scene at the right time. Their influence seems to be present in Israel's later legal codes. These prophets gave voice to the otherwise silent poor by articulating their cause so eloquently. They acted as advocates and spokespersons for the poor and oppressed. By criticizing oppression and injustice of any kind, (and by anyone), sometimes risking their own lives, the prophets are an additional source of hope and survival for the poor. Due to the lack of comparable data on the poor by the poor themselves, the prophetic account and witness is no doubt biased or one-sided.

Since the prophets were spokespersons of Yahweh, it follows that Yahweh becomes the ultimate advocate for the poor. Yahweh ultimately provides for, protects, and guarantees the rights of the poor and oppressed.

Socio-Ethical Implications

The prophets argue that the problem of poverty is a result of gross violations of justice and righteousness, indeed an abandonment of the divine mandate for Israel. Amos and Micah, both of whom are the fiercest defenders of the rights of the poor, highlight the issue of injustice in ancient Israelite society. True worship of Yahweh is characterized by the proper treatment of others, particularly the poor and other disadvantaged members of the community.[158] A study of the prophets also indicates that poverty is not something that defies explanation. On the contrary, poverty is a condition that human beings have created, both rulers and their subjects. Greed, exploitation, dishonest and unethical business practices, as well as other forms of injustice, all contribute to the problem.

So far, this study has shown that poverty and wealth are two sides of the same coin; one necessarily implies the other. This means that these subjects cannot be completely divorced from each other. In a sense, they are humanity's common destiny. A discussion of poverty inevitably brings up issues of inequality, injustice, oppression, and indeed wealth, as they affect all human beings.

The implication of the foregoing discussion is that in order to alleviate the problem of poverty, a change of heart and attitude is surely necessary. This change can take place only when human beings begin to treat each other with justice and equity. This is the basic meaning of the central teachings of the prophets, especially Amos and Micah. Essentially, it is obedience to the divine mandate, however idealistic it may be viewed. The continued existence of the poor and other oppressed people through prophetic times compounds the problem of poverty in the Bible. At the very least it demonstrates Israel's history of disobedience to the vision spelled out in the book of Deuteronomy. The problem is aggravated by the fact that despite the prophets playing an active role of brother's keeper, the poor continued to multiply. It is also worsened by the fact that injustice reigned and the poor proliferated when kingship was firmly in place. The conclusion is clear: Israel's kings had neglected their divinely instituted duty as protectors and defenders of the poor and oppressed.

NOTES

1. The Former Prophets are Joshua-Kings and the Latter Prophets are the "classical" prophets comprising the three major prophets (Isaiah, Jeremiah, and Ezekiel), and the twelve minor prophets (Hosea-Malachi).

2. The phrase "Deuteronomistic History" was first proposed by Martin Noth in 1943. See Martin Noth, *Uberlieferungsgeschichtliche Studien. Die sammelnden und bearbeitenden Geschichtswerke in alten Testament* (Tubingen: Max Niemeyer, 1943; 2d ed. 1957); idem, *The Deuteronomistic History,* JSOT Supplement 15 (Sheffield: University of Sheffield, 1981).

3. Cross, *CMHE,* 223. Kingship emerged roughly around 1000 BCE and ended in 587/6 BCE.

4. See Wilson, *Prophecy and Society in Ancient Israel.*

5. Ibid., 28, 51. Wilson derives the idea of intermediation from practices in modern societies which include Shamanism and concepts of mediumship, divination, spirit possession, and the interaction between two separate worlds (pp. 21-88). He characterizes intermediaries as "central" or "peripheral" so that the Hebrew prophets become either "central" or "peripheral" intermediaries.

6. In the 1920s and 1930s German scholars Albrecht Alt and Martin Noth proposed that the occupation of Canaan was due to a gradual, peaceful infiltration in two stages or immigration over time. In the 40s and 50s the American School (or archaeologists) of Albright, Wright, and Bright opposed the German scholars and instead proposed a unified military conquest. More modern scholars like Mendenhall and Gottwald have proposed the revolt or social revolution method, a thesis that has generally been welcomed by recent scholars. The endogenous model is gaining more acceptances among minimalist scholars with its suggestion that the Israelites were

Canaanites who were already in the land. See the following works: Albrecht Alt, "The Settlement of the Israelites in Palestine," in his *Essays on Old Testament History and Religion* (Garden City, NY: Doubleday, 1966), 173-221; Martin Noth, *The History of Israel,* 2d ed (New York: Harper & Row 1960), 53-84, 141-63; William Foxwell Albright, *The Archaeology of Palestine* (Baltimore: Penguin, 1949); idem, "Archaeology and the Date of the Hebrew Conquest of Palestine," *BASOR* 58 (1935): 10-18; idem, "Further Light on the History of Israel from Lachish and Megiddo," *BASOR* 68 (1937): 22-26; idem, "The Israelite Conquest of Canaan in the Light of Archaeology," *BASOR* 74 (1939): 11-23; George Ernst Wright, "The Literary and Historical Problem of Joshua 10 and Judges 1," *JNES* 5 (1946); Iain Provan, V. Philips Long, and Tremper Longman III, *A Biblical History of Israel* (Louisville: Westminster John Knox Press, 2003), 138-192; and Hershel Shanks, ed. *Ancient Israel: From Abraham to the Roman Destruction of the Temple,* Revised and Expanded (Upper saddle River, NJ: Prentiss Hall, 1999), 55-89.

7. Leslie J. Hoppe, *Being Poor: A Biblical Study* (Wilmington, DE: Michael Glazier, 1987), 37.

8. Bennett, *Injustice Made Legal,* 142.

9. Gnuse, *You Shall Not Steal,* 67.

10. Gnuse, *You Shall Not Steal,* 76; Hoppe, *Being Poor,* 50.

11. Gnuse,*You Shall Not Steal,* 74. Cross argues that Jeroboam's establishment of two rival shrines was an attempt to "out-archaize" David/Jerusalem (*CMHE,* 199, 279, n. 22).

12. Gnuse, *You Shall Not Steal,* 76-82; Hoppe, *Being Poor,* 60-88. Hanson proposes a triadic Yahwistic notion of community, based on the principles of righteousness, compassion, and worship. See *The People Called: The Growth of Community in the Bible,* especially pp. 70-86.

13. Gnuse, *You Shall Not Steal,* 77. See also Gerhard von Rad, *The Message of the Prophets,* trans. D. M. G. Stalker (New York, Hagerstown, San Francisco, London: Harper & Row Publishers, 1962), 100-101.

14. Gnuse, *You Shall Not Steal,* 77. See also James M. Ward, *Thus Says the Lord: The Message of the Prophets* (Nashville: Abingdon Press, 1991), 201; Gunther Wittenberg, "The Message of the O. T. Prophets During the Eighth Century B. C. Concerning Affluence and Poverty," in *Affluence, Poverty and the Word* of *God,* 141-52. Some scholars wonder if God favors the poor while others challenge that claim. For example, see Sam A. Potaro, "Is God Prejudiced in Favor of the Poor?" *Christian Century* 102 (April 1985): 404-405, and Ronald J. Sider, "Is God Really on the Side of the Poor?" *Sojourners* 6 (October 1977): 11-14. Sider argues: "God is not biased. But neither is he neutral in the struggle for justice. The Bible clearly and repeatedly teaches that God is at work in history casting down the rich and exalting the poor. Why? Because the rich have failed to aid the needy. Or because they have often become rich, as scripture points out, precisely because they have oppressed the poor. The God revealed in scripture is on the side of the poor precisely because he is *not* biased, precisely because he is a God of impartial justice. God longs for the salvation of the rich as much as for the salvation of the poor" (p. 14) [Sider's emphasis].

15. See Thomas D. Hanks, "Why People are Poor: What the Bible Says," *Sojourners* 10 (January 1981): 19-22; idem, "Oppressors on the Run: An In-depth Look at an Important Biblical Teaching that Most of Us Usually Miss," *Other Side* 113 (1981): 23-35. See also Frances Moore Lappé, "Who Benefits; Who Has the Power to Decide? The Cause and Relief of Poverty," *Currents in Theology and Mission* 7 (October 1980): 277-87.

16. For literature and commentaries on the Former Prophets, consult the following works: Robert G. Boling and George Ernst Wright, *Joshua: A New Translation with Notes and Commentary,* Anchor Bible 6 (Garden City, NY: Doubleday & Company, 1982); Robert G. Boling, *Judges,* AB 6a (Garden City, NY: Doubleday & Company, 1975; P. Kyle McCarter, *I Samuel: A New Translation with Introduction, Notes and Commentary,* AB 8 (Garden City, NY: Doubleday & Company, 1980); idem, *II Samuel: A New Translation with Introduction, Notes and Commentary,* AB 9 (Garden City, NY: Doubleday & Company, 1984); John Mauchline, *1 and 2 Samuel,* NCB (London: Oliphants, 1971); John Gray, *I & II Kings: A Commentary,* 2d fully revised ed., OTL (London: SCM, 1970); Mordechai Cogan and Hayim Tadmor, *II Kings: A New Translation with Introduction and Commentary,* AB 11 (New York: Doubleday & Company, 1988); John Gray, *Joshua, Judges, Ruth,* NCBC (Grand Rapids: Wm. B. Eerdmans Publishing Company / Basingstoke, England: Marshall Morgan & Scott Publications, 1986), and Terence E. Fretheim, *Deuteronomic History,* Interpreting Biblical Texts (Nashville: Abingdon Press, 1983).

17. Gray, *Joshua, Judges, Ruth,* 6; Boling and Wright, *Joshua,* 52-55.

18. See Norman Habel, "The Form and Significance of the Call Narratives," *ZAW* 77 (1965): 297-323.

19. *NBDB* translates the noun *maḥsôr* מחסור (from verb *ḥāsēr* חסר) as "need, things needed, poverty," (p. 341).

20. *'āšaq* עשק is defined as follows: "oppress, wrong, extort," (*NBDB,* 798); "oppress, wrong," (Holladay, 286). *NBDB* defines *rāṣaṣ* רצץ as "crush, oppress" (p. 954), and Holladay defines it as "smash up" in general, but "ill-treat, abuse," (p. 346), in this context (1 Sam 12:3-4). Driver remarks that *'šq* עשק means "*to oppress, in particular by defrauding a labourer or dependent of his due*" (*Notes on the Hebrew Text and the Topography of the Book of Samuel,* 88). Hertzberg argues that this text inquires if Samuel has used force or unjust dealings like his sons, but he agrees with Mauchline that it also shows the incorruptibility of Samuel as judge and administrator (Hertzberg, *I & II Samuel,* 98; Mauchline *1 and 2 Samuel,* 107-108). See also Joseph Kandathil, "Oppression/Liberation Experience of Israel in Exodus," *Jeevadhara* 17 (1987): 438-50; and George P. Kaniarakath, "Liberation in the Old Testament," *Bible Bashyam* 9, no. 3 (1983): 5-16.

21. From the verb *rûš* רוש or rîš ריש—to "be in want, poor" (*NBDB,* 930); "poor," Holladay, 336).

22. Hertzberg, *I & II Samuel,* 161; Hoppe agrees with Hertzberg (*Being Poor,* 47); see Pleins, "Poor, Poverty," 408.

23. Pleins, "Poor, Poverty," 408; McCarter, *II Samuel,* 305.

24. *NBDB* (p. 776) lightly translates *'nh* ענה in 2 Sam 13 as to "humble" a woman by cohabitation, as if to justify the act. Holladay (p. 278) views *'nh* ענה as denoting

a crime and correctly translates it as "violate, rape," although he does not cite this specific text.

25. Pleins, "Poor, Poverty," 405-407.

26. Ibid., 408.

27. Hoppe, *Being Poor,* 37-43. As a result, the books of Joshua and Judges present Israel's rise in Canaan as "a struggle against power and wealth . . . a struggle for justice." By defeating the Canaanites, the Israelites can take control of their own destiny (pp. 42-43).

28. Ibid., 45; see also Malchow, *Social Justice in the Hebrew Bible,* 59.

29. Hoppe outlines some of the oppressive measures under Saul, David, and Solomon (*Being Poor,* 48; see also Gnuse, *You Shall Not Steal,* 68-71). Malchow calls Nathan's parable "a story of social injustice" (*Social Justice in the Hebrew Bible,* 59). Instead of protecting the weak, David uses his power to oppress and eliminate Uriah (p. 60).

30. Hoppe, *Being Poor,* 51. He further notes that the land was always to be the inheritance of all Israelites since it was the basis of prosperity (p. 51).

31. Malchow, *Social Justice in the Hebrew Bible,* 60. See, also Gnuse, *You Shall Not Kill,* 74-75; Hoppe, *Being Poor,* 50-52; Richard D. Nelson, *First and Second Kings* (Atlanta: John Knox Press, 1987), 138-45; Gray, *I & II Kings,* 433-444. As noted above, this story is the central focus of the essays in *Plutocrats and Paupers.*

32. The six land ideologies are: royal, agrarian, theocratic, prophetic, ancestral household, and immigrant. Habel argues that the poor and the Canaanites have no right to land and therefore can be made slaves of the empire at the will of the monarchy. See *The Land is Mine,* 30-32.

33. Ferdinand Deist, "Biblical Studies, Wealth and Poverty in South Africa: Retrospect and Prospect," in *Plutocrats and Paupers,* 252 [Deist's emphasis]. Deist proceeds to illustrate two conflicting views of community, economy, law, religion, culture, and righteousness in the Naboth narrative (pp. 253-54).

34. I. G. Gous, "City and Countryside: A Sociopolitical Perspective on Wealth and Poverty in ancient Israel," in *Plutocrats and Paupers,* 169 [emphasis added]. Deist adds that 1 Kings 21 "shows the extent to which the peasant community was at the mercy of the crown and officialdom." See "The Historical Scene in which the Old Testament was Enacted," in *Plutocrats and Paupers,* 119.

35. Karen Lebacqz, *Justice in an Unjust World: Foundations for a Christian Approach to Justice* (Minneapolis: Fortress Press, 2007), 109.

36. Hoppe thinks that this story illustrates the situation of the poor (during this drought) and not only that of the widow of Zarephath (*Being Poor,* 50, n. 20). Malchow sees the story as a model of sharing with the poor (*Social Justice in the Hebrew Bible,* 60). Nelson views the three stories in 1 Kings 17 (Elijah and the ravens [vv. 1-7]; Elijah and the widow [vv. 8-16]; and Elijah and the widow's son [vv. 17-24] as stories about "life in the midst of death" (*First and Second Kings,* 107-114).

37. Nelson, *First and Second Kings,* 175. There are four such stories in this chapter: Elisha and the widow (2 Kgs 4:1-7); the Shunammite's son (vv. 8-37); the spoiled stew (vv. 38-41); and feeding a hundred (vv. 42-44). Nelson notes that the stories in 2 Kings 4 are part of a larger "paratactic" presentation of stories about Elisha's pro-

phetic power (2 Kgs 3:4 - 8:15). He defines parataxis as "the placing of short items side by side to build up larger wholes" (pp. 10, 171).

38. For more information on the Day of Yahweh, see von Rad, *The Message of the Prophets,* 95-99; Ernst Jenni, "Day of the Lord," *IDB* 1 (1962): 784-85; and A. Joseph Everson, "Day of the Lord," *IDBSup* (1990): 209-10.

39. For commentaries on Amos, see the following works: Francis I. Andersen and David Noel Freedman, *Amos: A New Translation with Introduction and Commentary,* AB 24A (New York, London, Toronto, Sydney, Auckland: Doubleday, 1989); Shalom M. Paul, *Amos,* Hermenia (Minneapolis: Fortress Press, 1991); Hans Walter Wolff, *Joel and Amos,* Hermenia (Philadelphia: Fortress Press, 1977); James Limburg, *Hosea-Micah,* Interpretation (Atlanta: John Knox Press, 1988), 79-126; James Luther Mays, *Amos: A Commentary,* OTL (Philadelphia: The Westminster Press, 1969); Robert B. Coote, *Amos among the Prophets: Composition and Theology* (Philadelphia: Fortress Press, 1981); James M. Ward, *Thus Says the Lord: The Message of the Prophets* (Nashville: Abingdon Press, 1991), 201-14; Gerhard von Rad, *The Message of the Prophets,* 102-109; and Hobart E. Freeman, *An Introduction to the Old Testament Prophets* (Chicago: Moody Press, 1968), 184-90. See also Joseph G. Bailey, "Amos: Preacher of Social Reform," *TBT* 19 (1981): 306-13.

40. Based on archaeological evidence, most scholars date Amos' activities between 760 and 750 BCE (see Limburg, *Hosea-Micah,* 84; Wolff, *Joel and Amos,* 124). Shalom Paul argues that Amos must have finished his mission prior to 745 (*Amos,* 1). Andersen and Freedman prefer the decade of 765-755 when Uzziah and Jeroboam II were at the height of their power (*Amos,* 19).

41. Gerhard von Rad, *The Message of the Prophets,* 102. Wolff asserts that Amos was "probably not exactly poor" (*Joel and Amos,* 90). Because there were no sycamore trees in Tekoa and sheep-breeding required a lot of travel, Wolff argues that Amos was well-traveled and well-educated (pp. 90-91). Malchow agrees that Amos was "wealthy" and "educated" (*Social Justice in the Hebrew Bible,* 32). See also Terry Giles, "A Note on the Vocation of Amos," *Journal of Biblical Literature* 111 (Winter 1992): 690-92.

42. Wilson, *Prophecy and Society in Ancient Israel,* 268.

43. Victor H. Matthews, *Social World of the Hebrew Prophets* (Peabody, MA.: Hendrickson Publishers, 2001), 73.

44. Malchow, *Social Justice in the Hebrew Bible,* 32.

45. Matthews, *Social World of the Hebrew Prophets,* 68.

46. Andersen and Freedman divide the book into four parts as follows: Part I: "The Book of Doom" (1:1 - 4:13); Part II: "The Book of Woes" (5:1 - 6:14); Part III: "The Book of Visions of Judgment" (7:1 - 9:6); and Part IV: "The Epilogue" (9:7-15). Paul R. Noble determines the structure of Amos through structural parallelism and thematic correspondence. He argues that the book consists of a superscription (1:1) plus three main parts: Part I: Yahweh's word to the nations (1:2 - 3:8); Part II: A palistrophic judgment oracle (3:9 - 6:14); and Part III: The destruction and reconstruction of Israel (7:1 - 9:15). See "The Literary Structure of Amos: A Thematic Analysis," *JBL* 114 (1995): 209-26, especially pp. 209-10, 226.

47. The distribution is as follows: *'ebyôn* אביון: 2:6; 4:1; 5:12; 8:4, 6; *dal* דל: 2:7; 4:1 (*dallîm* דלים); 5:11; 8:6 (*dallîm* דלים); *'ănāwîm* ענוים: 2:7; 8:4. All these words (with the variant *'ānî* עני for *'ănāwîm* ענוים) are used in the Law Codes of ancient Israel as we saw in chapter 2 above. Such an occurrence may suggest Amos' familiarity with Israel's legal tradition, especially the Covenant Code.

48. Bennett, *Injustice Made Legal,* 69. He further argues that the social location of the poor "trapped these persons in a web of injustice and mistreatment, and increased their susceptibility to oppression," 71.

49. The formula starts with an accusation, then an announcement of judgment, and ends with the words, "Says Yahweh." See Claus Westermann, *Basic Forms of Prophetic Speech,* trans. Hugh Clayton White (Cambridge: The Lutterworth Press / Louisville, Ky: Westminster / John Knox Press, 1991), 98-128; Gene M. Tucker, "Prophetic Speech," in *Interpreting the Prophets,* ed. James Luther Mays and Paul J. Achtemeier (Philadelphia: Fortress Press, 1987), 27-40. John T. Greene has criticized OT form-critical scholarship which has loosely called the prophets "messengers" and their speeches "messages." From his comparative study of ancient Near Eastern materials, these designations are better attributed to ancient Near Eastern messengers and messages. See "The Old Testament Prophet as Messenger in the Light of Ancient Near Eastern Messengers and Messages" (Ph.D. diss., Boston University, 1980).

50. Andersen and Freedman, *Amos,* 310.

51. Wolff, *Joel and Amos,* 164-65.

52. Andersen and Freedman, *Amos,* 310-13. Limburg (*Hosea-Micah,* 90-92) and Mays, (*Amos,* 45-46) also agree that this verse refers to debt-slavery.

53. Paul, *Amos,* 78.

54. See Wolff, *Joel and Amos,* 166; Paul, *Amos,* 79-80; Andersen and Freedman, *Amos,* 313-16; Mays, *Amos,* 46; and Limburg, *Hosea-Micah,* 91.

55. Mays, *Amos,* 46.

56. Ibid. See also Paul, *Amos,* 81-83.

57. Paul, *Amos,* 85. Paul cites other studies and instances where *hbl* הבל applies to distraints—persons or property—taken only when the loan falls due and the debt is defaulted (pp. 83-84). For the traditional interpretation, see Mays, *Amos,* 47; Limburg, *Hosea-Micah,* 91; Wolff, *Joel and Amos,* 167; Andersen and Freedman, *Amos,* 319.

58. Victor Matthews, *Social World of the Hebrew Prophets,* 70.

59. Andersen and Freedman, *Amos,* 321; Mays, *Amos,* 47.

60. Paul, *Amos,* 87. Wolff emphasizes the "exploitation of debtors" (*Joel and Amos,* 167).

61. Paul, *Amos,* 126. See also Wolff, *Joel and Amos,* 201-202; Andersen and Freedman, *Amos,* 411; and Mays, *Amos,* 70.

62. The verb *'āšaq* עשק means "to oppress, wrong, extort" (see Lev 5:21; 1 Sam 12:4; *NBDB,* 798). The verb *rāṣaṣ* רצץ means "to crush" (1 Sam 12:4; Isa 42:4; *NBDB,* 954). Thomas D. Hanks notes that *'āšaq* עשק occurs fifty-nine times in the Hebrew Bible. He translates it as "oppression, injustice" (see *God So Loved the Third World,* 5-8). Similarly, he interprets *rāṣaṣ* רצץ as "crush, grind, pound," figuratively, "oppress" (pp. 11-14). He remarks, "To be oppressed is like being sat on by a fat cow!" (p. 13). See also Elsa Tamez, *Bible of the Oppressed,* 22-30; Aloysius Pieris,

"Religion and the Liberation of the Oppressed," *Dialogue* 15, nos. 1-3 (1988): 101-110; Marie Augusta Neal, *The Just Demands of the Poor: Essays in Socio-Theology* (Mahwah, NY: Paulist Press, 1987).

63. Translation of Andersen and Freedman, *Amos,* 419.

64. Mays, *Amos,* 72.

65. Limburg, *Hosea-Micah,* 99. Robertson argues that Israel's women are excoriated "because the poor suffer exorbitant taxes that fund these women's opulent lifestyles." See Cleotha Robertson, "Amos," in *The Africana Bible: Reading Israel's Scriptures from Africa and the African Diaspora,* edited by Hugh R. Page, Jr., et al., 172-179 (Minneapolis: Fortress Press, 2010), 176.

66. Wolff, *Joel and Amos,* 205; Paul, *Amos,* 129. Andersen and Freedman who view the imagery as intended for both men and women, call it "a parody and an insult." It is also "sarcastic" (*Amos,* 421).

67. Wolf states: "The women, no less than the men, are held accountable for their attitudes and actions towards the poor" (*Joel and Amos,* 207). Limburg concurs: "Responsibility for what happens to . . . the poor in a society does not lie with the male segment of the population only. Exercising such responsibility is women's work too" (*Hosea-Micah,* 100-101).

68. Paul, *Amos,* 170-71.

69. Andersen and Freedman, *Amos,* 500. They note that the exact crime here cannot be determined but the sense is that of the rich neglecting to be generous to the poor (pp. 500-501; see also Wolff, *Joel and Amos,* 247).

70. *NBDB* translates *ṣrr* צרר as "bind, tie up, be restricted, narrow, scant, cramped" (p. 864). Amos' use of this verb gives one a sense of oppressive force that incapacitates someone. Paul rightly notes that "the poor and underprivileged are continually the victims of the local judiciary, who victimize them at the very place . . . where justice should be dispensed" (*Amos,* 174-75).

71. See Temba L. J. Mafico, "Just, Justice," in *ABD,* vol. 3, ed., David Noel Freedman (New York, London, Toronto, Sydney, Auckland: Doubleday, 1992), 1127-29, especially p. 1128. On the theme of justice in general, consult the following studies: Moshe Weinfeld, *Social Justice in Ancient Israel and the ANE,* especially chap. 1; León Epsztein, *Social Justice in the ANE;* Wright, *An Eye for an Eye,* 137-47; Henning Graf Reverentlow and Yair Hoffman, eds., *Justice and Righteousness: Biblical Themes and their Influence,* JSOTSup 137 (Sheffield, England: JSOT Press, 1994); Ronald Sider, *Cry Justice! The Bible Speaks on Hunger and Poverty* (New York: Paulist Press, 1980); John Sowada, "Let Justice Surge Like Water...," *TBT* 19 (1981): 301-305; Carroll Stuhlmueller, "Justice Toward the Poor," *TBT* 24 (November 1986): 385-90; Leslie J. Hoppe, "Biblical Faith and Global Justice," *Spirituality Today* 31, no. 1 (1979): 4-13; Christopher Rowlands, "In Dialogue with Itumeleng Mosala: A Contribution to Liberation Exegesis," *Journal for the Study of the New Testament* 50 (June 1993): 43-57; Stephen Charles Mott, *Biblical Ethics and Social Change* (New York / Oxford: Oxford University Press, 1982), 59-81; James Luther Mays, "Justice: Perspectives from the Prophetic Tradition," *Int* 37 (1983): 5-17; Dale Patrick, "The Rights of the Underprivileged," *SBLSP* 1 (1975): 1-6; and Calvin E. Beisner, "Justice and Poverty: Two Views Contrasted," *Transformation* 10 (January-April 1993): 16-22.

72. Mafico, *Yahweh's Emergence as "Judge" among the Gods*, 167.

73. Paul, *Amos,* 192. This theme of justice and righteousness is maintained in Amos: 5:7, 15; 6:12; so Jer 22:3, 15-16.

74. Ibid., 205. Limburg refers to it as *"individual affluence coupled with social Indifference"* (*Hosea-Micah,* 112 [Limburg's emphasis]). See also Mays, *Amos,* 116-17; Wolff, *Joel and Amos,* 276-77. Andersen and Freedman note that such a picture is only paralleled by the behavior of the participants at Belshazzar's feast in Daniel 5:2-4, 22-23 (*Amos,* 562-66).

75. The "end" is one of the thematic elements of the book of Amos. See David L. Petersen, *The Prophetic Literature: An Introduction* (Louisville, London: Westminster John Knox Press, 2002), 186-187.

76. Robert Wafawanaka, "Amos' Attitude toward Poverty: An African Perspective," in *African Journal of Biblical Studies*, edited by David Tuesday Adamo, Vol. XIX /2 (November 2003): 97-109.

77. Andersen and Freedman, *Amos,* 801.

78. Ibid., 807. Paul states: "The buyer was always deceived—he received too little and paid too much" (*Amos,* 258; see also Wolff, *Joel and Amos,* 327-28). Berthoud argues that "Amos never condemns prosperity that results from honest, hard work, or from wise investment of wealth. He attacks shameless business practices such as 'skimping the measure, boosting the price and cheating with dishonest scales' (Amos 8:5). He attacks those who ignore the misery around them and instead practice a superficial optimism, particularly in international relations." See Pierre Berthoud, "Prophet and Covenant," in *Freedom, Justice, and Hope: Toward a Strategy for the Poor and Oppressed,* ed. Marvin N. Olasky, Herbert Schlossberg, Pierre Berthoud, and Clark H. Pinnock (Westchester, IL: Crossway Books, 1988), 19-39, especially p. 29.

79. Bennett, *Injustice Made Legal,* 70.

80. Mays, *Amos,* 143. See Deist, "The Historical Scene," and Gous, "City and Countryside," in *Plutocrats and Paupers.*

81. *ANET,* 423 [author's emphasis]. In the "Protestation of Guiltlessness," or the so-called "Negative Confession," the deceased in the Egyptian Book of the Dead confesses his or her innocence: "I have neither increased or diminished the grain measure. I have not added to the weight of the balance. I have not *weakened* the plummet of the scales" (*ANET,* 34). Babylonian literature also deals with the same issue. Ur-Nammu standardized all measures (*ANET,* 523-24) and Ammisaduqa's reform-minded *misarum*-acts fixed weights and measures (*ANET,* 526-28). The Shamash Hymn states:

> The merchant who [practises] trickery as he holds the balances,
> Who uses two sets of weights,
> . . . .
> He is disappointed in the matter of profit and loses [his capital.]
> The honest merchant who holds the balances [and gives] good weight-
> Everything is presented to him in good measure [...]
> The merchant who practises trickery as he holds the corn measure,
> Who weighs out loans (or corn) by the minimum standard, but requires a large quantity in repayment,

The curse of the people will overtake him before his time,
. . . .
The honest merchant who weighs out loans (of corn) by
the maximum standard, thus multiplying kindness,
It is pleasing to Šamaš, and he will prolong his life.
He will enlarge his family, gain wealth,
And like the water of a never failing spring [his]
descendants will never fail (Lambert, *Babylonian Wisdom
Literature,* 133, lines 107-121; see also *ANET,* 388).

82. Mafico, "Just, Justice," 1128. See also Thomas J. Finley, "An Evangelical Response to the Preaching of Amos," *Journal of the Evangelical Theological Society* 28 (December 1985): 411-420; and Herbert B. Huffmon, "The Social Role of Amos' Message," in *The Quest for the Kingdom of God: Studies in Honor of George E. Mendenhall,* ed. Herbert B. Huffmon, Frank A. Spina, and A. R. W. Green (Winona Lake, IN: Eisenbrauns, 1983), 109-116.

83. Mays, *Amos,* 160.

84. Paul, *Amos,* 285.

85. Limburg, *Hosea-Micah,* 122. See also Ward, *Thus Says the Lord,* 205. Alistair Kee says that "the truly religious life apparently must be based on establishing justice and caring for the poor." See "Amos and Affluence," *The Furrow* 38, no. 1 (1987): 151-61, especially p. 159.

86. Hoppe, *Being Poor,* 63. Coote sees Amos' *only* concern as "socioeconomic Injustice" (*Amos among the Prophets,* 39).

87. Willy Schottroff, "The Prophet Amos: A Socio-Historical Assessment of His Ministry," in *God of the Lowly: Socio-Historical Interpretations of the Bible,* ed. Willy Schottroff and Wolfgang Stegemann (Maryknoll, NY: Orbis Books, 1984), 40.

88. For references, see the following books: James Limburg, *Hosea-Micah;* Delbert R. Hillers, *Micah: A Commentary on the Book of the Prophet Micah,* Hermeneia (Philadelphia: Fortress Press, 1984); Hans Walter Wolff, *Micah the Prophet,* tr. Ralph D. Gehrke (Philadelphia: Fortress Press, 1981); James Luther Mays, *Micah: A Commentary,* OTL (London: SCM, 1976); Gerhard von Rad, *The Message of the Prophets,* 118-144; James M. Ward, *Thus Says the Lord,* 233-40; Hobart E. Freeman, *An Introduction to the Old Testament Prophets,* 215-24; Klaus Koch, *The Prophets,* vol. 1 (Philadelphia: Fortress Press, 1982; 3d printing, 1987), 94-105; Abraham J. Heschel, *The Prophets,* vol. 1 (New York: Harper & Row, 1969), 98-102; and George V. Pixley, "Micah-A Revolutionary," in *The Bible and the Politics of Exegesis: Essays in Honor of Norman K. Gottwald on His Sixty-Fifth Birthday,* ed. David Jobling, Peggy L. Day, and Gerald T. Sheppard (Cleveland, Ohio: The Pilgrim Press, 1991), 53-60, 308.

89. Limburg, *Hosea-Micah,* 163-65; Matthews, *Social World of the Hebrew Prophets,* 99; and Petersen, *The Prophetic Literature,* 193-196.

90. Malchow, *Social Justice in the Hebrew Bible,* 33. Wilson argues that Micah was "a peripheral prophet in Jerusalem" (*Prophecy and Society in Ancient Israel,* 276).

91. Wolff, *Micah,* 99. Micah's language may also have been influenced by his rural background. As rural prophets, both Micah and Amos seem to have a different

vision or perspective from that of urban prophets like Isaiah of Jerusalem, a prophet of the establishment. Wilson suggests that Micah's sharp tone was because "the Jerusalemite establishment was unwilling to recognize his prophetic claims" (*Prophecy and Society in Ancient Israel*, 276).

92. See Pixley, "Micah-A Revolutionary."

93. Mays, *Micah*, 63. He interprets *ḥāmad* חמד as "self-centered desire" (p. 63).

94. Hillers, *Micah*, 37.

95. Mays, *Micah*, 71. He suggests that Mic 2:10b refers to avaricious creditors who were taking land in pledge for the slightest debt and seizing it if one failed to pay off a debt (p. 72). If so, this would be a great offense since the law only allowed small items, such as one's garment, to be taken as a pledge.

96. Limburg, *Hosea-Micah*, 175. Hillers calls it "hyperbole for their rapacity and cruelty," *Micah*, 43).

97. Mays, *Micah*, 89; see also Limburg, *Hosea-Micah*, 178.

98. Hillers, *Micah*, 51-53. Some scholars think this passage was edited after the exile. Compare and contrast Mic 4:4 with Zech 3:10 and Isa 11:6-9 for a vision of peace and harmony.

99. Mafico notes that Yahweh, like his ancient Near Eastern counterparts, 'El, Baal, Yamm, and Mot, was considered to be the judge of all the earth (*šōp̄ēṭ kol-hā'āreṣ* כל הארץ שפט [Gen 18:25]). In the Hebrew Bible the root *špṭ* שפט is "multifarious in meaning." See "Judge, Judging," in *ABD* 3 (1992): 1104-1106.

100. Limburg, *Hosea-Micah*, 191. Mays focuses on the character of the worshiper, as that which God wants (*Micah*, 136-43).

101. Limburg, *Hosea-Micah*, 192.

102. Mays, *Micah*, 142.

103. Hillers, *Micah*, 85.

104. See Waldemar Janzen, *Old Testament Ethics: A Paradigmatic Approach*, chap. 6.

105. I am adopting Katheryn P. Darr's approach and, unless otherwise specified, I am also using "Isaiah" or "Isaian" to refer to the biblical book, not to the eighth-century prophet. I prefer this approach for its clarity and focus on the entire book, Isaiah. See Darr, *Isaiah's Vision and the Family of God*, Literary Currents in Biblical Interpretation (Louisville, Kentucky: Westminster John Knox Press, 1994), 228, n. 1; idem, "Isaiah's Vision and the Rhetoric of Rebellion," *SBLSP*, Annual Meeting (Atlanta: Scholars Press, 1994), 847, n. 2.

106. For the discussion on Isaiah, see the following references: Wilson, *Prophecy and Society in Ancient Israel*, 270-74; Hoppe, *Being Poor*, 65-68; Malchow, *Social Justice in the Hebrew Bible*, 31-49; von Rad, *The Message of the Prophets*, 118-144; Heschel, *The Prophets*, vol. 1, 61-97; Koch, *The Prophets*, vol. 1, 105-156; Ward, *Thus Says the Lord*, 34-79; Freeman, *An Introduction to Old Testament Prophets*, 191-213; Blenkinsopp, *A History of Prophecy in Israel*, 106-118; J. J. M. Roberts, "Isaiah in Old Testament Theology," in *Interpreting the Prophets*, 62-74; Darr, *Isaiah's Vision and the Family of God*; idem, "Isaiah's Vision and the Rhetoric of Rebellion," 847-82; A. S. Herbert, *Isaiah 1-39*, The Cambridge Bible Commentary (Cambridge: Cambridge University Press, 1973); George Buchanan Gray, *A Critical*

and Exegetical Commentary on the Book of Isaiah I-XXXIX, ICC (New York: Charles Scribner's Sons, 1912); Otto Kaiser, *Isaiah 1-12: A Commentary,* 2d ed., OTL (Philadelphia: Fortress Press, 1983); John H. Hayes and Stuart A. Irvine, *Isaiah the Eighth-Century Prophet: His Times and His Preaching* (Nashville: Abingdon Press, 1987); John L. McKenzie, *Second Isaiah,* AB 20 (Garden City, NY: Doubleday & Company, 1968); Claus Westermann, *Isaiah 40-66: A Commentary,* OTL (Philadelphia: The Westminster Press, 1969); Roger N. Whybray, *Isaiah 40-66,* NCB (London: Oliphants, 1975); Bruce C. Birch, *Singing the Lord's Song: A Study of Isaiah 40-55* (Nashville: Abingdon Press, 1990); and Elizabeth Achtemeier, *The Community and Message of Isaiah 55-66: A Theological Commentary* (Minneapolis: Augsburg Publishing House, 1982).

107. Sometimes scholars use "Second Isaiah" to refer not only to chaps. 40-55, but also to 55-66, or simply, chaps. 40-66. My discussion presupposes the tripartite division of the book.

108. Edgar W. Conrad, *Reading Isaiah,* OBT (Minneapolis: Fortress Press, 1991), 6.

109. See Darr, *Isaiah's Vision;* idem, "Isaiah's Vision"; Conrad, *Reading Isaiah;* Wolfgang Roth, *Isaiah,* Knox Preaching Guides (Atlanta: John Knox Press, 1988); Christopher R. Seitz, "Introduction: The One Isaiah // The Three Isaiahs," in *Reading and Preaching the Book of Isaiah,* ed. C. R. Seitz (Philadelphia: Fortress Press, 1988), 13-22; idem, "Isaiah 1 - 66: Making Sense of the Whole," in *Reading and Preaching Isaiah,* 105-126; Ronald E. Clements, "The Unity of the Book of Isaiah," *Int* 36 (April 1982): 117-29; idem, "Beyond Tradition History: Deutero-Isaianic Development of First Isaiah's Themes," *JSOT* 31 (1985): 95-113; and Brevard S. Childs, *Introduction to the Old Testament as Scripture* (Philadelphia: Fortress Press, 1979; sixth printing, 1989), 311-38.

110. Darr, *Isaiah's Vision,* 14; Seitz, "The One Isaiah," 17.

111. Rolf Rendtorff, *The Old Testament: An Introduction,* trans. John Bowden (Philadelphia: Fortress Press, 1991), 190; Seitz, "The One Isaiah," 17. See also Clements, "Unity of Isaiah," 125-26. For Clements, "A striking instance of unity" in Isaiah is the fact that the prophetic message falls on deaf ears and on those who cannot comprehend what they see.

112. Seitz, "Isaiah 1 - 66," 109-116. Seitz adds that "the unity of the Book of Isaiah is not to be sought in issues of single authorship or uniform historical setting, but rather in the common witness of all sixty-six chapters to the one God of Israel, Isaiah's 'Holy One,' who casts down and raises up, whose justice shapes the cosmos itself, and whose promises extend into a future beyond the horizon of the book's own historical and literary world" ("The One Isaiah," 20-21). See also Clements, "Beyond Tradition History," 99; idem, "The Unity of Isaiah," 120-21. Rendtorff sees "many connections between the three parts of the book of Isaiah." He enumerates these as follows: references to the motifs of "comfort," the "guilt" of Israel, "Zion/Jerusalem," the *"kabod* of YHWH," the "Holy One of Israel," and the motif of "righteousness" (*The Old Testament,* 198-99).

113. Darr makes the excellent point that scrolls are "more sequential than books," and "one must unroll it sequentially, even if the goal is a particular pericope near the end" (*Isaiah's Vision,* 230, n. 17).

114. Darr, "Isaiah's Vision," 857.

115. For a detailed discussion, see Klaus Koch, *The Prophets,* vol. 1, 107-108; Hayes and Irvine, *Isaiah the Eighth-Century Prophet,* 17-66; McKenzie, *Second-Isaiah,* XV-LXXI; Westermann, *Isaiah 40-66,* 3-30, 295-308.

116. Wilson, *Prophecy and Society in Ancient Israel,* 271. Thus, he views him as "a peripheral prophet with a small support group" (p. 273).

117. The distribution is of these words is as follows: *'ebyôn* אביון: 14:30; 25:4; 29:19; 32:7; 41:17; *dal* דל: 10:2; 11:4; 14:30; 25:4; 26:6; *'ānî* עני /*'ānāwîm* ענוים: 3:14-15; 10:2, 30; 11:4; 14:32; 26:6; 29:19; 32:7; 41:17; 48:10; 49:17; 51:21; 54:11; 58:7; 61:1; 66:2.

118. See Isa: 1:17, 23; 9:16; 10:2; 47:8.

119. For example, *nāgaś* נגש: Isa 3:5, 12; 9:4; 14:2, 4; 53:7; *'āšaq* עשק: 23:12; 30:12; 33:15; 38:14; 52:4; 54:14; 59:13; *lahaṣ* לחץ: 19:20; *yānah* ינה: 49:26; *rāṣaṣ* רצץ: 58:6; *ṣārar* צרר: 63:9; *rāmas* רמס: 16:4; 26:6; and *ḥāmôṣ* חמץ: 1:17.

120. Kaiser, *Isaiah 1-12,* 35. The NRSV wrongly translates *ḥāmôṣ* חמץ as "rescue the oppressed." The NIV reads, "Encourage the oppressed," but in a note it correctly says, "Rebuke the oppressor." The *NBDB* translates the phrase correctly: "Set right the ruthless," (p. 330).

121. Hayes and Irvine, *Isaiah the Eight-Century Prophet,* 92.

122. See D. N. Premnath, "Latifundialization and Isaiah 5:8-10." *JSOT* 40 (1988): 49-60, especially p. 53. See also Kaiser, *Isaiah 1-12,* 100-101; Hayes and Irvine, *Isaiah the Eighth-Century Prophet,* 102-103.

123. Kaiser, *Isaiah 1-39,* 227. In this passage, widow and fatherless are grouped together with *'ānî* עני and *dal* דל.

124. Herbert, *Isaiah,* 100.

125. See the discussion by Hayes and Irvine, *Isaiah the Eighth-Century Prophet,* 237, and George Gray, *The Book of Isaiah,* 267-71.

126. *NBDB,* 864. The NRSV and NIV translate it as "distress."

127. Edward J. Young, *The Book of Isaiah,* The New International Commentary on the Old Testament (Grand Rapids, MI: William B. Eerdmans Publishing Company, 1969), 327. Pleins views them as those mistreated by rulers and evil doers ("Poor, Poverty," 403).

128. Pleins, "Poor, Poverty," 403.

129. Westermann, *Isaiah 40-66,* 336-337.

130. McKenzie, *Second Isaiah,* 171.

131. Matthews, *Social World of the Hebrew Prophets,* 83, 84.

132. For references, consult the following works: Klaus Koch, *The Prophets,* vol. 2, 13-80; Abraham Heschel, *The Prophets,* vol. 1, 103-139; Gerhard von Rad, *The Message of the Prophets,* 161-188; John Bright, *Jeremiah,* AB 21a (Garden City, NY: Doubleday & Company, 1965); Robert P. Carroll, *Jeremiah: A Commentary,* OTL (London: SCM, 1986); Douglas Rawlinson Jones, *Jeremiah,* NCBC (Grand Rapids, MI: William B. Eerdmans Publishing Company, 1992); Walter Brueggemann, "The Book of Jeremiah: Portrait of the Prophet," in *Interpreting the Prophets,* 113-129; William L. Holladay, "The Years of Jeremiah's Preaching," in *Interpreting the Prophets,* 130-142; idem, *Jeremiah 1,* Hermenia (Philadelphia: Fortress Press, 1986);

idem, *Jeremiah 2,* Hermenia (Minneapolis: Fortress Press, 1989); James M. Ward, *Thus Says the Lord,* 119-170; Hobart E. Freeman, *An Introduction to the Old Testament Prophets,* 237-250; and Joseph Blenkinsopp, *A History of Prophecy in Israel,* 153-176.

133. Klaus Koch (*The Prophets,* vol. 2, 13) and von Rad (*The Message of the Prophets,* 161) believe that Jeremiah began his career in 627/6 BCE. Heschel (*The Prophets,* vol. 1, 103) thinks that he received his call in 625 and was active during the reigns of the last kings of Judah—Josiah, Jehoiakim, Jehoiachin, and Zedekiah—and continued for some time after the fall of Jerusalem in 587 BCE. Holladay (*Jeremiah 1,* 1-9) contends that Jeremiah was born in 627 and he hesitantly says that he received his call in 615, when he was twelve years old. This may explain why Jeremiah doesn't pass much judgment on Josiah's reforms of 622 since he would have been only a boy of five years old.

134. Wilson, *Prophecy and Society in Ancient Israel,* 242. While his connection to the priesthood might make him a central prophet in the religious establishment, Wilson believes that nothing in the book suggests this claim (p. 241).

135. Koch, *The Prophets,* vol. 2, 17. Malchow notes that Amos, Micah, Isaiah, and Jeremiah were all educated, wealthy, and upper-class people who nevertheless identified with the cause of the poor at the risk of their own careers (*Social Justice in the Hebrew Bible,* 34).

136. Jeremiah makes reference to the *'ebyôn* אביון, *dal* דל / *dallâ* דלה, and *'ānî* עני. The distribution is as follows: *'ebyôn* אביון: 2:34; 5:28; 20:13; 22:16; *dal* דל: 5:4; 39:10; *dallâ* דלה: 40:7; 52:15-16; *'ānî* עני: 22:16; widow and/or fatherless child: 5:28, 7:6; 15:8; 18:21; 22:3; 49:11; the oppressor (*hayyônâ* היונה): 25:38; 46:16; 50:16; *'āšaq* עשק: 6:6; 7:6; 22:3; 50:33; *laḥaṣ* לחץ: 30:20; and *ṣārâ* צרה: 14:8.

137. Holladay, *Jeremiah 1,* 110; Jones, *Jeremiah,* 94; Carroll, *Jeremiah,* 140. Carroll adds that the oppression of the poor is not a main theme of Jeremiah so its appearance here is probably a secondary development (p. 140). This statement can only be evaluated after studying the book in its entirety.

138. Holladay, *Jeremiah 1,* 558.

139. Ibid., 594-97.

140. Ibid., 596.

141. Whereas Abraham stopped his wager at ten righteous people in order for Yahweh to save Sodom and Gomorrah, Yahweh is making it easy for Jeremiah by asking for only one person. See also the discussion by Temba L. J. Mafico in "A Study of the Hebrew Root Špṭ with Reference to Yahweh" (Ph.D. diss., Harvard University, 1979), 88-126; and Mafico, *Yahweh's Emergence as "Judge" among the Gods,* 144-172.

142. Holladay, *Jeremiah 1,* 178. He also makes the interesting point that while the leaders (*haggĕdōlîm* הגדלים [v. 5]) "are graced with the definite article," the poor (*dallîm* דלים) are not. Hence, "Even grammatically the poor remain anonymous" (p. 178). While the NRSV translates *haggĕdōlîm* הגדלים with "the rich," the NIV translates it with "the leaders." While writing about the poor in Latin America, Gustavo Gutiérrez echoes the same point. He notes that "the poor are insignificant, anonymous, nameless." See "Preferential Option for the Poor," 179. In a different article, he elaborates his argument:

"The poor person is the insignificant one who has no economic clout, who belongs to a spurned race, and who has been culturally marginalized. The poor are socially insignificant, except before God. They are always present through statistics, but they have no names." See "Option for the Poor: Assessment and Implications," 66. Gutiérrez cites an apt example to illustrate his point. He relates that during the funeral of Bishop Romero of El Salvador, forty people were killed but none was mentioned by name. They were identified through statistics while everyone knew Romero's name.

143. 2 Kings 25:12 refers to the *umiddallat hā-'āreṣ* ומדלת הארץ and 2 Kgs 24:14 to the *dallat 'am-hā'āreṣ* דלת עם הערץ. In the first case, "Some of the poorest of the land" are to be vinedressers and tillers of the soil. In the second, the "poorest of the people of the land" are not assigned any specific task. Thus, Jer 39:10 agrees with 2 Kgs 25:12 on the poor getting access to vineyards and fields. However, Bright (*Jeremiah*, 242-43) and Carroll *(Jeremiah*, 692) agree that the MT word for "fields" is of uncertain meaning.

144. Jones, *Jeremiah*, 465. Holladay suggests that Nebuchadrezzar's motive for redistributing some land to peasants was "both as an economic necessity and as a measure of pacification" (*Jeremiah 2*, 293).

145. Bright, *Jeremiah*, 253. These were "economically underprivileged classes" (p. 253). See also Jones, *Jeremiah*, 470; and Carroll, *Jeremiah*, 703.

146. Holladay, *Jeremiah 2*, 436.

147. Carroll, *Jeremiah*, 862; Jones, *Jeremiah*, 550. Holladay wonders if *dallôt* דלות (n. f. pl. of *dal* דל) in both vv. 15-16 (which is rendered *umiddallat* ומדלת in 2 Kgs 25:11-12) was an attempt to understand the expression as "the poor women" (*Jeremiah 2*, 437, n. 6). This is unlikely since no women are mentioned in these verses or in 2 Kgs 25:11-12. This would have been much more likely had the expression been used in Jer 40:7 where women are mentioned. Ralph W. Klein defines haplography as "a mistake in writing, when a copyist wrote once what should have been written twice; the opposite of dittography. Sometimes used to refer to any omission." See Klein, *Textual Criticism of the Old Testament: The Septuagint after Qumran*, Guides to Biblical Scholarship, ed. Gene M. Tucker (Philadelphia: Fortress Press, 1974; third printing 1981), p. x.

148. Pleins, "Poor, Poverty," 406.

149. Holladay, *Jeremiah 1*, 199. He also points out that the LXX has "widow" after the fatherless because these two are usually paired in the Bible. Here the fatherless are paired with the poor (p. 199). See also Bright, *Jeremiah*, 40; Carroll, *Jeremiah*, 188.

150. Matthews, *Social World of the Hebrew Prophets*, 120.

151. Refer to the familiar stories of Sarai/Sarah and Hagar (Gen 16:1-15; 21:1-21), Rachel and Leah (Gen 29:31 - 30:24), and Hannah and Peninnah (1 Sam 1:1 - 2:21). All these stories are interestingly characterized by despair/sorrow, jealousy, and conflict, but joy at the birth of a child, a male.

152. Matthews, *Social World of the Hebrew Prophets*, 126. Jerome Ross argues the thesis that Israel's history can better be understood as that of the "survival" of a dominated minority nation for most of its existence except for brief periods of time. See Ross, *The History of Ancient Israel and Judah: A Compilation* (Pittsburgh, PA.: Dorrance Publishing Co., 2003), ix, xi, xii, 2.

153. Carroll thinks this verse is "strange" because a Judean God offers to protect Edomite victims of his wrath. Such concern may also indicate a lack of serious hostility against Edom. He further observes that "Yahweh's role as a caring and protective figure is seldom applied to members of foreign nations" (*Jeremiah,* 803).

154. That is, first cousins, see Gen 25:30; 36:1, 8.

155. Carroll, *Jeremiah,* 140.

156. Hoppe, *Being Poor,* 87. Since the prophets mainly functioned within the establishment, Bailey even argues that they supported the system that oppressed the poor. The prophets addressed their words, not to the poor themselves, but to the rich, warning them what to do or not do in order to stay in power. Even the priests benefited from the system, for they received the tithe and offering and ate it. Private communication, January 6, 2010.

157. Iliffe, *The African Poor,* 4.

158. Mafico puts it thus: "Unless the Israelites practiced righteousness . . . and good neighborliness among themselves, as a covenant community, God would punish them for their iniquities (Amos 2:6-8). True worship of Yahweh demanded a change of heart in those who believed in the holy God (Jer 31:33). This would be evidenced by their showing justice toward the poor, who were being crushed economically by the unscrupulous rich (Amos 4:1-3)." See "Ethics (Old Testament)," in *ABD* 2 (1992): 652. Bruce C. Birch notes that responsibility for action to reduce poverty lay with the privileged, rather than with the poor themselves. See "Hunger, Poverty and Biblical Religion," *ChrCent* 92 (June 1975): 593.

Chapter Four

Poverty in the Writings

INTRODUCTION

This chapter concludes our study of the Hebrew Bible by focusing on the Writings especially the wisdom literature and the book of Psalms. As noted above, the problem of poverty continued to be paramount in both the legal materials and the prophetic literature despite the injunction of the divine mandate for Israel. As we trace the development of the Hebrew Bible, it becomes apparent that the problem of poverty had not yet been solved. While different explanations for poverty are given in each section of the Hebrew Bible, we encounter more perspectives on poverty in the Writings. While this section continues some of the perspectives in the earlier parts of the Bible, there is a development in the understanding of the problem of poverty. While the law codes and the prophetic literature have focused on what society can do for the poor, some of the new ideas in wisdom literature are the responsibility of the poor for themselves.

STRUCTURE AND CAUSES OF POVERTY IN THE WISDOM LITERATURE AND THE BOOK OF PSALMS

We thus turn our attention to the wisdom literature, specifically the book of Job, Proverbs, Qoheleth (Ecclesiastes), as well as in the book of Psalms, a poetic collection of Israel's cultic praises (Hebrew *tehillim* תהלים).[1] In these writings, poverty maintains some of the older characteristics yet at the same time develops new meanings. For example, Job makes uses of the language of poverty which is peculiar to the prophetic tradition and Israel's legal codes.

In this case, Job's understanding of poverty assumes a "prophetic character," in which poverty is primarily understood as the result of oppressive social structures.[2] This is also clear from the words Job uses to describe oppressive situations, for example '*āšaq* עשק, *laḥaṣ* לחץ, and *rāṣaṣ* רצץ. The widow and fatherless are also featured in the book of Job as victims of oppression.

Proverbs betrays several understandings about the nature and structure of poverty. Not only is poverty caused by the rich oppressing the poor (Prov 22:2, 7, 9, 16, 22-23; 28:3), but also it is caused by laziness (6:6-11; 10:4, 26; 12:24; 13:4; 15:19; 19:24); ignoring instruction or lack of discipline (11:18; 13:18); worthless pursuits (28:19); excessive pleasure (12:11, 21:17; 23:20-21; 28:19); excessive sleep (6:9-11; 10:5; 20:13; 24:33-34); drunkenness and gluttony (23:20-21); or love of pleasure (21:17). While wine and strong drink are prescribed for the poor in order that they may forget their misery and poverty, these drinks are forbidden for kings because they might make them pervert the duties of proper rule (31:4-7). Since Proverbs is thought to have been written by the elite circles of Israel, wealth is not seen as a necessarily bad thing (10:15; 14:20; 18:11, 16, 23). Yet the wise also caution others about the dangers of wealth (10:2; 11:28; 13:11; 15:6).[3] In the same light, generosity is also called for (11:24; 19:17; 21:26) and viewed as righteousness (11:23-24; 29:7). According to Dianne Bergant, "a kind of ambiguity toward wealth does appear in several places. For example, despite the high regard accorded good fortune, there is a warning about the peril that awaits those who covet riches."[4] Prov 13:21 claims that sinners are pursued by misfortune while the righteous are rewarded with prosperity. Verse 25 reads: "The righteous man eats to his heart's content, But the belly of the wicked is empty" (*Tanakh*). Proverbs further explores the connection between righteousness and wealth (or well-being) in 2:21-22; 10:22; 21:21; and 28:10, 20, 25.[5] These texts emphasize success through proper conduct and balance in life. According to Naomi Franklin, "In the biblical context, righteousness must be exercised in one's dealings both with God and one's fellow human beings."[6] Poverty is not necessarily viewed as estrangement from God since Yahweh defends the poor (22:23; 23:10f) and punishes oppressors. In addition, the rich are expected to use their wealth responsibly.[7]

The book of Qoheleth does not have much to say about poverty but some blame is placed on oppression. Due to his philosophy that "all is vanity," Qoheleth seems to see no difference between being rich or poor. However, because he values wisdom, he believes that it is better to be poor and wise than rich and foolish.

The Psalms are not only full of praises for the Lord but also laments from the worshippers. They appeal to Yahweh to rescue them from their predicament. The '*ānî* עני feature most prominently in the Psalms. In their supplications, they often describe their needs, condition, and hope for deliverance. The wicked and unjust people are frequently seen as the causes of the suffering of the worshipper.

JOB

The book of Job[8] revolves around the subject of Job's unjust suffering and Yahweh's apparent neglect of Job's innocence. Job and his friends attempt to unravel the mystery of his suffering, inevitably discussing the question of theodicy in their numerous dialogues.[9] His friends subscribe to the traditional doctrine of retribution that views suffering as the result of sin and blessings as a reward for righteousness. Throughout the dialogues, Job vehemently denies that he has sinned and continues to assert his innocence until he is vindicated yet humbled by the unpredictable nature of Yahweh's response. Kathryn Schifferdecker offers a fresh interpretation of the divine speeches in Job and argues that God puts Job "in his place," that is, as part of God's creation theology and ordering of the cosmos.[10]

While the problem of unmerited suffering pervades the book of Job, the writer still manages to offer perspectives on poverty and wealth in the dialogues between Job and his friends such that some critics have seen a prophetic character in the book. However, Bergant cautions that Job belongs "to the privileged class" for he ends up "a prosperous man" but his encounter with God brought him "new insight."[11]

The book of Job uses the traditional words for poverty that we have encountered elsewhere: *'ebyôn* אביון , *dal* דל, and *'ānî* עני .[12] In Eliphaz's first speech to Job (5:15), he claims that God saves the needy (*'ebyôn* אביון) from the clutches of the powerful (*ḥazaq* חזק). The *'ebyôn* אביון are here portrayed as "weak" people in the grip of the strong. In 24:4 Job asks Eliphaz why the Almighty (Shaddai) seems to abandon the poor (24:4). The wicked victimize the *'ebyôn* אביון by appropriating their property and possessions.[13] In verse 14, the *'ebyôn* אביון are victims of a nocturnal murderer.

In Job's final defense of his righteousness, he claims that he was father of the *'ebyônîm* אביונים and defender of the stranger (29:16). He ensured justice by representing them in court, because they had no one to do so.[14] The *'ebyônîm* אביונים are therefore plaintiffs without legal representation. By defending them, Job acts in a just and righteous manner. In addition, Job's soul grieves for the *'ebyôn* אביון (30:25), a statement that indicates Job's identification and sympathy with the condition of the *'ebyôn* אביון. The *'ebyôn* אביון are also portrayed as those without enough clothes (31:19), and in his goodness, Job sees to it that they are clothed.

In as much as Job protects the weak (5:15), he also gives hope to the *'ānî* עני (5:16) by protecting them from the injustice of the powerful. Yet this does not ring true with Job's accusers, who think that his suffering is a result of his misdeeds. Perdue comments, "In the world constructed by the opponents of Job, creation, itself corrupt, is the domain of sinful human beings, ruled over by a sovereign Lord of justice who brings the wicked to an ignoble end but also is willing to save the penitent who turn to him for mercy."[15] In his second speech (20:10), Zophar explains that the children of the wicked person are dependent upon the poor *(dallîm* דלים*)*. Though economically poor, the *dallîm* דלים in this text are not destitute. In 20:19 Zophar implies that Job has victimized the *dallîm* דלים by seizing their houses, thus making them homeless. Under oath, Job continues to uphold his innocence. He swears that he has fulfilled the desires of the *dallîm* דלים (31:16). Pope notes that Job's repudiation of evil in this chapter has been compared to the "negative confession" in the Egyptian Book of the Dead in which the deceased enumerates sins he or she has not committed.[16] In Elihu's second speech, he attempts to show Job that God shows no partiality to the rich or poor *(dal* דל*)* for they are all God's creatures (34:19; see Deut 10:17; 2 Chron 19:7; Prov 22:2). That the *dal* דל are mentioned alongside the rich indicates that they are the material poor, the opposite of the rich. In 34:28, Elihu charges that the wicked cause the *dal* דל to cry out to God (see Exod 22:21-24). These victimized individuals are oppressed members of the community who seek solace in God.[17]

The word *'ānî* עני appears several times in the book of Job. The first occurrence is in Job's reply to Eliphaz (24:4). Just as the wicked victimize the *'ebyôn* אביון, so also do they oppress the *'ăniwwê-'āreṣ* עני ארץ by seizing their property and possessions. Job chronicles the height of cruelty by the wicked in 24:9. They seize the children of the *'ānî* עני like a pledge for a debt (see Deut 24:7). Habel describes this "most heartless crime of all" as follows: "The poor possess only their children, yet these are torn from the poor until they pay their petty debts."[18] The context clearly shows that the *'ānî* עני are insolvent debtors whose children become debtor slaves. Moreover, just as the *'ebyôn* אביון are nocturnal murder victims (24:14), so also are the *'ānî* עני.

The *ānî* עני are also depicted as the helpless who cry for help (29:12). Job claims to have assisted them in their time of need. In 34:28, God hears and responds not only to the cry of the oppressed *dal* דל but also to that of the *'ăniyyîm* עניים (Kethib form of *Qere 'ănāwîm* עניים). Elihu's fourth speech also portrays God as the advocate of the *'ăniyyîm* עניים or those who are deprived of their rights (36:6). Similarly, God delivers the *'ānî* עני (36:15) from their suffering. In Job, *'ānî* עני clearly possesses an element of suffering and anguish.

Pleins makes the interesting observation that in the book of Job, *'ebyôn* אביון is used mostly by Job, whereas *dal* דל is almost always used by Job's accusers. This is so because *dal* דל is the preferred word of the conventional wisdom tradition (fifteen times in Proverbs) which the accusers represent.[19]

The book of Job also makes reference to the widow *('almānâ* אלמנה*)* and fatherless *(yātôm* יתום*)* who frequently appear together in legal and prophetic texts. In 6:27 Job accuses Eliphaz of casting lots over a fatherless child (see 2 Kgs 4:1), an action showing how vulnerable and defenseless the fatherless were. By contrast, Job protected such persons (31:17, 21) as the law required. However, the accusations and counter-accusations continue throughout the dialogues. Despite Job's assertion of his innocence, Eliphaz still accuses him of not being charitable to the widow and fatherless, an action that reaches "the depths of degradation and perversity."[20]

Further abuse of the widow and fatherless is evident from Job's speech about the actions of the wicked (24:3, 9, 21). The wicked take away the animals of the widow and fatherless as pledge items (cf. Deut 24:17). These animals were essential for their livelihood; to seize them was to remove the basic means of survival for the defenseless.[21] Moreover, as we saw in the Law Codes of ancient Israel, a pledge item was supposed to be something as small as a piece of clothing. Yet even that little item had to be returned at the end of the day as a source of warmth for the poor. By seizing the animals of the widow and fatherless, the wicked not only violate the law but also prove to be heartless. Snatching away a suckling child from a widow was further victimization (v. 9). The wicked, while showing no kindness to the widow (v. 21), may suffer the same fate as the widow (27:15). These verses therefore show gross violations of the rights of the widow and fatherless. The wicked not only oppress the widow and fatherless but they also reduce them to a state of destitution.

In his final defense, Job replies to Eliphaz's charges by stating how he had advocated for the widow and fatherless such that the widow's heart was gladdened (29:12-13). This passage depicts Job as the ideal ancient Near Eastern ruler who administers justice for the oppressed. Verse 7 states that Job sat at the gate of the city, the traditional seat of justice.[22] Job stands by his conviction that he has acted rightly with regard to the widow and fatherless while he judged their cases at the gate (31:16-17, 21). Habel argues that Job would not even think of abusing a fatherless child because it "would be like abusing his own children."[23]

Although the discussion about the widow and fatherless consists of both alleged abuses and proper treatment, three things are clear: (1) the book of Job narrates potential forms of injustice and exploitation to which the widow and fatherless were susceptible; (2) it also indicates how they were accorded proper justice in accordance with the law; and (3) the references to the widow and fatherless and their close association with the *'ānî* עני*, dal* דל*,* and *'ebyôn*

אביון (24:3-4, 9, 14; 29:12-13, 16; 31:16-17, 19, 21) indicate that they are viewed in the same light. Being mentioned in the same context as the poor shows that to the author of the book of Job, the widow and fatherless were classified as poor and subject to the same treatment, just or unjust.

The book of Job also makes brief reference to oppression *(rāṣaṣ רצץ)* as something which the poor could be subjected to (20:19). Zophar accuses Job of having done this; hence his suffering. Elihu also claims that God delivers sufferers from their affliction (*laḥaṣ* לחץ [36:15]). To him, Job's suffering is a sign of his guilt.

The use of *'ebyôn* אביון, *dal* דל, *'ānî* עני, *'almānâ* אלמנה, and *yātôm* יתום (and avoidance of the term *rāš* רש) gives the book of Job not only a "prophetic character," but also one immersed in ancient Israelite and ancient Near Eastern value-systems and beliefs. Such usage suggests the author's familiarity with the traditions of the ancient Near East in general. Though privileged, Job is the personification of a true arbiter of justice to the poor and oppressed.

PROVERBS

The book of Proverbs[24] is usually divided into the following literary blocks: 1 - 9; 10 - 29; and 30 - 31. Chapters 1 - 9 consist of educational material corresponding to the international wisdom genre or the "Instruction" in Egyptian materials. Proverbs 22:17 - 24:22 closely resemble the Egyptian Instruction of Amen-em-opet. In fact, some scholars have suggested a literary dependence of some sort.[25] McKane refers to Prov 10 - 29 as "sentence literature" and 30 - 31 as poems and numerical sayings.[26] This structural division of the book is even supported by words for "poor" and "poverty" in the book of Proverbs.[27]

Proverbs uses the familiar words for the poor and a couple of new ones. These are: *dal* דל, *'ānî* עני/*'ănāwîm* ענוים, *'ebyôn* אביון, *rāš* רש, and *maḥsôr* מחסור.[28]

A variety of perspectives are evident in the use of the word *dal* דל in Proverbs. Chapter 10:15 states that wealth (*hôn* הון) is the fortress of the rich (*'āšîr* אשיר) while poverty (*rāš* רש) is the ruin of the poor (*dallîm* דלים). This is quite a departure from our previous understandings of poverty. Here wealth is being glorified and poverty derided. In this context, the *dallîm* דלים are obviously the financially poor, the opposite of the rich. The same view is evident in some of the sayings. For example, wealth attracts many friends but a poor man (*dal* דל) is deserted by friends (19:4). According to these verses, wealth is something more desirable than poverty. However, a sympathetic reading is given in other sayings. Proverbs 14:31 states that oppressing the *dal* דל is showing contempt for the *dal's* creator. The *dal* דל here is a powerless person being afflicted.

Proverbs 22:22 echoes the same sentiment. It advises the reader against exploiting *(gāzal* גזל*)* the *dal* דל on account of their status. These individuals are victims of oppression because they are either not powerful or cannot defend themselves. This sense of helplessness is captured in the imagery of the roaring lion and a destructive storm (28:3, 15). Bergant comments insightfully that while Proverbs does not condemn the poor, concern for them "may in fact be condescending and not at all disinterested, because reward is often promised for following this advice."[29] Genuine assistance to the poor must be given without expecting something in return. This is why the law urged assisting the poor even as the *šĕmiṭṭâ* שמטה year approached (Deut 15:7-11).

The oppression of the *dal* דל in order to increase one's wealth is viewed negatively, especially if the aim is to give gifts to the rich (22:16). Both practices are frowned upon, and the perpetrators are threatened that they could end up being poor themselves. This reversal of fortune is also evident in 21:13. The one who ignores the cry of the poor will end up in that position and his or her cry will be ignored as well. Proverbs 28:8 attacks those who enrich themselves by charging high interest rates *(néšek* נשך*)*. The wealth acquired in this way may be inherited by someone who will be generous to the poor.[30] Proverbs attacks the practice of usury which was forbidden in the Law Codes (Exod 22:25; Lev 25:36; Deut 23:19). Again, the *dal* דל are portrayed as victims of economic oppression.

A few references specifically recommend kindness and justice to the *dal* דל (19:17; 29:7, 14). Such behavior leads to divine reward (19:17). In 22:9, one is blessed for sharing one's food with the *dal* דל or those who are hungry. In fact, practicing justice on behalf of the *dallîm* דלים is called righteousness (29:7). By contrast, the evil have no concern for the poor. Similarly, a king who judges the *dallîm* דלים with fairness secures his throne (29:14). This was the traditional expectation of the duty of the good king. Proverbs 28:11 has a unique use of *dal* דל as compared to the above discussion. A rich man may think that he is wise but actually a poor man may be wiser. In this single text, the writer focuses attention not so much on the poverty of the *dal* דל as on the possibility that the *dal* דל is more intelligent than the rich person. Proverbs therefore uses *dal* דל in several ways, but this word has also acquired new meaning. It is also notable that *dal* דל is used only in Proverbs 10 – 29, the so-called "sentence literature."

Proverbs also uses the word *'ānî* עני in some distinctive ways. In 15:15 the *'ānî* עני are portrayed as those who spent a lifetime of wretchedness. They are contrasted with those who are continually cheerful. Proverbs 22:22 instructs the listener not to mistreat the *'ānî* עני in court, giving the implication that there was a possibility of legal abuse for this group. While 30:14 portrays the *'ănāwîm* ענוים (*'ănniyîm* עניים) as those who are devoured from the earth, 3:34 portrays them as those who are blessed by God. A religious connotation is presented here; hence the term is often translated as "the humble ones."

The Instruction for King Lemuel from his mother (31:9) urges him to practice the proper duty of the king by defending the rights of the *'ānî* עני and delivering fair legal judgments.[31] Verse 20 describes the ideal wife as one who is charitable to the poor. Such kindness to the poor assures one of blessings (14:21). Finally, Prov 16:19 states that it is better to be like a lowly person than to share in the aggression of war. Proverbs is somewhat "frank" about its portrayal of the condition of the poor. So far, it is clear that being either a *dal* דל or *'ānî* עני is not desirable. But the book also calls for charity even as it praises wealth.

Proverbs uses the term *'ebyôn* אביון on only four occasions. The *'ebyôn* אביון are the oppressed poor, but kindness to them honors God (14:31). Moreover, like the *'ănāwîm* ענוים, they are also devoured from the earth (30:14). In the King Lemuel Instruction, the king is instructed to be fair and just to the *'ebyôn* אביון (31:9). In addition, the ideal wife is to be as charitable to the *'ebyôn* אביון as she is to the *'ănāwîm* ענוים. The relationship of the *'ebyôn* אביון to the *'ānî* עני in these texts is unmistakable. The author views them in the same light as individuals susceptible to oppression.

A variety of perspectives on poverty are also evident in Proverb's use of the word *rāš* רש.[32] Perhaps the most remarkable usage of *rāš* רש is the statement that poverty is something people bring upon themselves. The legendary sluggard of Proverbs is a case in point here (Prov 6:6-11, see also 20:4, 13; 30:25). In the success-driven culture of the rich elite, laziness, love of sleep, and fecklessness are major causes of poverty (6:10-11; 24:33-34; 10:4; 20:13). In these texts *rāš* רש is used to describe someone who becomes poor essentially because of a poor work ethic. Thus Prov 28:19 appreciates hard work lest one become a *rāš* רש. Similarly, Proverbs 13:18 attributes poverty to a lack of discipline.

Two sayings seem to teach contradictory lessons. According to Prov 23:21, the only fate of drunkards and gluttons is to become poor (*rāš* רש). However, in 31:7 the queen mother instructs King Lemuel to give strong drink to the poor so that they may forget their misery.[33]

Another glaring perspective is that poverty is an undesirable condition. The poor person is shunned by his or her neighbors, while the rich person has many friends (14:20). In 19:7 the poor person is shunned by his or her family. One can only ask how much more by friends? These considerations serve to heighten the unenviable condition of the poor. Indeed, poverty is seen as the ruin of the poor (10:15).

Some contrasting statements are also given concerning the *rāš* רש. While poverty causes no threat to the poor person (13:8), the rich rule over the poor (22:7) or the poor plead for mercy from the rich (18:23). In 30:8, the speaker desires neither riches nor poverty, but only to have enough. Thus poverty is an undesirable extreme, as wealth also can be. This saying teaches about the importance of finding balance in life.

The *rāš* רשׁ are also seen as the opposite of the rich. The *'āšîr* אשׁיר and the *rāš* רשׁ have nothing in common except only one thing: God made them both (22:2). They are opposite sides of the same coin. This is also clear in 29:13 where the oppressor and the *rāš* רשׁ have their "createdness" as their common link. Here the *rāš* רשׁ is being described as a powerless victim of the oppressor. Such an oppressor is compared to a destructive storm (28:3). Solfrid Storøy argues that the use of "polar word pairs and other poetic devices" in Proverbs helps to illuminate the true meaning of these word pairs. He writes:

> What is good cannot be fully known until the bad has been tasted. Poverty is measured on its counterpart. The words for "poor" must be seen in relation to their polar words when wanting to come to grips with them.[34]

A few "better-than" sayings, however, describe poverty as the more preferable of two conditions. Hence, it is better to be a good poor person than a perverse fool or rich person (19:1; 28:6). Similarly, it is better to be poor than a liar (19:22). Giving to the poor is still seen as a worthy exercise (28:27); mocking them is tantamount to mocking God (17:5). Raymond C. Van Leeuwen remarks that these types of sayings "overturn the usual evaluation of wealth as simply good and poverty as bad."[35]

In one saying, someone who pretends to be rich may actually be a *rāš* רשׁ whereas the one who pretends to be a *rāš* רשׁ may actually be rich (13:7). Another saying portrays the condition of the *rāš* רשׁ as fated (13:23). No matter how prosperous this person may be, misfortune will always visit him or her.[36] Proverbs therefore expands the definition of the poor in a significant way.

Proverbs also uses the word *maḥsôr* מחסור to describe the condition of poverty. The basic meaning that emerges from the context is that *maḥsôr* מחסור is basically a "lack" of something.[37] In 6:11 (see also 28:27), the sluggard who loves to sleep will have nothing. His or her poverty is a lack of goods due to indolence. Conversely, hard work and diligent planning are seen as profitable (14:23, 21:5), but the absence of these qualities leads to the condition of *maḥsôr* מחסור. Likewise the lover of pleasure or wine (21:17) will become a *maḥsôr* מחסור; in fact, the text says he or she will not be rich. The *maḥsôr* מחסור in this context is therefore someone who lacks money. Finally, oppressing the poor or giving to the rich (instead of the poor) leads one to become a *maḥsôr* מחסור (22:16). This understanding is clearly evident in 28:27, where the one who gives to the poor lacks (*maḥsôr* מחסור) nothing. There is also an element of personal responsibility in Proverbs' use of the word *maḥsôr* מחסו. The lack that these persons experience is basically because of their own actions. According to Norman Habel, the book of Proverbs has "a number of apparently discrete paradigms for life" such as the paradigm of success in life, the hard work paradigm, and the harsh reality paradigm, among others.[38]

Several references to the widow and fatherless indicate that they deserve special protection because of their vulnerability. Proverbs 15:25 states that Yahweh preserves the boundaries of the widow while tearing down the house of the proud. McKane observes:

> The boundary of the widow's piece of land is maintained by Yahweh, when otherwise she might be defenseless before the cupidity of her neighbours. This optimistic assertion contrasts with the realism of the prophetic preaching.[39]

Whybray further observes that what is striking in this verse is the assertion (as in much of Old Testament teaching) "that Yahweh himself will act directly to defend widows from exploitation and to root out the offenders."[40] Proverbs 23:10 also teaches one not to move the boundary stones or encroach on the fields of the fatherless. These actions against the widow and fatherless were specifically prohibited by ancient Israelite laws (see Deut 19:14; 27:17). As in most of the laws and the prophets, the widow and fatherless are here paired as persons in need of special protection because of their vulnerability.

Proverbs also uses words for oppression like *'āšaq* עשק (14:31; 22:16) and *dakā'* דכא (22:22) to signify the exploitation of the poor. Those who oppress (*'ōšeq* עשק) the poor (*dal* דל) disrespect their creator, but those who are kind to the needy (*'ebyôn* אביון) honor God (14:31). Moreover, oppressing the *dal* דל to enrich oneself or giving to the rich (*'āšîr* אשיר) leads one to the same state of poverty (*maḥsôr* מחסור [22:16]). Finally, Proverbs instructs one not to rob (*gāzal* גזל) the *dal* דל because of their condition, or crush (*dakā'* דכא) the afflicted (*'ānî* עני) at the gate, because Yahweh defends their cause (*kî Yahweh yārîb rîbām* כי יהוה יריב ריבם; 22:22-23).

It is also clear from the preceding discussion that Proverbs frequently discusses the poor and the rich in the same context. This is intended to show that the poor are often portrayed as the opposite of the rich. In general, Proverbs has enriched our understanding of poverty by using a variety of meanings for words pertaining to poverty and the poor.

QOHELETH

Biblical scholars have referred to the book of Qoheleth[41] as "strange," "cynical," and "nihilistic," among other characterizations. Its "negative stance toward all of life and the created order seems to be at considerable variance with the central themes of the Hebrew Bible."[42]

A wealthy man (2:4-10), Qoheleth's perspective is from that of wealth, power, and privilege. However, he is disillusioned by the futility of questing after wealth and the indifference of death to social status of rich or poor.[43] He sees everything as vanity, or a chasing after the wind. His reflections on wealth and poverty are governed by the same skepticism he holds toward life. Yet he is aware of the power of privilege and wealth.

Qoheleth uses two typical wisdom words for poverty, namely, *miskēn* מסכן, *rāš* רש, and the word *'ānî* עני which appears in all the literary blocks of material under consideration.[44] In the first occurrence of the word *miskēn* מסכן, Qoheleth argues that it is better to be a poor (*miskēn* מסכן) but wise youth than an old and foolish king who cannot take advice. Crenshaw believes that Qoheleth is reversing ancient wisdom's traditional view of age as signifying wisdom and honor, and being better than youth and foolishness.[45] The word *miskēn* מסכן is used twice in 9:15. A powerful king surrounds a small city which is ultimately saved by a poor (*miskēn* מסכן) but wise man. Ironically, nobody remembered the wise deeds of that poor man. In fact, his actions were not acknowledged (v. 16). Either the poor man's advice was unheeded or despised.[46] In any case this story proves Qoheleth's philosophy that wisdom is better than folly. Because of the poor wise man's great deeds, Qoheleth implies that poverty with wisdom is better than strength with foolishness.

In the first use of the word *rāš* רש Qoheleth ties it to another king. After stating that it is better to be poor (*miskēn* מסכן) and wise than a foolish king, Qoheleth describes the circumstances of the youthful king's poverty. He may have been born poor (*rāš* רש) but rises to be a king. Whybray believes that this poor young man has supplanted the king, possibly by revolution.[47]

The second and last use of *rāš* רש occurs in 5:8 (Heb 5:7). Qoheleth argues that one should not be surprised to see a poor person being oppressed because it is a sign of administrative corruption. One cannot do anything about such a state of affairs except to accept it.[48] In the rest of this chapter, Qoheleth goes on to prove that wealth is meaningless anyway. One never gets enough of it (5:10); moreover, it can be a source of sorrow (5:13-14). These two texts therefore describe two forms of poverty—one acquired at birth and the other resulting from the exploitation of others.

The word *'ānî* עני appears in 6:8 only. Qoheleth asks what the *'ānî* עני gains by knowing proper conduct. This question is parallel to his first question: "What advantage does a wise person have over a fool?" Scholars generally agree that this verse is problematic and some suggest that it is corrupt.[49]

Finally, Qoheleth describes the act of oppression as at least contributing to poverty. He makes three claims in 4:1: (a) he saw all the oppression (*hā'ăšûqîm* העשוקים) under the sun; (b) he saw the tears of the oppressed; and (c) the oppressors ('*ōšeqêhem* עשקהם) are powerful. In 5:8, the oppression ('*ōšeq* עשק) of the officials is making people poor (*rāš* רש). Here, Qoheleth makes a direct connection between poverty and oppression. In 7:7, extortion and bribery corrupt the wise person.

By using the unique word *miskēn* מסכן, Qoheleth also extends the definition of poverty. The writer betrays a sense of social justice by his criticism of the powerful and corrupt government officials who worsen the condition of the poor through unjust practices.

THE BOOK OF PSALMS

The book of Psalms[50] contains Israel's songs of praise to Yahweh. Scholars have identified at least five types of psalms, namely: hymns, laments, thanksgivings, songs of trust, and wisdom meditations.[51]

The book of Psalms uses six words to describe poverty: '*ānî* עני, '*ănāwîm* עניים, '*ebyôn* אביון, *dal* דל, *maḥsôr* מחסור, and *rāš* רש.[52] These words occur in all of the types of psalms mentioned above.

The '*ānî* עני are portrayed as facing various situations for which they send a communication to Yahweh. In many cases the wicked cause them to suffer. In one lament, the '*ānî* עני are hunted down by the wicked, who are always devising evil plans to catch them (10:2, 9; see also 14:6; 37:14; 109:16). Sometimes these evil-doers frustrate the plans of the '*ānî* עני (14:6). They are also portrayed as using a sword to oppress the poor. In some cases, they hound the poor to death. The '*ānî* עני are thus helpless victims of evil people.

In their suffering, they express hope that Yahweh will deliver them, or they directly petition God to do so (12:5, 68:10). Psalm 40:17 (see 70:5) shows a sufferer acknowledging his or her condition and asking God for help and deliverance. One personal lament indicates that the speaker is in pain (69:29). A speaker petitions God to listen (86:1), while another says he or she has been suffering for a long time (88:16). Psalm 102:1 portrays the speaker as crying out to God for deliverance.

Some Psalms also express the belief that God will judge in favor of the '*ānî* עני (18:27). Yahweh provides justice (*dîn* דין, *mišpāṭ* משפט) for the '*ānî* עני (140:12). Similarly, Yahweh will defend the cause of the '*ānî* עני and all who are deprived of their rights (82:3). Psalm 82 shows the superiority of Yahweh over other gods who cannot provide justice for the poor and suffering.[53]

The book of Psalms also uses '*ānî* עני in close association with '*ebyôn* אביון (35:10; 40:17; 70:5; 72:12; 82:3; 86:1; 107:41, 109:22). The picture that emerges is of the *'ānî* עני as those who are poor and suffering a variety of misfortunes and seeking solace in Yahweh.

The word *'ănāwîm* עניים, which has generally been assigned a "religious" connotation by some scholars, appears a few times in the Psalms. Psalm 9:12 portrays Yahweh as the avenger of blood who listens to the cry of the *'ănāwîm* עניים whose hope in Yahweh does not fade (v. 18). For the moment, the *'ănāwîm* עניים seem to be those who have suffered an injustice of some kind.

In Ps 22:26 the *'ănāwîm* עניים are obviously the hungry poor, for they shall eat and be satisfied. Psalm 25:9 does seem to have a religious flavor: Yahweh is the one who guides and teaches the *'ănāwîm* עניים what is right. True, they lack proper understanding of God's ways. In 34:2 they rejoice and exult in the Lord. Psalm 37:11 describes the *'ănāwîm* עניים as those who will inherit the earth and enjoy great peace. These are the traditional "meek." Weiser calls them "the humiliated." Presently, "They are still the humiliated and oppressed . . . but because of their hope, assured by their faith, they are more blessed than those who are without hope."[54] Therefore, when the *'ănāwîm* עניים behold the acts of God on their behalf, they are bound to praise God (69:32).

This sense of God's magnanimity and just acts is evident in Ps 76:9. Here, the use of the phrase *'ănwê-'ereṣ* עני ארץ is both unique and peculiar. It symbolizes all the poor and other victims of injustice and oppression. Weiser remarks that Yahweh's benevolent activity "shines like a sunbeam through the storm-clouds of the impending judgment."[55] The perpetrators of these crimes are abandoned by Yahweh who saves the *'ănāwîm* עניים (147:6; 149:4).

Although a few texts give a religious connotation to the word *'ănāwîm* עניים, it is clear that most of the texts view them as victims of evil persons who oppress them. Yahweh always comes to their rescue as Yahweh has done historically.

The Psalmist also uses the word *'ebyôn* אביון to refer to the poor. This word is often translated "needy." In several instances, *'ebyôn* אביון is used in the same context with *'ānî* עני indicating that their situation is similar. In fact, some of the worshippers refer to themselves as being both the *'ānî* עני and *'ebyôn* אביון (40:17; 70:5; 86:1; 109:22). These seem to be the very desperate ones, perhaps the very destitute or even beggars. The wicked and oppressors are viewed as contributing to their current predicament (37:14; 72:4; 82:4). According to W. Eugene March, the poor and needy suffer in a very real sense:

> These people experience real, material difficulties . . . a spiritual interpretation should never replace or diminish the primary point of reference: these people are without means or power. The poor and needy, as with the others mentioned, are especially vulnerable and defenseless. The poor and needy are the impoverished living on the edge of life.[56]

In 35:10, the *'ebyôn* אביון are sheer victims of robbery. Yahweh will rescue them just as Yahweh has rescued the weak from the strong. The *'ebyôn* אביון, like the other victims of injustice, have abiding faith in Yahweh and confidence that Yahweh will deliver them from their distressful situations (40:17; 69:33).

A wisdom psalm (49:2) portrays the *'ebyôn* אביון as the opposite of the rich. This intended contrast is evident in the Psalmist's use of opposite words. As a result, the contrast between "high" and "low" parallels that between "rich" and "poor." The psalm (c.f., Ps 73) goes on to explain that wealth is fleeting and the rich have no advantage over the poor because when they die, they will leave their wealth behind. They should not trust in their wealth and the poor need not envy them.[57] Bergant adds that while the poor may hope to improve their circumstances, they may also be heartened by the realization that the "dissociation of virtue from wealth releases them from acceding to the contentions of any prejudicial stereotyping."[58]

Psalm 72:4 seems to contain a reference to the exploited poor who are threatened with losing their children to unscrupulous people. Yahweh is said to save the children of the *'ebyôn* אביון and crush the oppressor (lit. "crush the crusher"). Dahood's reference to extortion[59] strengthens my argument. I think there is a strong likelihood that this reference can actually be to the poor who fail to pay their debts. In that case the creditor responds by seizing the debtor's children.

This chapter is also loaded with references to several descriptions of poor people—the *dal* דל, *'ebyôn* אביון, and *'ānî* עני (72:4, 12-13). Moreover, this categorization of the poor is duplicated and expanded in 82:3-4. Herein are the *dal* דל, *'ebyôn* אביון, *'ānî* עני, *rāš* רש, and *yātôm* יתום. McPolin observes that "the focus is people who are materially, socially poor."[60] It is not surprising that the wicked are mentioned in this context. The concentration of these types of vulnerable persons suggests that they share the same fate. The *'ebyôn* אביון are part of those deprived of justice. In the divine council that Yahweh convenes, Yahweh asks the gods when they will extend proper justice to these groups of the poor (82:1-2).[61] Obviously, the gods are guilty of this miscarriage of justice. The sheer multiplicity of the victims of injustice is an indication of the extensive nature of the problem.

Psalm 113:7 presents Yahweh as a very compassionate God. Yahweh is described anthropomorphically as raising the *dal* דל from the dust and the *'ebyôn* אביון from the ash heap. Weiser argues that this may be a reference to "the sick" who face a predicament reminiscent to that of Job (see Job 2:8).[62] In 132:15, the poor of Jerusalem will be provided for by Yahweh, hence the *'ebyôn* אביון in this context are those who are hungry.

As with other types of the poor, the *'ebyôn* אביון also express hope that Yahweh will deliver them from their predicament (140:12). According to Dahood, "Yahweh will uphold the cause of justice by rewarding the persecuted and the poor in the future life."[63]

The Psalmist portrays the *dal* דל as those who are also in need of divine help because of their perceived physical weakness. In 41:1, the one who cares for the *dal* דל is fortunate. The context (v. 3) indicates that the word *dal* דל refers to a sick person.[64] Psalm 113:7 strengthens this interpretation since in that case, Yahweh raises the *dal* דל (or sick person) from the dust (and the *ebyôn* אביון from the ashes). Yahweh will have compassion on the *dal* דל (72:13). Psalm 83:3-4 groups the *dal* דל with other vulnerable persons. The *dal* דל are also part of those who are deprived of their rights. Moreover, they are victims of those who scheme evil plans. However, Yahweh will fight for their rights. Significantly, *dal* דל is also grouped with *'ebyôn* אביון, *'ānî* עני, and *rāš* רש . In addition to *dal* דל standing for a victim of evil and oppression, this word particularly connotes physical sickness in the Psalter.

The Psalmist uses the word *maḥsôr* מחסור only once in a thanksgiving psalm (34:10). As in the case of Proverbs, this word also means to "lack" something. The Psalter confirms this by stating that those who fear or seek Yahweh will lack nothing. This sense is strengthened by the imagery of the lion that may become hungry and weak because of lack of food.

The word *rāš* רש is also used once in the book of Psalms (82:3). It connotes material poverty. This word is grouped with *dal* דל, *'ebyôn* אביון, and *'ānî* עני in a context of oppression and evil deeds. The *rāš* רש are therefore the economically poor due to exploitation and perversity.

The fact that the author is concerned about poverty and injustice is also clear from several references to the traditionally "poor" people and the language of oppression. God protects the rights of the widow and fatherless (10:14, 18). In fact, Ps 68:5 describes God as the father of the fatherless and the judge or defender (*dayyîn* דיין) of the widows. God assumes the role of both father and husband. As noted above, Job claimed the same status. Also, as already stated, these two were particularly vulnerable since they lacked a male kinsman to protect them. In 82:3 the widow and fatherless are grouped with other precarious persons. An interesting reference appears in Ps 146:9, which portrays Yahweh as watching over the widow, the fatherless, and the *gērîm* גרים—all of whom are victims of evil people. The mention of the *gērîm* גרים here completes the circle of the traditionally dependent people.

That the author is serious about poverty is also clear from the several references to words signifying oppression and exploitation. Yahweh is a refuge for those who are oppressed (*dak* דך [9:9]). The *'ānî* עני and *'ebyôn* אביון of 35:10 are those who are robbed (*gāzal* גזל). The word *lahaṣ* לחץ is used to describe personal suffering that the worshipper is experiencing (42:9; 43:2; 56:1). The sufferer feels as if Yahweh has abandoned him or her in this misfortune. In these instances, an enemy is responsible for the misery.

The word '*āšaq* עשׁק is used several times in the book of Psalms. In 73:8, the wicked are the agents of oppression. Psalms 103:6 and 146:7 use '*āšaq* עשׁק to explain the absence of justice and righteousness. The latter text also refers to those who suffer due to lack of food. In both cases, Yahweh will provide the missing element. In Ps 119:121-22 the petitioner has acted properly and expects Yahweh's protection from oppressors. Verse 134 portrays the worshipper as apparently bargaining with God in order to be protected from oppression.

The over-arching sense in the book of Psalms is that of a serious confrontation with material poverty as evidenced by the plight and petitions of the worshippers. They trust that Yahweh will deliver them from their poverty, afflictions, and other forms of misfortune that they are experiencing.

SUMMARY AND CONCLUSIONS

The wisdom literature and the book of Psalms were shown to be concerned primarily with material poverty. The books of Job and Proverbs were considered to possess a "prophetic" character because of their interest in the subject of the poor. Even in the book of Psalms, the socio-economic meaning of poverty overrides its spiritualizing tendencies.

Coping Mechanisms

What is evident in this collection of wisdom literature is the persistence of the issue of poverty. From the legal corpus through the Prophets and the Writings, it is apparent that the problem of poverty in ancient Israelite society had obviously not been solved. The question of the divine mandate for Israel was still as relevant as it had been at the pronouncement of this injunction. We can conclude that Israel continued to disregard its mandate through the different periods of its history. Although we witness a variety of efforts to deal with the problem, the critical issue is that there was no end to the existence of poverty. Oppression continued to compound the problems of the poor despite vehement prophetic denunciations of oppressors. For their part, the wise rationalized the problems of the poor and saw it as either continuing oppression or a result of one's lack of industry or the inability to take advantage of the system that kept them wealthy and powerful.

The books of Job, Proverbs, Qoheleth, and Psalms all deal with the question of the persistence of poverty in some distinctive ways. The foregoing study indicates that they all confront the question of material poverty in its manifold manifestations. What is the wise way to deal with poverty? How do the poor cope in these books?

The book of Job offers a few explanations including the prescribed mandate of the rich to the poor. The poor can expect to cope with poverty through the generosity of the rich. Job himself goes on to do these acts as a way of proving his innocence and righteousness. By describing himself as a father of the needy, Job shows that the poor can depend on his just actions at the city gate (29:12-20). The friends think differently, but they are proven to be wrong. The poor also survive through God's compassionate caring (5:15-16; 36:6).

Proverbs offers several explanations for the existence of poverty in human societies. In addition, the book makes several recommendations for alleviating poverty. Perhaps the most memorable cause of poverty according to the book of Proverbs is one's own laziness, signified by the legendary sluggard of 6:6-11. The lesson is that the poor can cope by abandoning their indolent habits, having a good work ethic, and planning carefully, just as the little ant does. A practical piece of advice: avoiding strong drink and excessive pleasure, as well as good planning, can protect one from poverty.[65] Proverbs also presents charity as a coping mechanism for the poor. Since wealth is desirable in Proverbs, one is encouraged to acquire it but share it with the poor. As for rulers, they ought to judge with equity and care for the poor. The ideal wife of Proverbs 31 is also portrayed as a charitable person.

Qoheleth has very little advice to give. For him, riches are largely meaningless, as is fighting oppression. For this writer, the pursuit of wisdom is a better option than accumulating wealth which is ephemeral in nature.

The Psalms overwhelmingly present Yahweh as the pillar of support for the poor and oppressed. The poor in the psalms were shown to be confronting concrete situations of miserable existence. In various ways they appeal to God for deliverance from suffering, oppression, and indeed poverty. To use Iliffe's categories, the wisdom literature presents the poor as the "structural poor" whose poverty is due to both personal and social circumstances. While an other-directed ethic is suggested, individual effort is largely preferred as demonstrated by Proverbs' call for a good and responsible work ethic.

SOCIO-ETHICAL IMPLICATIONS

The wisdom literature presents a number of lessons on the subject of poverty. Caring for the poor is recommended as exemplified by Job. This can be done through the administration of proper justice in society. Proverbs teaches that charity is one way of caring for the poor. While God cares for the poor, individual responsibility is called for as well. Qoheleth seems to suggest that the pursuit of wisdom is a better way of dealing with poverty than trying to "fight the system." While the book of Psalms calls for social justice, it also shows that such justice ultimately resides with Yahweh and is available for those who petition Yahweh.

This book has sought to demonstrate that the problem of poverty in ancient Israel would have been idealistically resolved if Israel had adhered to its divine mandate. However, what we have uncovered is a perpetual system of the oppression and abuse of the poor throughout. Israel's violation of its divine mandate largely explains the persistence of poverty through the different periods of its history. Despite the intentions of the Mosaic Torah, poverty proved to be a timeless problem. The lessons from this study can be instructive for us as we continue to wrestle with the problem of poverty in modern societies. What can we glean from a study of ancient Israel's approach to the problem of poverty? How might we appropriate some of the lessons from this study? What can we learn from the mistakes of an ancient agrarian society? To these and other questions we now turn as we conclude this study.

NOTES

1. The dates of these books are generally as follows: Scholars commonly date the book of Job in the post-exilic era. See Norman C. Habel, *The Book of Job,* OTL (London: SCM, 1985), 42; Marvin Pope suggests the Persian period, see *Job,* AB (Garden City, NY: Doubleday & Company, 1965), XXXII-XLIII. A mid-sixth century date is suggested by H. H. Rowley in *Job,* The Century Bible (Ontario, Trinidad: Nelson, 1970), 19. Hanson suggests a date around 500 BCE (*The People Called,* 212, 252). Proverbs is given a "court origin" date before 587 BCE to the post-exilic era. See Roger N. Whybray, *Proverbs,* NCBC (Grand Rapids MI: William B. Eerdmans Publishing Company, 1994), 9, 28-30. Whybray gives Qoheleth a third century BCE date: *Ecclesiastes,* NCBC (Grand Rapids, MI: Wm B. Eerdmans Publishing Company, 1989), 4-12. James L. Crenshaw puts the date "between 225 and 250." See *Ecclesiastes,* OTL (London: SCM, 1988), 50. Sigmund Mowinckel dates the Psalms in the monarchic or pre-exilic period. See *The Psalms in Israel's Worship,* vols. 1-2 (Nashville, New York: Abingdon Press, 1962), 35, 46-47. Artur Weiser prefers a pre-exilic date for most Psalms and a post-exilic date for a few. See *The Psalms,* OTL (Philadelphia: Westminster, 1962), 91. See also Mitchell Dahood, *Psalms I: 1-50,* AB (Garden City, NY: Doubleday & Company, 1966), XXIV-XXX.

2. Pleins, "Poor, Poverty," 410.

3. See Roger N. Whybray, "The Social World of the Wisdom Writers," in *The World of Ancient Israel,* ed. Ronald E. Clements, 227-50.

4. Dianne Bergant, *Israel's Wisdom Literature: A Liberation-Critical Reading* (Minneapolis: Fortress Press, 1997), 100.

5. The question of whether riches are a blessing or not has been debated by scholars and theologians. The view of riches as a blessing for obedience to God has given rise to so-called "prosperity teaching." Other scholars, however, view this form of teaching as a heresy. While wisdom literature has a number of explanations for the existence of poverty, some social scientists or anthropologists such as Oscar Lewis have attributed it to what they term the "culture of poverty." This is the belief that poverty is inherited and passed on from generation to generation without hope of overcoming it. This theory tends to blame the victims for their poverty without addressing institutional and other causes of poverty. The "culture of poverty" idea compares favorably to the concept of the "feminization of poverty." For further discussion, see the following works: Sunard Sumithra, "Prosperity, Property and Poverty," *EvRTh* 11 (July 1987): 195-272; Calvin E. Beisner, "Prosperity and Poverty: The Compassionate Use of Resources in a World of Scarcity," *Christian Scholar's Review* 21, no. 2 (1991): 212-13; Jose M. Bonino, "Poverty as Curse, Blessing, and Challenge," *The Iliff Review* 34 (Fall 1977): 3-13; Walter C. Kaiser, "The Old Testament Promise of Material Blessings and the Contemporary Believer," *Trinity Journal* 9 (Fall 1988): 151-70; Irving Hexham, *The Bible, Justice and the Culture of Poverty: Emotive Calls to Action versus Rational Analysis* (London: Social Affairs Unity, 1985); Julius K. Muthengi, "The Culture of Poverty: Implications for the Urban Ministry," *Africa Journal of Evangelical Theology* 11, no. 2 (1992): 90-104; H. G. M. Williamson, "The Old Testament and the Material World," *Evangelical Quarterly* 57, no. 1 (1985): 5-22; Walter Vogels, "Biblical Theology for the 'Haves' and 'Have-Nots.'" *Science et esprit* 39, no. 2 (1987): 193-210; Jurie Le Roux, "God Also Loves the Rich: An Allegorical Reading of the Old Testament," in *Plutocrats and Paupers,* 85-95; William Domeris, "God Cares for His Chosen Ones: A Prosperity Reading," in *Plutocrats and Paupers,* 25-32; and David T. Williams, "The Heresy of Prosperity Teaching: A Message for the Church in its Approach to Need," *JTSA* 61 (December 1987): 33-44.

6. Naomi Franklin, "Proverbs," in *The Africana Bible: Reading Israel's Scriptures from Africa and the African Diaspora,* edited by Hugh R. Page, Jr., 244-248 (Minneapolis: Fortress Press, 2010), 247.

7. Bergant, *Israel's Wisdom Literature,* 100.

8. For further references, see the following works: Habel, *The Book of Job;* Pope, *Job;* James L. Crenshaw, *Old Testament Wisdom: An Introduction* (Atlanta: John Knox Press, 1981), 100-125; J. David Pleins, "Poverty in the Social World of the Wise," *JSOT* 37 (1987): 61-78; T. P. Townsend, "The Poor in Wisdom Literature," *Bible Bhashyam* 14 (1988): 5-25; Bruce V. Malchow, "Social Justice in the Wisdom Literature," *BTB* 12 (October 1982): 120-24; John W. Olley, "'Righteous' and Wealthy? The Description of the Ṣaddiq in Wisdom Literature," *Colloquium* 22 (May 1990): 38-45; and Gerhard von Rad, *Wisdom in Israel* (Nashville, New York: Abingdon Press, 1972).

9. According to Crenshaw, "Theodicy is the attempt to defend divine justice in the face of aberrant phenomena that appear to indicate the deity's indifference or hostility toward virtuous people." See "Theodicy," in *ABD,* vol. 6, ed. David Noel Freedman (New York, London, Toronto, Sydney, Auckland: Doubleday, 1992), 444-47, especially p. 444.

10. Kathryn Schifferdecker, *Out of the Whirlwind: Creation Theology in the Book of Job.* Harvard Theological Studies 61 (Cambridge, MA: Harvard University Press, 2008), 2-3.

11. Bergant, *Israel's Wisdom Literature*, 39. One insight is that the doctrine of retribution can prejudice our perception of life to believe that prosperity is a sign of goodness while deprivation is a sign of sin, concepts which are proved to be inadequate in the book of Job.

12. The distribution is as follows: *'ebyôn* אביון: Job 5:15; 24:4, 14; 29:16; 30:25; 31:19; *dal* דל: 5:16; 20:10, 19; 31:16; 34:19, 28; *'ānî* עני: 24:4, 9, 14; 29:12; 34:28; 36:6, 15. Job also refers to the *'almānâ* אלמנה and *yātôm* יתום: 6:27; 22:9; 24:3, 9, 21; 27:15; 29:12-13; 31:16-17, 21. Twice he uses *dal* דל with *rāṣaṣ* רצץ (20:19) and *'ānî* עני with *laḥaṣ* לחץ (36:15).

13. Habel, *The Book of Job,* 359.

14. Ibid., 411.

15. Leo G. Perdue, "Wisdom in the Book of Job," In *In Search of Wisdom: Essays in Memory of John G. Gammie,* edited by Leo G. Perdue, Bernard B. Scott, and William J. Wiseman, 73-98 (Louisville, KY: Westminster / John Knox Press, 1993), 88. Dianne Bergant puts it this way: "The righteous will enjoy the fruits of their virtue, and the wicked will suffer the consequences of their sin," *Israel's Wisdom Literature,* 25. She also highlights the lessons of the book: success is ephemeral and is not a true sign of moral integrity; disaster can strike anyone at anytime and setbacks are not foolproof indications of moral frailty, ibid., 37.

16. Pope, *Job,* 227.

17. Ibid., 259; Habel, *The Book of Job,* 485.

18. Habel, *The Book of Job,* 359-60.

19. Pleins, "Poor, Poverty," 404, 406.

20. Habel, *The Book of Job,* 339.

21. Ibid., 359. See also 2 Sam 12:1-6. Pope refers to this crime as "doubly heinous" *(Job,* 175, n. 3).

22. Both Pope *(Job,* 212) and Habel *(The Book of Job,* 410) agree that Job's role is similar to that of King Dan(i)el who sits at the gate judging the case of the widow and fatherless in the Aqhat Epic. In the Keret Legend King Keret's rule is threatened because he has neglected his duty to the widow *(ANET,* 142-55).

23. Habel, *The Book of Job,* 435. Job had described himself as "father" of the poor in 29:16. Habel also suggests that Job was never intimidated into compromising his administration of justice at the city gate (p. 436).

24. For further discussion, consult the following works: William McKane, *Proverbs: A New Approach,* OTL (Philadelphia: The Westminster Press, 1970); Roger N. Whybray, *Proverbs,* NCBC (London: Marshall Pickering / Grand Rapids: William B. Eerdmans Publishing Company, 1994); R. B. Y. Scott, *Proverbs. Ecclesiastes,* AB (Garden City, NY: Doubleday & Company, 1965); R. N. Whybray, *Wealth and Poverty in the Book of Proverbs,* JSOTSup 99 (Sheffield: JSOT Press, 1990); idem, "Poverty, Wealth, and Point of View in Proverbs," *ExpTim* 100 (June 1989): 332-36; idem, "Some Literary Problems in Proverbs I-IX," *VT* 16 (1966): 482-96; Crenshaw, *Old Testament Wisdom,* 66-99; idem, "Poverty and Punishment

in Proverbs," *Quarterly Review* 9, no. 3 (1989): 30-43; G. H. Wittenberg, "The Lexical Context of the Terminology for 'Poor' in the Book of Proverbs," *Scriptura* S 2 (1986): 40-85; idem, "The Situational Context of Statements Concerning Poverty and Wealthy in the Book of Proverbs," *Scriptura* 21 (1987): 1-23; Norman C. Habel, "Wisdom, Wealth and Poverty Paradigms in the Book of Proverbs," *Bible Bhashyam* 14 (1988): 26-49; idem, "The Symbolism of Wisdom in Proverbs 1 - 9," *Int* 26 (1972): 131-57; Gordon A. Chutter, "'Riches and Poverty' in the Book of Proverbs," *Crux* 18, no. 2 (1982): 23-28; Raymond C. van Leeuwen, "Wealth and Poverty: System and Contradiction in Proverbs," *Hebrew Studies* 33 (1992): 25-36; Solfrid Storøy, "On Proverbs and Riddles. Polar Word Pairs and Other Poetic Devices, and Words for 'Poor and Needy' in the Book of Proverbs," *Scandinavian Journal of the Old Testament* 7, no. 2 (1993): 270-84; T. Donald, "The Semantic Field of Rich and Poor in the Wisdom Literature of Hebrew and Accadian," *Oriens Antiquus* 3 (1964): 27-41; Brian W. Kovacks, "Is there a Class-Ethic in Proverbs?" in *Essays in Old Testament Ethics,* ed. James L. Crenshaw and John T. Willis (New York: Ktav Publishing House, 1974), 173-89; Harold C. Washington, *Wealth and Poverty in the Instruction of Amenemope and the Hebrew Proverbs,* SBLDS 142 (Atlanta, GA: Scholars Press, 1994).

25. See Washington, *Wealth and Poverty in the Instruction of Amenemope and the Hebrew Proverbs,* 135-46. Washington contends that "close affinities between Proverbs and Amenemope indicate a relationship of literary dependence" (p. 203). He also adds that "it is clear that Proverbs is dependent upon the Instruction of Amenemope" (p. 203).

26. McKane, *Proverbs,* 1-261; see also Scott, *Proverbs. Ecclesiastes,* XV-LIII, 1-30; and Whybray, *Proverbs,* 3-20.

27. Pleins, "Poor, Poverty," 407. He notes that except for only one case (Prov 6:11), the word *maḥsôr* מחסור occurs in Proverbs 10 - 29. The terms *dal* דל and *rāš* רש only occur in these chapters as well. While chapters 1-9 are "largely unconcerned with the topic of poverty," Proverbs 30 - 31 predominantly use words *'ānî* עני and *'ebyôn* אביון. Thus, Pleins argues that "this vocabulary distribution serves to bind together chaps. 10-29 and isolate them from chaps. 1-9 and 30-31" (p. 407).

28. The distribution of these words is as follows: *dal* דל: 10:15; 14:31; 19:4, 17; 21:13; 22:9, 16, 22; 28:3, 8, 11, 15; 29:7, 14; *'ānî* עני: 15:15; 22:22; 30:14; 31:9, 20; *'ānāwîm* עניים: 3:34; 14:21; 16:19; *'ebyôn* אביון: 14:31; 30:14; 31:9, 20; *rāš* רש: 6:11; 10:4, 15; 13:7-8, 18, 23; 14:20; 17:5; 18:23; 19:1, 7, 22; 20:13; 22:2, 7; 23:21; 24:34; 28:3, 6, 19, 27; 29:13; 30:8; 31:7; *maḥsôr* מחסור: 6:11; 11:24; 14:23; 21:5, 17; 22:16; 24:34; 28:27. Proverbs also refers to other significant words: *'almānâ* אלמנה / *yātôm* יתום: 6:27; 15:25; 22:9; 23:10; 24:3, 9; 29:12; 31:17, 21; *'āšîr* עשיר : 10:15; 13:8; 14:20; 18:11, 23; 22:2, 7, 16; 28:6, 11; *'āšaq* עשק: 14:31; 22:16; 28:3, 16; *dakā'* דכא: 22:22; *ḥéser* חסר (poverty): 28:22; *'ōšer* עשר (wealth): 11:16, 28; 13:8; 14:24; 22:1, 4; *hôn* הון (wealth): 10:15; 11:4; 12:27; 13:7, 11; 18:11; 19:4, 14; 28:8, 22; 29:3. See also Whybray, (*Wealth and Poverty,* 11-31) for other words describing wealth and poverty in various forms and states.

29. Bergant, *Israel's Wisdom Literature,* 103.

30. Whybray, *Proverbs,* 391.

31. Ibid., 424.

32. *NBDB* defines *rāš* רשׁ as to "be in want, poor" (p. 930). An analysis of this word will give more substance to this brief definition.

33. The soporific effect of alcohol is similar to Karl Marx's claim that religion is the opium of the people.

34. Storøy, "On Proverbs and Riddles," 275. Storøy adds that this device also expresses the idea of completion or totality, for example, "Upper and Lower Egypt" mean "(the whole of) Egypt" (p. 275). R. N. Whybray makes a similarly eloquent statement about how poverty cannot be discussed adequately without reference to its counterpart. He states: "Very frequently in the Old Testament itself the poor are mentioned in close association with their counterparts, the rich. *To ignore this association is a methodological error.* If the two extremes of social and economic status formed a natural pair in the minds of the ancient Israelites, this is a significant datum which affects the interpretation of the Old Testament texts" [emphasis mine]. See "Poverty, Wealth, and Point of View in Proverbs," 332-33.

35. Van Leeuwen, "Wealth and Poverty," 31. Furthermore, he adds that "these 'better-than' sayings set material wealth and poverty in an ultimate normative context which utterly reverses their usual worth . . . . Wealth which may *appear* as a blessing of the Creator is not intrinsically and invariably good." [author's emphasis] (p. 31). Finally, he notes that these sayings "reveal an awareness of situations which contradicted the usual character-consequence connections [eg., good leads to good and bad to bad]" (p.32).

36. The Shona people of Zimbabwe have a typical proverb which aptly describes this situation. It says, *"Murombo haarovi chine nguo"* (A poor man never kills [a big animal] with skin). The explanation goes: "Irony has it that people in want are rarely successful in satisfying their real needs. The rich seem to get richer without much effort." See Mordikai A. Hamutyinei and Albert B. Plangger, *Tsumo-Shumo: Shona Proverbial Lore and Wisdom,* 174, proverb #549.

37. Whybray describes *maḥsôr* מחסור as "want" (*Proverbs,* 219; *Wealth and Poverty,* 15-16).

38. Habel, "Wisdom, Wealth and Poverty Paradigms in the Book of Proverbs." G. H. Wittenberg argues that the four major terms for "poor" in Proverbs—*rāš* רשׁ, *dal* דל, *'ebyôn* אביון, and *'ānî* עני, belong to two lexical fields, namely that of poverty and wealth, as well as that of justice (See "The Lexical Context"). In a different article, Wittenberg also contends that the shifting perspectives of statements pertaining to wealth and poverty in the book of Proverbs are due to the corresponding changing social, political, and economic situation of Israel (See "The Situational Context"). J. David Pleins refers to "practical guidelines for meeting the challenges of the world" in the wisdom writers' vocabulary of poverty ("Poverty in the Social World of the Wise," 66).

39. McKane, *Proverbs,* 485. Whybray adds that the loss of land or livelihood was a misfortune that could befall a family in ancient Israel. Exploitation of the widow and fatherless was "a particularly heinous crime." He also notes that this crime is denounced in the Instruction of Amen-em-opet (*ANET,* 422). See *Proverbs,* 235-36.

40. Whybray, *Proverbs,* 235. Van Leeuwen argues that Proverbs has "a prophet-like concern for social justice" (See "Wealth and Poverty," 30).

41. For further study, see the following works: R. B. Y. Scott, *Proverbs. Ecclesiastes;*James L. Crenshaw, *Ecclesiastes,* OTL (London: SCM, 1988); R. N. Whybray, *Ecclesiastes,* NCBC (Grand Rapids, MI: Wm B. Eerdmans Publishing Company / London: Marshall, Morgan & Scott, 1989); and Frank Anthony Spina, "Qoheleth and the Reformation of Wisdom," in *The Quest for the Kingdom of God: Studies in Honor of George E. Mendenhall,* ed., Herbert B. Huffmon, Frank Anthony Spina, and A. R. W. Green (Winona Lake, IN: Eisenbrauns, 1983), 267-79.

42. Spina, "Qoheleth and the Reformation of Wisdom," 267. Spina argues that Qoheleth's wisdom stance is reformist in the sense that he is revolting against Israel's betrayal of its ancient Yahwistic/Mosaic value-system. Thus, "Qoheleth may actually be thought of as a thoroughgoing 'conservative'" (p. 277). Consequently, "Qoheleth is unorthodox only from the point of view of those who translated Mosaic religion into primarily ritualistic forms and transformed with the addition of their traditions the idea of the kingdom of Yahweh into the idea that the Israelite state was that kingdom" (p. 278).

43. Michael V. Fox, "Wisdom in Qoheleth," in *In Search of Wisdom,* 124-127. C.f., Bergant, *Israel's Wisdom Literature,* 110. She adds that Qoheleth observed that "society does not seem to operate according to laws of equity," 112. Hopkins argues that for Qoheleth, even oppression is a form of vanity. See Jamal-Dominique Hopkins, "Ecclesiastes," in *The Africana Bible,* 264.

44. The distribution is as follows: *miskēn* מִסְכֵּן: 4:13; 9:15a, b, 16; *rāš* רָשׁ: 4:14; *5:8* (Heb 5:7*); 'ānî* עָנִי: 6:8. The author also uses the word *'āšaq* עָשַׁק to describe oppression: 4:1a, b, c; 5:8; 7:7.

45. Crenshaw, *Ecclesiastes,* 112-113. He also adds that the word *miskēn* מִסְכֵּן (occurring only in Qoheleth in the Hebrew Bible) appears in Sirach 4:3; 30:14 and the Tulmud. Whybray deduces that it is a "late word" probably composed closer to Qoheleth's time (*Ecclesiastes,* 88).

46. Crenshaw, *Ecclesiastes,* 166-67; Whybray, *Ecclesiastes,* 148-49. Scott says no one remembered the poor man "because he was little regarded" (*Proverbs. Ecclesiastes,* 247, n. 15).

47. Whybray, *Ecclesiastes,* 89.

48. Crenshaw (*Ecclesiastes,* 118-119) and Whybray (*Ecclesiastes,* 97) eloquently describe the nature of this form of corruption. Bergant adds that Qoheleth neither has much sympathy for the disadvantaged, nor does he want to change the social structured that may have disadvantaged them, *Israel's Wisdom Literature,* 120.

49. Whybray, *Ecclesiastes,* 107-108; Crenshaw, *Ecclesiastes,* 128-29.

50. For further reading, see the following references: Bernhard W. Anderson, *Out of the Depths: The Psalms Speak for Us Today,* rev. and exp. ed. (Philadelphia: The Westminster Press, 1983); Sigmund Mowinckel, *The Psalms in Israel's Worship,* vols. 1-2. trans. D. R. Ap-Thomas (Nashville, New York: Abingdon Press, 1967); Mitchel Dahood, *Psalms I: 1-50;* idem, *Psalms II: 51-100,* AB (Garden City, NY: Doubleday & Company, 1968); idem, *Psalms III: 101-150,* AB (Garden City, NY: Doubleday & Company, 1970); Artur Weiser, *The Psalms: A Commentary,* OTL (Philadelphia: The Westminster Press, 1962); James Luther Mays, *Psalms,* Interpretation (Louisville: John Knox Press, 1994; Sue Gillingham, "The Poor in the Psalms,"

ExpTim 100 (1988): 16-19; James McPolin, "Psalms as Prayers of the Poor," in *Back to the Sources: Biblical and Near Eastern Studies* (Dublin: The Glendale Press, 1989), 79-103; Walter Brueggemann, "Psalms 9-10: A Counter to a Conventional Social Reality," in *The Bible and the Politics of Exegesis,* 3-15, 297-301; idem, "Psalm 109: Three Times 'Steadfast Love,'" *WW* 5 (Spring 1985): 144-154; W. Eugene March, "Psalm 86: When Love is not Enough," *Austin Bulletin: Faculty Edition* 105 (Spring 1990): 17-25; Erhard S. Gerstenberger, "Singing a New Song: On Old Testament and Latin American Psalmody," *WW* 5 (Spring 1985): 155-67; Claus Westermann, *Praise and Lament in the Psalms,* trans. Keith R. Crim and Richard N. Soulen (Atlanta: John Knox Press, 1981).

51. Anderson, *Out of the Depths,* 39-62; idem, *Understanding the Old Testament,* 4th ed (Englewood, NJ: Prentice-Hall, 1986), 546-47. Anderson also refers to Psalms 78, 105 - 106, 135 - 136 as "story-telling (or historical) psalms" or "psalms of sacred (or salvation) history." He notes that the hymn celebrates the majesty of God; the lament or petition presupposes a problem which God seems not to be addressing; and thanksgiving psalms are praises for divine deliverance from trouble. These are closely related to the lament and sometimes may overlap with the hymn (pp. 546-47). For other types of psalms see also Weiser, *Psalms,* 52-91; Mowinckel, *The Psalms in Israel's Worship,* vol. 1 and 2; Mays, *Psalms,* 19-29.

52. The distribution is as follows: *'ānî* עני: 10:2, 9; 12:5 [Heb 12:6]; 14:6; 18:27 [Heb 18:28]; 25:16; 34:6 [Heb 34:7]; 35:10; 37:14; 40:17 [Heb 40:18]; 68:10 [Heb 68:11]; 69:29 [Heb 69:30]; 70:5 [Heb 70:6]; 72:2, 4, 12; 74:19, 21; 82:3; 86:1; 88:16; 102:1; 107:41; 109:16, 22; 140:12 [Heb 140:13]; *'ănāwîm* ענוים: 9:12 [Heb 9:13]; 9:18 [Heb 9:19]; 22:26 [Heb 22:27]; 25:9; 34:2 [Heb 34:3]; 37:11; 69:32 [Heb 69:33]; 76:9 [Heb 76:10]; 147:6; 149:4; *'ebyôn* אביון: 9:18 [Heb 9:19]; 35:10; 37:14; 40:17 [Heb 40:18]; 49:2 [Heb 49:3]; 69:33 [Heb 69:34]; 70:5 [Heb 70:6]; 72:4, 12-13; 74:21; 82:4; 86:1; 107:41; 109:16, 22, 31; 112:9; 113:7; 132:15; 140:12 [Heb 140:13]; *dal* דל: 41:1 [Heb 41:2]; 72:13; 82:3, 4; 113:7; *maḥsôr* מחסור: 34:10; *rāš* רש: 82:3. Psalms also refers to the *yātôm* יתום, *'almānâ* אלמנה, or *gēr* גר: 10:14, 18; 68:5; 78:64; 82:3; 94:6; 109:9; 146:9. It also uses other significant words: *dak* דך: 9:9 [Heb 9:10]; 10:18; 74:21; *laḥaṣ* לחץ: 42:9 [Heb 42:10]; 43:2; 44:24 [Heb 44:25]; 56:1 [Heb 56:2]; 106:42; *'āšaq* עשק: 62:10; 73:8; 103:6; 119:121, 122, 134; 146:7; *gāzal* גזל: 35:10; and *'ōšer* עשר: 107:39.

53. Mays, *Psalms,* 269-70. See also Dahood, *Psalm II,* 269; Weiser, *The Psalms,* 559.

54. Weiser, *The Psalms,* 319. This interpretation suggests in part that the *'ănāwîm* ענוים are suffering in a very real and concrete sense, so they look to God for liberation.

55. Ibid., 528.

56. March, "Psalm 86: When Love is Not Enough," 21.

57. Bergant, *Israel's Wisdom Literature,* 59.

58. Bergant, *Israel's Wisdom Literature,* 67.

59. Dahood, *Psalm II,* 180. He also compares such extortion to the story of King Keret, who failed to drive away exploiters.

60. McPolin, "Psalms as Prayers of the Poor," 94. He adds that "the poor are those who have been reduced to poverty and misery by various misfortunes of life. Also the

poor are simply those materially needy to whom the 'just' person distributes wealth freely" (p. 95).

61. See Mays' discussion of "The trial of the gods" in *Psalms*, 268-71.

62. Weiser, *The Psalms*, 707.

63. Dahood, *Psalms III*, 301. It is interesting to notice an eschatologizing tendency in this comment. The persecuted and the poor are seeking relief from their *present* predicament, not bliss in some uncertain future.

64. Mays, *Psalms*, 171-72. He argues that sickness is connected with sin and this is the occasion of this prayer.

65. Washington warns against the possible misuse of the book of Proverbs "to blame victims of oppression and exploitation" (see *Wealth and Poverty in the Instruction of Amenemope and the Hebrew Proverbs*, 185).

Part III

CONCLUSION

Chapter Five

Summary and Conclusions

AN OVERVIEW OF THE STUDY

This book has argued that Israel's divine mandate was to ensure the eradication of poverty among its members by playing the role of brother's keeper faithfully. The text of Deuteronomy 15 presupposes adherence to this mandate with the stern instruction, "but there will be no poor among you" (v. 4, RSV). However, verse 11 anticipates disobedience on the part of Israel and states, "for the poor will never cease out of the land" (RSV). Because of disobedience to the divine mandate, the text goes on to specify the nature of Israel's responsibility toward its poor: "Therefore I command you, You shall open wide your hand to your brother, to the needy and to the poor, in the land" (v. 11b, RSV).

This study has revealed that despite strong social legislation in the legal codes, the poor continued to exist because Israel did not fully extend her hand to the poor as mandated. Indeed, one study argues that Deuteronomic law regarding widows, strangers and orphans was nothing but legalized injustice.[1] Additionally, much of biblical evidence points to a history of continual oppression on the part of the poor. This is especially the case in the prophetic corpus wherein representative Major and Minor Prophets all rail against injustice and the oppression of the poor. The wisdom writers also wrestled with the problem of the poor in peculiar ways. The problem of poverty in antiquity has ironically carried into the modern era. Despite human development and scientific advancement, this ancient conundrum continues to plague humanity although in different ways. Poverty in an agrarian economy has become poverty in an industrialized world. However, poverty is still poverty no matter where or when it occurs. Its terms and conditions might differ but the basic lack of enough resources to sustain a livelihood is a connecting thread. This study compels us to draw some parallels between ancient and modern forms of poverty. Since poverty has become a global phenomenon, we need to ask ourselves if we can glean any useful lessons and paradigms to address the same problem in our contemporary society. To this task we now turn.

My basic approach has been to analyze poverty in the different parts of the Hebrew Bible by focusing on the structure and causes of poverty, the coping mechanisms of the poor, and social programs that were designed to alleviate this condition. I have also attempted to determine the socio-ethical implications of the problem of poverty and what it means for us today.

To accomplish these tasks, I have utilized a comparative, cross-cultural, and sociological analysis of several sets of materials. I have derived source material from ancient Near Eastern evidence and from the Hebrew Bible. In all these cases, poverty is primarily seen as material need or deprivation. My contention is that this approach sheds considerable light and insight on the problem of poverty in ancient Israel, as reflected in the Hebrew Bible. This in turn contributes to our understanding of poverty not only in ancient Israel, but also in modern societies on a historical continuum. Such an approach as used by Wilson has yielded considerable insights.[2]

I have also made use of what Iliffe terms "structural" and "conjunctural" poverty[3] in his study of the African poor from the thirteenth to the twentieth century. While these categories apply to a modern agrarian economy, they are also applicable to an ancient agrarian economy.

Poverty in ancient Israel and traditional Africa, both land-based economies, reveals similar patterns.[4] The history of Israel, especially the oppressive measures of the early monarchy and the rise of latifundialization during the eighth-century BCE, is truly the history of the structural poor, victims of the social and political circumstances of the day.

Throughout my analysis of the major parts of the Hebrew Bible, I have endeavored to determine Israel's compliance with the divine mandate. What has emerged from this survey is however a pattern of systemic abuses, injustice, and the oppression of the poor. Far from the biblical vision of a society without poverty, the evidence suggests an inability to fulfill this mandate. Despite strong legal and social legislation to provide for the poor, we find numerous infractions and abuses in the literature under investigation. In fact such strong legislation seems to mask a deep underlying social problem in ancient Israel. The mandate suggests a society without poverty but the evidence points to a persistent class of the poor and dependent in ancient Israel.

I began my biblical analysis by examining three legal codes in the Pentateuch: the Covenant Code (Exodus 20:22 - 23:33); the Deuteronomic Code (Deuteronomy 12 - 26); and the Holiness Code (Leviticus 17 - 26). In these codes, the poor were shown to be persons in dependent positions or vulnerable situations, and whose existence was often precarious. These were identified as slaves, resident aliens, widows, fatherless minor children, as well as those designated by specific Hebrew terms for "poor." To use Iliffe's model, these groups of people fall into the category of the "structural" poor whose poverty is due to personal or social circumstances.

While these groups were not always identified as poor, studies of specific Hebrew words for "poor" and "poverty" were more revealing. Peter D. Miscall argues that the typical "Israelite concept" of poverty is enshrined in the description of the poor as the *'ebyôn* אביון, *dal* דל, *'ānî* עני, and *rāš* רש.[5] My analysis showed that the first three of these terms are used in legal materials and often in the same context with dependent persons, especially the widow, the fatherless, and the resident alien. Such usage was deemed to be an attempt by the authors to classify these groups as poor. This argument was substantiated by a consideration of ancient Near Eastern materials, which share a concern for the widow, the fatherless, and the poor.[6]

An analysis of the coping mechanisms of the poor in the legal materials revealed an apparent wealth of resources intended to benefit them. The Law Codes of ancient Israel appear to be the central expression of Israel's value systems and attitudes toward poverty. These laws, especially the Deuteronomistic Code and the Holiness Code, are probably better viewed as the distillation of the prophetic passion for social justice. In these Law Codes, poverty was not only an important but persistent theme. Specific laws were legislated not only to protect the poor but also to prevent forms of abuse to which they were susceptible. Moreover, specific groups of people were accorded special rights and protection under the law. However, a critical reading of this material is troubling because the problem was never solved despite the persistent call to care for the poor and other dependent persons.

The text however outlines certain deliberate measures in the form of an ancient social welfare system to ensure that the poor would always be provided for. For example, the Fallow or Sabbatical Year and the Jubilee Year contained specific provisions for the poor and needy. The regulations of the Fallow Year directly benefited the poor and animals (both wild and domestic), while at the same time guaranteeing the sustenance of the general populace. Perhaps the Jubilee ought to be seen as a classic example of release from debt, return of property, and rehabilitation of poor families. This research also showed that laws concerning wages, loans, business transactions, buying, and selling, were all legislated to promote fairness and protect the rights of the poor and other vulnerable groups of people. However, many biblical scholars question the practicality of these measures. In fact it can be argued that these measures were put in place because of the reality of various forms of abuse.

The prophets railed against oppressors precisely because the poor were being oppressed despite the biblical mandate or evidence of a flourishing economy especially in 8[7] century Israel.[7] Due to systemic abuses, the text also points to other coping mechanisms available for the poor.

One such mechanism is the role of the family in the context of poverty and deprivation. In both ancient Israel and the African context, the family was shown to be central in the fight against poverty. Like the traditional African family, the ancient Israelite family was an "extended family" or a "larger family."[8] It consisted of the father's house (*bêt 'āb* בית אב), the clan (*mišpāḥâ* משפחה), and the tribe (*šēbeṭ* שבט/*maṭṭeh* מטה). The members of such an Israelite family had socio-economic, military, and judicial/legal responsibilities to one another. As in the case of the African context where "everybody is related to everybody else,"[9] the Israelites viewed each other as brothers and sisters, or "a member of your community, whether a Hebrew man or a Hebrew woman" (Deut 15:12; NRSV). The Israelites had a particular and divinely-mandated responsibility, especially towards the less fortunate members of the community. I have tried to demonstrate that if Israel had obeyed Yahweh's commandments (and taken care of its poor), then there would have been no poor person in Israel (Deut 15:1-18). The alleviation of poverty (ideally, its removal), was one task expected of the extensive Israelite family.

Research in the prophetic corpus demonstrated that the prophets addressed the problem of poverty from a different social setting and perspective. During the prophetic era, there were gross violations of the rights of the poor, especially in eighth-century Israel. The Former Prophets barely dealt with the subject of poverty. In fact, words pertaining to "poor" or "poverty" do not really have an economic sense in this setting. The classical or writing prophets are the ones who dealt with the problem of poverty as a social, political, and economic issue.

Two representative Minor Prophetic books (Amos and Micah) and two Major Prophets (Isaiah and Jeremiah) were considered. Word studies of these books indicated that the prophets upheld Israel's legal traditions including the divine mandate. These four books employ the words for "poor" and "poverty"—*'ebyôn* אביון, *dal* דל, *'ānî* עני/*'ănāwîm* ענוים—which are found in Israel's Law Codes, a total of sixty-one times. The context and usage of these terms is primarily socio-economic. This suggests a great deal of concern for the welfare of the poor on the part of the prophets.

Further analysis showed that the prophets were significant advocates for the poor because they were being consistently oppressed by the rich and powerful landowners of the day. Amos and Micah led the fight against social, political, and economic injustice with memorable oracles of doom. They were not afraid to criticize even the king, the divine representative on earth and guardian of justice and morality, for violating the rights of the poor. Isaiah and Jeremiah followed closely in their footsteps. In general, the prophets denounced oppression and exploitation which they viewed as the major cause of poverty. In eighth-century Israel, social structures collapsed and the poor were subjected to the worst forms of injustice. Hence the prophets called for justice and righteousness, or simply "a fair deal" in human relationships.[10] This is the essence of the prophetic call to the proper worship of God (Amos 5:21-24; Mic 6:6-8). After all, the practice of justice and righteousness, being our brother's keeper, models God-pleasing behavior.[11]

Iliffe's model helps us to understand the nature of poverty during the prophetic era. Based on that model, we can safely argue that the great majority of the poor in the prophetic books under consideration were the "structural" poor whose poverty was due to social circumstances. This is evident from the rampant practice of latifundialization which deprived many Israelite peasants of their land, their basic means of survival.[12] Hence, the book of Isaiah pronounces judgment on the perpetrators of this great injustice. The RSV reads as follows: "Woe to those who join house to house, who add field to field, until there is no more room" (Isa 5:8). Biblical evidence shows that the poor of the prophetic times coped with their situation presumably through the advocacy of the prophets. However, we should be mindful of the one-sided nature of the prophetic witness and the lacunae that exist in some of the material. In the prophetic literature, one searches in vain for the voice of the poor themselves, or any other voice concerning the condition of the poor. We are left to wonder what the poor might have said about their situation. As is true with most of the Bible, the stories of the marginalized are often not in their own words. These considerations point to the larger question of who wrote the Bible and with what intention.[13] Karen Lebacqz captures this dilemma when she argues that "social programs designed for the poor must be judged and assessed from the perspective of the poor. Similarly, they must be designed *by* as well as *for* the poor."[14] In light of these arguments, a cautious evaluation of poverty in the prophetic literature is necessary.

The final part of this book focused on the wisdom literature (Job, Proverbs, and Qoheleth/Ecclesiastes), as well as the book of Psalms. Word studies in this section demonstrated that the wisdom writers had a tacit awareness of the problem of poverty in Israel's legal history and in the prophetic tradition. In fact, the book of Job was shown to have a "prophetic character" because of its usage of the vocabulary of poverty and its reference to people traditionally associated with the poor, namely, the widow (*'almānâ* אלמנה) and the fatherless child (*yātôm* יתום). In his personal life and by his exemplary character and care for the poor, Job himself was shown as the arbiter of justice par excellence. I contended that the wisdom books and the book of Psalms are largely concerned with the socio-economic meaning of poverty, as opposed to its spiritual meaning as some scholars have claimed. I argued that the supplicants of the book of Psalms, traditionally viewed as the "humble" or "pious" poor, were actually concerned about their own material poverty, suffering, and deprivation. In this manner, the Writings confront the problem of poverty with a sense of Israel's past. While the Writings (most of which were written during the post-exilic period) may be aware of Israel's past, it is evident that they are dealing with a different set of circumstances. This is so because at this time in Israel's history, most of the social structures had already been dismantled due to the ravages of the exile. Moreover, the office of the king no longer existed, and some of those wielding authority were foreign rulers. These factors may have contributed to the wisdom writers' understanding of poverty and presentation of new alternatives. This is evident from the new words for poverty—*rāš* רשׁ, *miskēn* מסכן, and *maḥsôr* מחסור—which they utilize. Although the word *rāš* רשׁ appears four times in the Deuteronomistic History and *maḥsôr* מחסור once in the Pentateuch, these contexts have nothing to do with poverty as an economic problem. Moreover, these terms do not appear at all in the Law Codes of ancient Israel. Thus, the wise present new interpretations in their understanding of poverty.

The new element is a rather philosophical understanding of poverty. Departing from the traditional view of poverty as caused by oppression, the wise tended to view poverty as a result of one's own moral failings. They interpreted it as a result of a poor work ethic, love of sleep, the pursuit of pleasure, strong drink, lack of planning, or simply a lack of wisdom. In keeping with Israel's prophetic and ancient traditions, they viewed God as the greatest defender of the poor. They even recommended charity for the poor, just as the Law Codes did. However, new realities and experiences may have caused them to value individual effort and hard work more. As writers whose work was based on experiential knowledge and keen observation of "the way things work," it is feasible to assume that this lens may have colored their view of poverty and the poor. In addition, as writers from an elite circle of Israel, the wise betray their dualistic approach to the problem of poverty by openly cherishing riches even as they caution others about the dangers of such wealth.

Overall, this research shows that the problem of poverty is pervasive in the Hebrew Bible. It appears in the Law Codes masked under massive social legislation and in the Prophets reflected as rampant systemic abuse and oppression. In the Writings, the problem of poverty also appears in a newly rationalized and "up-by-your-bootstraps" mentality. Yet the essence of this study is that the problem of poverty is timeless and cannot be ignored because it has serious implications for humanity.

IMPLICATIONS OF THE STUDY

This study shows that poverty is a serious and immense problem which is destined to plague humankind unless all humanity fights against it. This subject deserves our utmost attention, cooperation, and resourcefulness. My hope is that our journey through the ancient past will provide us with some useful models and paradigms for confronting this massive issue today.

This study has serious implications for those interested in the subject of poverty. The research showed that those adversely affected by poverty were often the powerless, weak, dependent, handicapped, unemployed, homeless, women, fatherless minor children, as well as others who were exploited and oppressed. The least affected and often the cause of such suffering and poverty were shown to be the powerful and often heartless rich, land-grabbers, unscrupulous or dishonest merchants, as well as corrupt public officials. As noted in the introduction, poverty has become a global problem in need of a global solution.

The existence of poverty affects all humanity, whether poor or rich. The biblical evidence outlined the many responsibilities of the rich to the poor; it also pointed out the responsibilities of the poor to themselves. The irony of poverty in the midst of plenty may be summed up by the Deuteronomist's simple requirement, "Open your hand to the poor and needy neighbor in your land" (Deut 15:11; NRSV). Hamilton suggests that this Deuteronomic imperative is for the powerful who can really make a difference in the life of the poor. He states, "The obligation falls, as it does in Deuteronomy, on those who have the capacity, the resources, to see that such a change from dependent living to good living is carried out."[15]

Consequently, poverty is a serious issue that can either unite or divide people, for it has as much to do with wealth as it has with the lack of wealth. While it may unite the rich with a false sense of security or even self-righteousness, it also may unite the poor with a sense of solidarity, yet still it will divide the rich and the poor along economic lines. Obviously, the complacent attitude of "it doesn't affect me" is null and void. Hence, issues of inequality, injustice, and oppression cannot be divorced from an honest discussion of poverty. All human beings need to be involved in a concerted fight against it. The biblical witness points to oppression as the major cause of poverty. This lesson pertains to our contemporary situation. As Hoppe puts it, "Poverty just does not happen; it happens because people make it happen."[16] Since the problem of poverty is a global crisis, it is fitting that a global response is needed as well.

RECOMMENDATIONS

From the foregoing study of poverty in the biblical word and its implications for us today, we can make several observations by way of recommendations that might assist us in our struggle against poverty in modern societies. While there are many differences between the ancient world and ours, there are enough similarities to warrant drawing out some conclusions based on this study. The reality of poverty has been a consistent theme in both settings and we might do well to glean some useful lessons from a biblical analysis of poverty.

One way to address the issue is to consider history and derive a few lessons. Since the history of poverty is so broad, there are many resources for us to rely on. The history and development of poverty in ancient Israel leaves us with some relevant lessons. Charity is one option if given properly, but as the wisdom writers teach, hard work and self-discipline are important means of avoiding poverty. However, in today's economy, poverty is exacerbated by the structural poor, those able-bodied persons who are unable to sell their labor power at sufficient prices to meet their minimum needs, or because of the lack of work opportunities. This reality also translates into creating meaningful social welfare programs that are designed to help the poor help themselves. Poverty is in no way desirable, nor does it give the victims any special status. I agree with Hoppe that the idealization of poverty in order to maintain the status quo of oppression ought to be rejected on the basis of biblical teaching.[17]

This study also teaches us that we must not institutionalize poverty because we benefit from the system. The rulers of ancient Israel benefited from the existence of poverty while the majority of poor peasants suffered even while there were laws designed to assist them.[18] But what is the point of having relief laws when those very laws were constantly being violated? As modern persons who have the advantage of benefiting from this rich legacy, we can learn to avoid legislating laws that we don't intend to follow. In other words, if we promise to take care of those disadvantaged persons in our midst, we must do so in word and in deed.

When the poor are disenfranchised or otherwise oppressed because we have neglected our duties and obligations, who are they to turn to for help? Our study has demonstrated that the poor always had God as their primary advocate, but some of them also had the prophets who spoke on behalf of

Yahweh. In contemporary terms, this means that God is believed always to be on the side of the poor and oppressed. However, the poor also need modern Isaiahs and Jeremiahs who can represent them and give voice to them. Such modern prophets must have the interests of the poor at heart and be prepared to fight for social justice by unmasking oppression, exploitation, and confronting authority when necessary. This is the "prophetic character" of modern advocates for the poor and oppressed, such as Martin Luther King Jr., or Mahatma Gandhi.[19]

Another recommendation for us is to reevaluate the value of family in the fight against poverty. Our analysis also shows that the institution of the extended family was an invaluable source of support for the poor. This has direct implications for modern families and how they can assist the poor in their midst. Simply put, when families support, share with, and care for one another, they stand a better chance of defeating poverty. Therefore, the concept of "family values" should not be taken lightly.[20] In the case of Africa as noted at the beginning of this work, the institution of the family is confronting severe challenges due to the prevalence of poverty, underdevelopment, and preventable diseases. The demise of the family can only exacerbate an already difficult situation.

"But who is my family?" one may ask. This question is reminiscent of the lawyer's question, "And who is my neighbor?" in the parable of The Good Samaritan (Luke 10:29-37). In this parable, Jesus tells the story of the man who fell into the hands of robbers who beat him and left him for dead. While the priest and Levite passed by, the Samaritan stopped and assisted this helpless victim. Jesus uses this story to illustrate that the true neighbor to the wounded Jew was the compassionate Samaritan (considered an outsider), not the priest or Levite (considered insiders and hence family) who failed to help the wounded man. This parable implies that one's family is not only the traditional nuclear family but is extended to embrace those who would normally be considered outsiders, the community at large. This concept of family encourages us "to see the neighbor or kin to whom obligation is due in the widest possible terms."[21] This is the sense one gets about the nature of the family in traditional Africa and ancient Israel. One's family therefore starts with the nuclear family and goes out in concentric circles to include the extended family, the neighbor, and the whole community. Any needy person in these circles is a family member who should be assisted. Consequently, we too are challenged to expand our traditional definition of family.

The next recommendation is intended for those who wield the power to liberate the poor or to keep them in oppressive situations. While the poor are encouraged to do as much as they can to rescue themselves from poverty and want, this research has shown that what the poor can do is but limited. Oftentimes the poor are struggling against systems that are designed to keep them in perpetual poverty. For example, insolvency was one of the major causes of poverty in the ancient world because of high interest rates. In that context those who could not pay off their debts sometimes ended up in slavery. That is why the biblical text recommended debt reduction or cancellation altogether. This crisis of insolvency is not uncommon in our own world. Many have assumed debts they can no longer pay because of job loss or compounded interest rates. Such measures do not ease the burden of the poor but rather worsen their situation. In a similar way, developing nations are groaning under debt that they can never repay in full. That is why some have suggested cancelation of such debt in order to ensure the economic viability of poor nations. This debt relief, however, would be viewed as a form of aiding the poor.[22]

Since the poor can only deal with their situation in a limited way, the heart of this study has shown that the challenge of the biblical mandate lies on the shoulders of those persons with the means to impact the situation of the poor negatively or positively. Hamilton states, "the powerful are reminded that the health of society is defined both by the absoluteness of its allegiance to YHWH and by its treatment of the dependent in its midst. The responsibility, the moral imperative, is . . . on the powerful who can make . . . that society a just one."[23] Given the evidence of persistent poverty in biblical context and mounting cases of poverty in global context, Gutiérrez articulates what it means to take an option for the poor. He remarks, "The ideal, what we should strive for, is that there be no poor; if there must be some, the conduct of the believer should be that of opening one's heart and one's hand to the poor."[24] The global ramifications of such an act are enormous. Sachs has already projected the end of poverty in our times if we follow what amounts to the biblical mandate in economic terms.[25] Among his suggestions are that rich nations should help poor nations to get out of "the poverty trap" through debt cancellation, global trade, economic development, and eradication of disease, among others. These suggestions have enormous potential to achieve their purpose if only the global community would adhere to them just as the biblical mandate challenged Israel.

Deuteronomy 15:4 mandates that "there will be no poor among you" as long as members are responsible for one another's well-being. The evidence reveals a history of infractions and the persistence of poverty throughout the biblical period. This pattern is replicated in our own world where poverty continues unabated despite our advancement and progress. When those with the means play the role of brother's and sister's keeper faithfully, the vision of the biblical mandate may yet be transformed from vision to reality.

NOTES

1. See Bennett, *Injustice Made Legal.*
2. See Wilson, *Prophecy and Society in Ancient Israel.*
3. Iliffe, *The African Poor,* 4.
4. See Wafawanaka, "Poverty in the Old Testament in African Perspective," in *Biblical Interpretation in African Perspective,* ed. David Tuesday Adamo.
5. Miscall, "The Concept of the Poor in the Old Testament."
6. See especially Havice, "The Concern for the Widow and the Fatherless in the Ancient Near East."
7. See Michael Joseph Brown, *What They Don't Tell You: A Survivor's Guide to Biblical Studies* (Louisville, KY: Westminster John Knox Press, 2000), 75-79.
8. Asana, "Problems of Marriage and Family Life in an African Context," 8, 33; Hugo A. Kamya, "The Interrelationship of Stress, Self-Esteem, Spiritual Well-Being and Coping Mechanisms among African Immigrants," Ph.D. diss., Boston University, 1994; Mbiti, *African Religions and Philosophy,* 81-89, 104-106; Porter, *The Extended Family in the Old Testament,* 1-21; Wright, *An Eye for an Eye,* 174-96; idem, *God's People in God's Land,* 3-114; idem, "Family," 761-69; and Baab, "Family," 238-41.
9. Mbiti, *African Religions and Philosophy,* 102.
10. Mafico, "Just, Justice," 1128.
11. See Janzen, *Old Testament Ethics: A Paradigmatic Approach.*
12. Premnath, "Latifundialization," 49-60. Premnath argues that "the worst form of Latifundialization" is witnessed in the eighth-century BCE (p. 54).
13. In a nutshell, biblical literature is literature of the rich and elite, written from their perspective and for their counterparts. It is much like history which has traditionally been written from the perspective of the powerful or the conquerors. Only recently have scholars and historians started to write history from "the underside," or from the perspective of those who were otherwise marginalized. The critical task for biblical scholars is to reconstruct the history of the biblical poor from what has been said or left unsaid about them. According to Gustavo Gutiérrez, scholars must reconstruct "the other history" or "the history of the other" (See *The Power of the Poor in History,* 201). He argues that history must be read from the "underside," that is, "*reread from the side of the poor*" (p. 201). See also the ground-breaking book by Elisabeth Schüssler Fiorenza, *In Memory of Her: A Feminist Theological Reconstruction of Christian Origins* (New York: Crossroad, 1983).
14. Lebacqz, *Justice in an Unjust World,* 107. Her emphases.
15. Hamilton, *Social Justice and Deuteronomy,* 150. He adds that the book encourages those who can shape society for the better to do so.
16. Hoppe, *Being Poor,* 175. In the same direct language, he concludes: "People have created poverty; they ought to be able to end it" (p. 179). See also Jim Wallis, "Poverty is a Scandal," *Sojourners* 14, no. 10 (1985): 4-5.
17. Ibid., 177. Hope also rejects any institutionalization of poverty (pp. 177-78). With regard to charity, Maimonides articulated one of the greatest statements when he stated that the best charity is that which helps the poor dispense with charity (see Sacks, *Wealth and Poverty: A Jewish Analysis,* 5). Bennett's argument that the legal-

ization of injustice in the Deuteronomic law benefited the rulers and drafters of this law thereby maintaining the status quo of oppression during the Omride administration is well taken here. See Bennett, *Injustice Made Legal.*

18. Bailey insightfully observes that Israelite kings are judged by whether they did good or bad, not whether they took care of the poor or ended poverty. Private communication, January 6, 2010.

19. See Wafawanaka, "Preaching in the Context of Poverty, Economic Marginalization, and the Ideal of Social Justice," in *Born to Preach: Essays in Honor of the Ministry of Henry & Ella Mitchell,* edited by Samuel K. Roberts, 40-54 (Valley Forge, PA: Judson Press, 2000).

20. See Julie Wortman, "Family Values: Only for the Privileged?" *The Witness* 77 (December 1994): 11-13. Wortman states that "society tends to believe that families in which members take care of one another in times of need are to be valued. A family, after all, is supposed to be where, no matter what, you know they will take you in" (p. 11). She also describes how social, economic, and political forces sometimes perpetuate poverty. She remarks that oftentimes the poor lose their children simply because they are poor and often stereotyped as irresponsible and unfit. Raymond Fung argues that families may defeat poverty by simply eating together, whereas rich families having no one to eat with are truly poor. See "Come to the Table," *Other Side* 134 (November 1982): 10-13.

21. Hamilton, *Social Justice and Deuteronomy,* 145.

22. See Sachs, *The End of Poverty, 126-127,* 280-81, 296-298, 342-343.

23. Hamilton, *Social Justice and Deuteronomy,* 150.

24. Gutiérrez, "Memory and Prophecy," in *The Option for the Poor,* ed. Groody, 23. See the rest of the essays in this book on what it means to take an option for the poor.

25. See Sachs, *The End of Poverty.*

Bibliography

Abesamis, Carlos H. "Good News to the Poor." In *Diakonia: Church for Others.* Edited by Norbert Greinacher and Norbert Mette, 25-32. Edinburgh: T. & T. Clark, 1988.

Achebe, Chinua. *The Education of a British-Protected Child: Essays.* New York: Alfred A. Knopf, 2009.

Achtemeier, Elizabeth. *The Community and Message of Isaiah 55-66: A Theological Commentary.* Minneapolis: Augsburg Publishing House, 1982.

Adamo, David Tuesday, ed. *Biblical Interpretation in African Perspective.* Lanham, Boulder, New York, Toronto, Oxford: University Press of America, 2006.

Albright, William Foxwell. "Archaeology and the Date of the Hebrew Conquest of Palestine." *Bulletin of the American Schools of Oriental Research* 58 (1935): 10-18.

————. "Further Light on the History of Israel from Lachish to Megiddo." *Bulletin of the American Schools of Oriental Research* 68 (1937): 22-26.

————. "The Israelite Conquest of Canaan in Light of Archaeology." *Bulletin of the American Schools of Oriental Research* 74 (1939): 11-23.

————. *The Archaeology of Palestine.* Baltimore: Penguin, 1949.

————. *The Biblical Period from Abraham to Ezra.* New York: Harper and Row, 1963.

Alexander, John F. "God's Preferential Option for the Poor." *The Other Side* 6 (March-April): 49-52; (May-June 1990): 51-53; (August 1990): 53-54.

Alt, Albrecht. *Essays on Old Testament History and Religion.* Garden City, NY: Doubleday, 1966.

Andersen, Francis, and David Noel Freedman. *Amos: A New Translation with Introduction and Commentary.* Anchor Bible 24A. New York, London, Toronto, Sydney, Auckland: Doubleday, 1989.

Anderson, Bernhard W. *Out of the Depths: The Psalms Speak for Us Today.* Rev. and expanded ed. Philadelphia: The Westminster Press, 1983.

————.*Understanding the Old Testament.* 4th ed. Englewood Cliffs, NJ: Prentice-Hall, 1986.

Araya, Victorio. "Toward a Church in Solidarity with the Poor." In *Faith Born in the Struggle for Life: A Re-Reading of Protestant Faith in Latin America Today,* 265-76. Grand Rapids, MI: William B. Eerdmans Publishing Company, 1988.

Azevedo, Marcello de Carvallo. "Semantics of the Option for the Poor." *SEDOS Bulletin* 25 (December 1993): 313-16.

Baab, Otto J. "Widow." In *The Interpreter's Dictionary of the Bible.* Vol. 4. Edited by George Arthur Buttrick, 842-43. New York, Nashville: Abingdon Press, 1962.

———. "Fatherless." In *The Interpreter's Dictionary of the Bible.* Vol. 2. Edited by George Arthur Buttrick, 245-46. New York, Nashville: Abingdon Press, 1962.

———. "Family." In *The Interpreter's Dictionary of the Bible.* Vol. 2. Edited by George Arthur Buttrick, 238-41. New York, Nashville: Abingdon Press, 1962.

Bailey, Warner M. "I Was Hungry: The Bible and Poverty." *Journal of Presbyterian History* 59 (Summer 1981): 181-96.

Bailey, Joseph G. "Amos: Preacher of Social Reform." *The Bible Today* 19 (1981): 306-13.

Ballard, Bruce. "On the Sin of Usury: A Biblical Economic Ethic." *Christian Scholar's Review* 24 (December 1994): 210-28.

Baltzer, K. "Liberation from Debt Slavery after the Exile in Second Isaiah and Nehemiah." In *Ancient Israelite Religion: Essays in Honor of Frank Moore Cross.* Edited by Patrick D. Miller, Paul D. Hanson, and S. Dean McBride, 477-84. Philadelphia: Fortress Press, 1987.

Bammel, Ernst. "*Ptōchós, Ptōcheia, Ptōchéuō.*" In *Theological Dictionary of the New Testament.* Vol. VI. Edited by Gerhard Friedrich. Translated by Geoffrey W. Bromiley, 885-915. Grand Rapids, MI: Wm. B. Eerdmans Publishing Company, 1968.

Barbour, Robin. *The Kingdom of God and Human Society: Essays by Members of the Scripture, Theology and Society Group.* Edinburgh: T. & T. Clark, 1993.

Barkay, Gabriel. "Your Poor Brother: A Note on an Inscribed Bowl from Beth Shemesh." *Israel Exploration Journal* 41 (1991): 239-241.

Barrick, W., and J. Spencer, eds. *In the Shelter of Elyon: Essays on Palestinian Life and Literature in Honour of G. W. Ahlström.* Sheffield, England: JSOT Press, 1984.

Barton, John. "Understanding Old Testament Ethics." *Journal for the Study of the Old Testament* 9 (1978): 44-64.

———. "Ethics in Isaiah of Jerusalem." *Journal of Theological Studies* 32 (1981): 1-18.

———. "Approaches to Ethics in the Old Testament." In *Beginning Old Testament Study.* Edited by J. Rogerson, 113-30. Philadelphia: Westminster Press, 1982.

Bauer, P. T., and Yamey, B. S. "Foreign Aid: Rewarding Impoverishment?" *Commentary* 80, no. 3 (1985): 38-40.

Bauer, Walter, William F. Arndt, and F. Wilbur Gingrich. *A Greek-English Lexicon of the New Testament and Other Early Christian Literature.* Chicago: The University of Chicago Press, 1957.

Baum, Gregory. "Taking Issue with Kenneth Westhues' 'The Option for (and Against) the Poor.'" *Grail* 3, no. 2 (1987): 6-8.

Beals, Art, and Larry Lebby. *Beyond Hunger: A Biblical Mandate for Social Responsibility*. Portland, OR: Multinomah Press, 1985.

Beckman, David M. "The Politics of Hunger: An Interview." *The Christian Century* 110 (April 1993): 452-56.

Beisner, Calvin E. "Prosperity and Poverty: The Compassionate Use of Resources in a World of Scarcity." *Christian Scholar's Review* 21, no, 2 (1991): 212-13.

———. "Justice and Poverty: Two Views Contrasted." *Transformation* 10 (January-April 1993): 16-22.

Benne, Robert. *The Preferential Option for the Poor: Essays*. Grand Rapids, MI: Eerdmans, 1988.

Bennett, Harold V. *Injustice Made Legal: Deuteronomic Law and the Plight of Widows, Strangers, and Orphans in Ancient Israel*. Grand Rapids, MI./ Cambridge, UK: William B. Eerdmans Publishing Company, 2002.

Bergant, Dianne. *Israel's Wisdom Literature: A Liberation-Critical Reading*. Minneapolis: Fortress Press, 1997.

Berthoud, Pierre. "Prophet and Covenant." In *Freedom, Justice, and Hope: Toward a Strategy for the Poor and Oppressed*. Edited by Marvin Olasky, Herbert Schlossberg, Pierre Berthoud, and Clark H. Pinnock, 19-39. Westchester, IL: Crossway Books, 1988.

Birch, Bruce C. "Hunger, Poverty and Biblical Religion." *The Christian Century* 92 (June 1975): 593-99.

———. *Singing the Lord's Song: A Study of Isaiah 40-55*. Abingdon Lay Bible Studies. Nashville: Abingdon Press, 1990.

———. *Let Justice Roll Down: The Old Testament, Ethics, and Christian Life*. Louisville, KY: Westminster and John Knox Press, 1991.

Birch, Bruce, and Larry Rasmussen. *The Predicament of the Prosperous*. Philadelphia: Westminster Press, 1978.

Blenkinsopp, Joseph. *A History of Prophecy in Israel: From the Settlement in the Land to the Hellenistic Period*. 1st ed. Philadelphia: Westminster Press, 1983.

Boecker, Hans Jochen. *Law and the Administration of Justice in the Old Testament*. Translated by Jeremy Moiser. Minneapolis: Augsburg, 1980.

Boerma, Conrad. *Rich Man, Poor Man and the Bible*. London: SCM, 1979.

———. *The Rich, the Poor, and the Bible*. Translated by John Bowden. Philadelphia: Westminster Press, 1979.

Boff, Leonardo. *When Theology Listens to the Poor*. Translated by Robert R. Barr. San Francisco: Harper & Row, 1988.

Boff, Leonardo, and Virgil Elizondo, eds. *Option for the Poor: Challenge to the Rich Countries*. Edinburgh: T. & T. Clark, 1986.

Boling, Robert G. *Judges: Introduction, Translation, and Commentary*. Anchor Bible 6a. Garden City, NY: Doubleday & Company, 1975.

Boling, Robert G., and George Ernst Wright. *Joshua: A New Translation with Notes and Commentary*. Anchor Bible 6. Garden City, NY: Doubleday & Company, 1982.

Bonino, Jose M. "Poverty as Curse, Blessing, and Challenge." *The Iliff Review* 34 (Fall 1977): 3-13.

Bonk, Jonathan J. "Missions and Mammon: Six Theses." *International Bulletin of Missionary Research* 13 (October 1989): 174-81.

Bosman, Hendrik L., I. G. P. Gous, and Izak J. J. Spangenberg, eds. *Plutocrats and Paupers: Wealth and Poverty in the Old Testament.* Pretoria: J. L. van Schaik, 1991.

Botterweck, G. Johannes. *"ebhyôn."* In *Theological Dictionary of the Old Testament.* Vol. III. Edited by G. Johannes Botterweck and Helmer Ringgren. Translated by John T. Willis, Geoffrey W. Bromiley and David E. Green, 27-41. Grand Rapids, MI: William B. Eerdmans Publishing Company, 1978.

Breastead, James Henry. *Ancient Records of Egypt: Historical Documents from the Earliest Times to the Persian Conquest.* 5 vols. Chicago, IL: The University of Chicago Press, 1927.

Bright, John. *Jeremiah.* Anchor Bible 21A. Garden City, NY: Doubleday & Company, 1965.

———. *A History of Israel.* Fourth Edition. Louisville, KY: Westminster John Knox Press, 2000.

Bromiley, Geoffrey W. ed. *The International Standard Bible Encyclopedia.* Vol. 3. Grand Rapids, MI: William B. Eerdmans Publishing Company, 1986.

Brown, Francis, Samuel R. Driver, and Charles A. Briggs, eds. *The New Brown, Driver and Briggs Hebrew and English Lexicon of the Old Testament, Based on the Lexicon of William Gesenius as Translated by Edward Robinson.* Lafayette, IN: Associated Publishers and Authors / Grand Rapids, MI: Baker Book House, 1907 and 1981.

Brown, Michael Joseph. *What They Don't Tell You: A Survivor's Guide to Biblical Studies.* Louisville, KY: Westminster John Knox Press, 2000.

Brown, Robert McAffe. *Unexpected News: Reading the Bible with Third World Eyes.* Philadelphia: Westminster Press, 1984.

Brueggemann, Walter. *The Land: Place as Gift, Promise, and Challenge in Biblical Faith.* Overtures to Biblical Theology. Philadelphia: Fortress Press, 1977.

———. "Psalm 109: Three Times 'Steadfast Love.'" *Word and World* 5 (Spring 1985): 144-54.

———. "The Book of Jeremiah: A Portrait of the Prophet." In *Interpreting the Prophets.* Edited by James Luther Mays and Paul J. Achtemeier, 113-29. Philadelphia: Fortress Press, 1987.

———. "The Book of Exodus." In *The New Interpreter's Bible.* Vol. 1. Edited by Leander E. Keck, 675-981. Nashville: Abingdon Press, 1994.

Budd, Philip J. *Leviticus: Based on the New Revised Standard Version.* London: Marshall Pickering / Grand Rapids, MI: W.B. Eerdmans Publishing Company, 1996.

Buvinić, Mayra, Margaret A. Lycette, and William Paul McGreevey, eds. *Women and Poverty in the Third World.* Baltimore and London: The Johns Hopkins University Press, 1983.

Byong-suh, Kim, "A Sociological Understanding of Poverty: The Asian Context." In *Mission in the Context of Endemic Poverty.* Papers of a Consultation on Mission in the Context of Poverty and in Situations of Affluence, Manila, Philippines, December 10-14, 1982. Edited by Lourdino A. Yuzon, 44-61. Toa Payoh, Singapore: Christian Conference of Asia, 1983.

Campbell, E. F., and David Noel Freedman. *The Biblical Archaeologist Reader.* Vol. 3. Garden City: Doubleday, 1970.

Carroll, Robert P. *Jeremiah: A Commentary.* Old Testament Library. London: SCM, 1986.

———. "Prophecy and Society." In *The World of Ancient Israel: Sociological, Anthropological and Political Perspectives: Essays by Members of the Society for Old Testament Study.* Edited by R. E. Clements, 203-225. Cambridge, New York, New Rochelle, Melbourne, Sydney: Cambridge University Press, 1989.

Cassuto, Umberto. *A Commentary on the Book of Exodus.* Jerusalem: The Magnes Press / The Hebrew University, 1967.

Cathcart, Kevin J., and John F. Healey, eds. *Back to the Sources: Biblical and Near Eastern Studies in Honor of Demot Ryan.* Dublin: Glendale Press, 1989.

Chaney, Marvin L. "Debt Easement in Israelite History and Tradition." *In The Bible and the Politics of Exegesis.* Edited by David Jobling, 127-39; 325-29. Cleveland: Pilgrim Press, 1991.

Chicago Tribune Editorial. "Eisegesis." *The Christian Century* 83 (July 1966): 856.

Chigwida, Max T. "Wealth, Poverty, and Justice: The Relationship between Traditional Understanding and Christian Teaching." *Transformation* 6, no. 1 (1989): 1-2.

Childs, Brevard S. *The Book of Exodus: A Critical Theological Commentary.* Old Testament Library. Philadelphia: The Westminster Press, 1962.

———. *Exodus: A Commentary.* Old Testament Library. London: SCM, 1974.

———. *Introduction to the Old Testament as Scripture.* Philadelphia: Fortress Press, 1979. Sixth Printing, 1989.

Chutter, Gordon A. "'Riches and Poverty' in the Book of Proverbs." *Crux* 18, no. 2 (1982): 23-28.

Cleary, Edward L., ed. *Born of the Poor: The Latin American Church Since Medellin.* Notre Dame: University of Notre Dame Press, 1990.

Clements, Ronald E. "The Unity of the Book of Isaiah." *Interpretation* 36 (April 1982): 117-29.

———. "Beyond Tradition-History: Deutero-Isaianic Development of First Isaiah's Themes." *Journal for the Study of the Old Testament* 31 (February 1985): 95-113.

———, ed. *The World of Ancient Israel: Sociological, Anthropological and Political Perspectives: Essays by Members of the Society for Old Testament Study.* Cambridge, New York, New Rochelle, Melbourne, Sydney: Cambridge University Press, 1989.

———. "Poverty and the Kingdom of God—An Old Testament View." In *The Kingdom of God and Human Society: Essays by the Members of the Scripture, Theology, and Society Group,* 13-27. Edinburgh: T. & T. Clark, 1993.

Clobus, Robert. "Justice and Peace: Option for the Poor; What More?" *SEDOS Bulletin* 88 (October 1988): 314-317.

Clouse, Robert G., ed. *Wealth and Poverty: Four Christian Views of Economics.* Downers Grove, IL: Intervarsity Press, 1984.

Cogan, Mordechai, and Hayim Tadmor. *II Kings: A New Translation with Introduction and Commentary.* Anchor Bible 11. New York: Doubleday & Company, 1988.

Coggins, Richard J. "The Old Testament and the Poor." *The Expository Times* 99 (October 1987): 11-14.

Collins, Adela Yarbro, ed. *Feminist Perspectives on Biblical Scholarship.* Chico, CA: Scholars Press, 1985.

Cone, James H. "Christian Theology and Scripture as the Expression of God's Liberating Activity for the Poor." *Bangalore Theological Forum* 22, no. 2 (1990): 26-39.

Conrad, Edgar W. *Reading Isaiah.* Overtures to Biblical Theology. Minneapolis: Fortress Press, 1991.

Coogan, Michael David, ed. and trans. *Stories from Ancient Canaan.* Louisville: The Westminster Press, 1978.

Coote, Robert B. *Amos among the Prophets: Composition and Theology.* Philadelphia: Fortress Press, 1981.

———. *Early Israel: A New Horizon.* Minneapolis: Fortress Press, 1990.

Cormie, Lee. "On the Option for the Poor and Oppressed in Doing Social Ethics." *Toronto Journal of Theology* 7, no.1 (1991): 19-34.

Coudere, H., and S. Marijsse. "'Rich' and 'Poor' in Mutoko Communal Area." *Zimbabwe Journal of Economics* 2, no. 1 (1988): 1-25.

Crenshaw, James L., ed. *Studies in Ancient Israelite Wisdom.* New York: Ktav Publishing House, 1976.

———. *Old Testament Wisdom: An Introduction.* Atlanta: John Knox Press, 1981.

———. *Ecclesiastes.* Old Testament Library. London: SCM, 1988.

———. "Poverty and Punishment in the Book of Proverbs." *Quarterly Review* 9, no. 3 (1989): 30-43.

———. "Theodicy." In *The Anchor Bible Dictionary.* Vol. 6. Edited by David Noel Freedman, 444-47. New York, London, Toronto, Sydney, Auckland: Doubleday, 1992.

Crenshaw, James L., and John T. Willis, eds. *Essays in Old Testament Ethics.* J. Philip Hyatt, In Memorium. New York: Ktav Publishing House, 1974.

Cross, Frank Moore. *Canaanite Myth and Hebrew Epic: Essays on the History of the Religion of Israel.* Cambridge, MA: Harvard University Press, 1973.

Cross, Frank Moore, Werner E. Lemke, and Patrick D. Miller, eds. *Magnalia Dei: The Mighty Acts of God: Essays on the Bible and Archaeology in Memory of George Ernst Wright.* Garden City, NY: Doubleday, 1976.

Cubitt, Verity S., and Roger C. Riddell. *The Urban Poverty Datum Line in Rhodesia: A Study of the Minimum Consumption Needs of Families.* Salisbury: Sebri Printers, 1974.

———. *Supplement to: The Urban Poverty Datum Line in Rhodesia: A Study of the Minimum Consumption Needs of Families (1974).* Salisbury: University of Rhodesia, 1979.

Curran, Charles E., and Richard A. McCormick, eds. *Official Catholic Social Teaching.* New York: Paulist Press, 1986.

Cuthbertson, Malcolm. "The Kingdom and the Poor." *Scottish Bulletin of Evangelical Theology* 4 (Autumn 1986): 123-33.

Dahood, Mitchell. *Psalms I: 1-50.* Anchor Bible. Garden City, NY: Doubleday and Company, 1966.

————. *Psalms II: 51-100*. Anchor Bible. Garden City, NY: Doubleday and Company, 1968.

————. *Psalms III: 101-150*. Anchor Bible. Garden City, NY: Doubleday and Company, 1970.

Darr, Katheryn Pfisterer. "Breaking Through the Wilderness: References to the Desert in Exilic Prophecy." Ph.D. diss., Vanderbilt University, 1984.

————. *Far More Precious than Jewels: Perspectives on Biblical Women*. Gender and the Biblical Tradition. Louisville, KY: Westminster / John Knox Press, 1991.

————. *Isaiah's Vision and the Family of God*. Literary Currents in Biblical Interpretation. Louisville, Kentucky: Westminster John Knox Press, 1994.

————. "Isaiah's Vision and the Rhetoric of Rebellion." *Society of Biblical Literature Seminar Papers*. Annual Meeting, 847-82. Atlanta: Scholars Press, 1994.

Davids, Peter H. "God and Mammon, Part 1: The Old Testament and the Teachings of Jesus." *Sojourners* 7 (February 1978): 11-17.

————. "God and Mammon, Part 2." *Sojourners* 7 (March 1978): 25-29.

Davidson, Benjamin. *The Analytical Hebrew and Chaldee Lexicon*. 3d Printing. Peabody, MA: Hendrickson Publishers, 1984.

Davies, Eryl W. "Land: Its Rights and Privileges." In *The World of Ancient Israel: Sociological, Anthropological and Political Perspectives: Essays by Members of the Society for Old Testament Study*. Edited by R. E. Clements, 349-69. Cambridge, New York, New Rochelle, Melbourne, Sydney: Cambridge University Press, 1989.

Davies, John T. "Poverty: Justice, Compassion, and Personal Responsibility." *Fundamentalist Journal* 4, no. 4 (1985): 27-30.

Davies, Paul Ewing. "Poor You Have With You Always: The Biblical View of Poverty." *McCormick Quarterly* 18 (January 1965): 37-48.

Davies, Philip R. *In Search of "Ancient Israel."* Journal for the Study of the Old Testament Supplement Series 148. Sheffield: JSOT Press, 1992.

Dawsy, James M. "The Biblical Authority of the Poor." *The Expository Times* 101 (July 1990): 295-98.

Day, Peggy L., ed. *Gender and Difference in Ancient Israel*. Minneapolis: Fortress Press, 1989.

De Vaux, Roland. *Ancient Israel: It's Life and Institutions*. Translated by John McHugh. New York, Toronto, London: McGraw-Hill Book Company, 1961.

————. *The Early History of Israel*. Translated by David Smith. Philadelphia: The Westminster Press, 1978.

Dearman, Andrew J. *Property Rights in the Eighth-Century Prophets*. Atlanta, GA: Scholars Press, 1988.

Deist, Ferdinand. "The Historical Scene in Which the Old Testament was Enacted." In *Plutocrats and Paupers: Wealth and Poverty in the Old Testament*. Edited by Hendrik L. Bosman, I. G. P. Gous, and Izak J. J. Spangenberg, 110-30. Pretoria: J. L. van Schaik, 1991.

DeLange, Harry M. "The Jubilee Principle: Relevant Today?" *The Ecumenical Review* 36 (1986): 437-43.

Dickinson, Richard D. N. "The Cry of the Poor." *International Review of Mission* 73 (April 1984): 173-84.

Domeris, W. R. "Biblical Perspectives on the Poor." *Journal of Theology for Southern Africa* 57 (December 1986): 57-61.

———. "God Cares for His Chosen Ones: A Prosperity Reading." In *Plutocrats and Paupers: Wealth and Poverty in the Old Testament.* Edited by Hendrik L. Bosman, I. G. P. Gous, and Izak J. J. Spangenberg, 25-32. Pretoria: J. L. van Schaik, 1991.

Donald, T. "The Semantic Field of Rich and Poor in the Wisdom Literature of Hebrew and Accadian." *Oriens Antiquus* 3 (1964): 27-41.

Driver, Samuel R. *Notes on the Hebrew Text and the Topography of the Books of Samuel.* 2d ed., rev. and enl. Oxford: Clarendon Press, 1966.

———. *A Critical and Exegetical Commentary on Deuteronomy.* International Critical Commentary. New York: Charles Scribner's Sons, 1895.

Elizondo, Virgil. "Unmasking the Idols." *SEDOS Bulletin* 24 (May 1992): 131-40.

Ellacuria, Ignacio, and Jon Sobrino, eds. *Mysterium Liberationis: Fundamental Concepts of Liberation Theology.* 2 vols. Maryknoll, NY: Orbis Books, 1993.

Elliott, Charles. *Patterns of Poverty in the Third World: A Study of Social and Economic Stratification.* New York: Praeger, 1975.

———. "Rural Poverty in Africa." Occasional Paper No. 12. Centre for Development Studies, 1-43. Swansea, United Kingdom: University College of Swansea, 1980.

———. "Poverty 2000." *Study Encounter* 7, no. 3 (1971): 1-8.

Emmerson, Grace I. "Women in Ancient Israel." In *The World of Ancient Israel: Sociological, Anthropological and Political Perspectives: Essays by Members of the Society for Old Testament Study.* Edited by R. E. Clements, 371-94. Cambridge, New York, New Rochelle, Sydney: Cambridge University Press, 1989.

Ensminger, Douglas, and Paul Bomani. *Conquest of World Hunger and Poverty.* Ames, Iowa: Iowa State University Press, 1980.

Epsztein, León. *Social Justice in the Ancient Near East and the People of the Bible.* Translated by John Bowden. London: SCM Press, 1986.

Everson, A. Joseph. "Day of the Lord." In *The Interpreter's Dictionary of the Bible.* Supplementary Volume. Ninth Printing. Edited by Keith Crim, 209-10. Nashville, Abingdon Press, 1990.

Fabry, Heinz-Josef. *"dal; dālal; dallāh; zālal."* In *Theological Dictionary of the Old Testament* Vol. III. Edited by G. Johannes Botterweck and Helmer Ringgren. Translated by John T. Willis, Geoffrey W. Bromiley, and David E. Green, 208-30. Grand Rapids, MI: William B. Eerdmans Publishing Company, 1978.

Fager, Jeffrey A. "Land Tenure in the Biblical Jubilee: A Moral World View." *Hebrew Annual Review* 11 (1987): 59-68.

———. *Land Tenure in the Biblical Jubilee: Uncovering Hebrew Ethics through the Sociology of Knowledge.* Sheffield, England: JSOT Press, 1993.

Feliciano, Juan G. "Gustavo Gutiérrez' Liberation Theology: Toward a Hispanic Epistemology and Theology of the Suffering of the Poor." *Apuntes* 13 (Summer 1993): 151-61.

Fensham, F. Charles. "Widow, Orphan, and the Poor in Ancient Near Eastern Legal and Wisdom Literature." *Journal of Near Eastern Studies* 21 (1962): 129-39.

Fernando, Kenneth. "Opting for the Poor—The Challenge to the Universal Religions." *Dialogue* (Colombo) 15, nos. 1-3 (1988): 28-35.

Ferré, Frederick, and Rita H. Mataragnon, eds. *God and Global Justice: Religion and Poverty in an Unequal World.* New York: Paragon House, 1985.

Finley, Thomas John. "An Evangelical Response to the Preaching of Amos." *Journal of the Evangelical Theological Society* 28 (December 1985): 411-20.

Freeman, Hobart E. *An Introduction to the Old Testament Prophets.* Chicago: Moody Press, 1968.

Fretheim, Terrence E. *Deuteronomistic History.* Interpreting Biblical Texts. Nashville: Abingdon Press, 1983.

———. *Exodus.* Interpretation. Louisville: John Knox Press, 1991.

Fry, John R. "There Will Be No Poor among You." *Renewal* 6 (March 1966): 22-23.

Frykenberg, Robert E. "Rising Expectations among the World's Poor." *Christianity Today* 30, no. 1 (1986): 61-71.

Fung, Raymond. "Come to the Table." *The Other Side* 134 (November 1982): 10-13.

Gaillot, Jacques. "Option for the Poor." In *Synod 1985: An Evaluation.* Edited by Guiseppe Alberigo and James Provost, 124-30. Edinburgh: T. & T. Clark, 1986.

Gamoran, Hillel. "The Biblical Law against Loans on Interest." *Journal of Near Eastern Studies* 30 (April 1971): 127-134.

Gelfand, Michael. *The Genuine Shona: Survival Values of an African Culture.* Salisbury: Mambo Press, 1973.

George, Augustine. "Poverty in the Old Testament." In *Gospel Poverty: Essays in Biblical Theology.* Translated and edited by Michael Guinan, 3-24. Chicago: Franciscan Herald Press, 1977.

Gerstenberger, Erhard S. "Singing a New Song: On Old Testament and Latin American Psalmody." *Word and World* 5 (Spring 1985): 155-67.

———. *Leviticus: A Commentary.* Old Testament Library. Louisville, KY: Westminster John Knox Press, 1996.

Giles, Terry. "A Note on the Vocation of Amos." *Journal of Biblical Literature* 111 (Winter 1992): 690-92.

Gill, Robin. *A Textbook of Christian Ethics.* Edinburgh: T. & T. Clark, 1985.

Gillingham, Sue. "The Poor in the Psalms." *The Expository Times* 100 (October 1988): 15-19.

Gnuse, Robert K. "Jubilee Legislation in Leviticus: Israel's Vision of Social Reform." *Biblical Theology Bulletin* 15, no. 2 (1985): 43-48.

———. *You Shall Not Steal: Community and Property in the Biblical Tradition.* Maryknoll, NY: Orbis Books, 1985.

Gonzalez, Justo L., and Anthony L. Dunnavant. *Poverty and Ecclesiology: Nineteenth-Century Evangelicals in the Light of Liberation Theology.* Collegeville, Minnesota: Liturgical Press, 1992.

Gonzalez, Justo L., and Anthony L. Dunnavant. "The Option for the Poor in Latin American Liberation Theology." In *Poverty and Ecclesiology: Nineteenth-Century Evangelicals in the Light of Liberation Theology.* Edited by Justo L. Gonzalez and Anthony L. Dunnavant, 9-26. Collegeville, Minnesota: The Liturgical Press, 1992.

Gottwald, Norman K. *The Tribes of Yahweh: A Sociology of the Religion of Liberated Israel, 1250-1050 BCE.* Third Printing. Maryknoll, NY: Orbis Books, 1985.

Gous, I. G. "City and Countryside: A Sociopolitical Perspective on Wealth and Poverty in Ancient Israel." In *Plutocrats and Paupers: Wealth and Poverty in the Old Testament.* Edited by Hendrik L. Bosman, I. G. P. Gous, and Izak Spangenberg, 159-69. Pretoria: J. L. van Schaik, 1991.

Gowan, Donald E. "Wealth and Poverty in the Old Testament: The Case of the Widow, the Orphan, and the Sojourner." *Interpretation* 41 (October 1987): 341-53.

Gower, Joseph F., ed. *Religion and Economic Ethics.* Lanham, MD: University Press of America, 1990.

Gray, George Buchanan. *A Critical and Exegetical Commentary on the Book of Isaiah I-XXXIX.* International Critical Commentary. New York: Charles Scribner's Sons, 1912.

Gray, John. *I and II Kings: A Commentary.* 2d. fully rev. ed. Old Testament Library. London: SCM, 1970.

———. *Joshua, Judges, Ruth.* New Century Bible Commentary. Grand Rapids, MI: William B. Eerdmans Publishing Company / Basingstoke, England: Marshall Morgan & Scott Publications, 1986.

Green, Reginald Herbold. "Sub-Saharan Africa: Poverty of Development, Development of Poverty." Discussion Paper 218. Institute of Development Studies, 1-42. Brighton, England: University of Sussex, 1986.

———. "Reduction of Absolute Poverty: A Priority Structural Adjustment." Discussion Paper 287. Institute of Development Studies, 1-40. Brighton, England: University of Sussex, 1991.

Greenberg, Harold I. *Poverty in Israel: Economic Realities and the Promise of Social Justice.* New York: Praeger, 1977.

Greene, John T. "The Old Testament Prophet as Messenger in the Light of Ancient Near Eastern Messengers and Messages." Ph.D. diss., Boston University, 1980.

Gremillion, Joseph B. "World Poverty, World Misery." *Social Action* (US) 33 (February 1967): 12-22.

Groody, Daniel G. ed. *The Option for the Poor in Christian Theology.* Notre Dame, IN: University of Notre Dame Press, 2007.

Grosz, Katarzyna. "Some Aspects of the Position of Women in Nuzi." In *Women's Earliest Records: From Ancient Egypt and Western Asia.* Proceedings of the Conference on Women in the Ancient Near East held at Brown University, Providence, RI 5-7 November 1987. Edited by Barbara S. Lesko, 167-89. Atlanta, GA: Scholars Press, 1989.

Guinan, Michael, ed. *Gospel Poverty: Essays in Biblical Theology.* Chicago: Franciscan Herald Press, 1977.

Gutiérrez, Gustavo. *A Theology of Liberation: History, Politics, and Salvation.* Maryknoll, NY: Orbis Books, 1972.

———. *The Power of the Poor in History: Selected Writings.* Translated by Robert R. Barr. Maryknoll, NY: Orbis Books, 1983.

———. "Church of the Poor." In *Born of the Poor: The Latin American Church since Medellin.* Edited by Edward L. Cleary, 61-71. Notre Dame: University of Notre Dame Press, 1990.

———. "Preferential Option for the Poor." *SEDOS Bulletin* 24 (June-July 1992): 176-81.

————. "Option for the Poor." In *Mysterium Liberationis: Fundamental Concepts of Liberation Theology*. Edited by Ignacio Ellacuria and Jon Sobrino, 235-50. Maryknoll, NY: Orbis Books, 1993.

————. "Option for the Poor: Assessment and Implications." *ARC* 22 (Spring 1994): 61-71.

Gutton, Jean-Pierre. *Lasociete et pauvres: l'exemple de la generalite de Lyons 1534-1789*. Paris: Privately Printed, 1971.

Habel, Norman C. "The Form and Significance of the Call Narratives." *Zeitschrift fur die alttestamentliche Wissenschaft* 77 (1965): 297-323.

————. "The Symbolism of Wisdom in Proverbs 1-9." *Interpretation* 26 (1972): 131-57.

————. *The Book of Job*. Old Testament Library. London: SCM, 1985.

————. "Wisdom, Wealth, and Poverty Paradigms in the Book of Proverbs." *Bible Bhashyam* 14 (1988): 26-49.

————. *The Land is Mine: Six Biblical Land Ideologies*. Minneapolis: Fortress Press, 1995.

Halloway, James Y. "For Three Transgressions, and for...." *Katallagete* 1 (December 1965): 3-10.

Halpern, Baruch. "The Exodus from Egypt: Myth or Reality?" In *The Rise of Ancient Israel*. By Hershel Shanks, William G. Dever, Baruch Halpern, and P. Kyle McCarter. Symposium held in Washington DC. 26 October 1991, 86-117. Washington, DC: Biblical Archaeology Society, 1992.

Hamel, Gildas. *Poverty and Charity in Roman Palestine, First Three Centuries C.E.* Berkeley: University of California Press, 1990.

Hamilton, Jeffries M. *Social Justice and Deuteronomy: The Case of Deuteronomy 15*. Society of Biblical Literature Dissertation Series 136. Atlanta, GA: Scholars Press, 1992.

————. "*Hā'āreṣ* in the Shemitta Law." *Vetus Testamentum* 42 (April 1992): 214-22.

Hamlin, E. John. "Foreigner." In *The Interpreter's Dictionary of the Bible*. Vol. 2. Edited by George Arthur Buttrick, 310-11. New York, Nashville: Abingdon Press, 1962.

Hamutyinei, Mordikai A., and Albert B. Plangger. *Tsumo-Shumo: Shona Proverbial Lore and Wisdom*. Shona Heritage Series Vol. 2. Gweru: Mambo Press, 1974.

Hanawalt, Emily Albu, and Carter Lindberg, eds. *Through the Eye of a Needle: Judeo-Christian Roots of Social Welfare*. Kirksville, MO: The Thomas Jefferson University Press at Northeast Missouri State University, 1994.

Hanks, Thomas D. "Why People are Poor: What the Bible Says." *Sojourners* 10 (January 1981): 19-22.

————. "Oppressors on the Run—An In-depth Look at an Important Biblical Teaching that Most of Us Usually Miss." *The Other Side* 113 (1981): 23-35.

————. *God So Loved the Third World: The Biblical Vocabulary of Oppression*. Translated by James C. Dekker. Maryknoll, NY: Orbis Books, 1984.

Hanson, Paul D. *The People Called: The Growth of Community in the Bible*. San Francisco: Harper & Row, 1986.

————. "The Ancient Near Eastern Roots of Social Welfare." In *Through the Eye of a Needle: Judeo-Christian Roots of Social Welfare*. Edited by Emily Albu

Hanawalt and Carter Lindberg, 7-28. Kirksville, MO: The Thomas Jefferson University Press at Northeast Missouri State University, 1994.

Harris, Rivkah. "Independent Women in Ancient Mesopotamia?" In *Women's Earliest Records: From Ancient Egypt to Western Asia.* Proceedings of the Conference on Women in the Ancient Near East held at Brown University, Providence RI 5-7 November 1987. Edited by Barbara S. Lesko, 145-65. Atlanta, GA: Scholars Press, 1989.

Harris R. Laird, Gleason L. Archer, and Bruce K. Waltke, eds. *Theological Wordbook of the Old Testament.* Vols. 1 and 2. Chicago: Moody Press, 1980.

Harrison, Paul. *The Third World Tomorrow: A Report from the Battlefront in the War Against Poverty.* New York: Penguin, 1980.

Hauck, Friedrich. *"Pénēs; Penichrós."* In *Theological Dictionary of the New Testament.* Vol. VI. Edited by Gerhard Friedrich. Translated by Geoffrey W. Bromiley, 37-40. Grand Rapids, MI: Wm. B. Eerdmans Publishing Company, 1968.

Hauser, Alan J. "The Revolutionary Origins of Ancient Israel: A Response to Gottwald *JSOT* 7 [1978] 37-52." *Journal for the Study of the Old Testament* 8 (July 1978): 46-49.

Havice, Harriet Katherine. "The Concern for the Widow and the Fatherless in the Ancient Near East: A Case Study in Old Testament Ethics." Ph.D. diss., Yale University, 1978.

Hayes, John H., and Irvine A. Stuart. *Isaiah the Eighth-Century Prophet: His Times and Preaching.* Garden City, NY: Doubleday and Company, 1968.

Heard, Warren. "Luke's Attitude toward the Rich and the Poor." *Trinity Journal* 9 (Spring 1988): 47-80.

Hendel, Kurt K. "The Care of the Poor: An Evangelical Perspective." *Currents in Theology and Mission* 15 (December 1988): 526-32.

Henriot, Peter J. *Opting for the Poor: A Challenge for North Americans.* Washington, DC: Center of Concern, 1990.

Herbert, A. S. *Isaiah 1-39.* The Cambridge Bible Commentary. Cambridge: Cambridge University Press, 1973.

Herron, Roy Brasfield. "The Land, the Law, and the Poor." *Word and World* 6, no. 1 (1986): 76-84.

———. "Evangelize the Poor (Lk 4:18)." *Religious Studies Bulletin* 1, no. 4 (1981): 101-109.

Hertzberg, Wilhelm. *I & II Samuel: A Commentary.* Old Testament Library. Philadelphia: The Westminster Press, 1964.

Heschel, Abraham J. *The Prophets.* Vols. 1 and 2. New York: Harper & Row, 1962.

Hexham, Irving. *The Bible, Justice and the Culture of Poverty: Emotive Calls to Action versus Rational Analysis.* London: Social Affairs Unit, 1985.

Hiebert, Paula S. "Whence Shall Help Come to Me? The Biblical Widow." In *Gender and Difference in Ancient Israel.* Edited by Peggy L. Day, 125-41. Minneapolis: Fortress Press, 1989.

Hillers, Delbert R. *Micah: A Commentary on the Book of the Prophet Micah.* Translated by Ralph D. Gehrke. Philadelphia: Fortress Press, 1984.

Hobbs, T. R. "Reflections on 'The Poor' and the Old Testament." *The Expository Times* 100 (May 1989): 291-94.

Hoffner, Harry A. *"'almānāh;'almānûth."* In *Theological Dictionary of the Old Testament.* Vol. I. Edited by G. Johannes Botterweck and Helmer Ringgren. Translated by John T. Willis, 287-91. Grand Rapids, MI: William B. Eerdmans Publishing Company, 1974. Rev. ed. 1977.

Holladay, William Lee, ed. *A Concise Hebrew and Aramaic Lexicon of the Old Testament, Based Upon the Lexical Work of Ludwig Koehler and Walter Baumgartner.* Grand Rapids, MI: William B. Eerdmans Publishing Company / Leiden, Netherlands: E. J. Brill, 1971.

————. "Jeremiah 2:34—A Fresh Approach." *Vetus Testamentum* 25 (April 1975): 221-25.

————. *Jeremiah 1: A Commentary on the Book of the Prophet Jeremiah.* Hermenia. Edited by Paul D. Hanson. Philadelphia: Fortress Press, 1986.

————. "The Years of Jeremiah's Preaching." In *Interpreting the Prophets.* Edited by James Luther Mays and Paul J. Achtemeier, 130-42. Philadelphia: Fortress Press, 1987.

————. *Jeremiah 2.* Hermenia. Minneapolis: Fortress Press, 1989.

Hollenbach, Paul. "Defining Rich and Poor Using Social Sciences." *Society of Biblical Literature Seminar Papers* 26 (1987): 50-63.

Hollyday, Joyce. "You Shall Not Afflict...." *Sojourners* 15, no. 3 (1986): 27-29.

Holwerda, David E. "Poor." In *The International Standard Bible Encyclopedia.* Vol. 3. Edited by Geoffrey W. Bromiley, 905-908. Grand Rapids, MI: William B. Eerdmans Publishing Company, 1986.

Hoppe, Leslie J. "Biblical Faith and Global Justice." *Spirituality Today* 31, no. 1 (1979): 4-13.

————. "Deuteronomy and the Poor." *The Bible Today* 24 (1986): 371-75.

————. *Being Poor: A Biblical Study.* Wilmington, DE: Michael Glazier, 1987.

————. *There Shall Be No Poor among You: Poverty in the Bible.* Nashville: Abingdon Press, 2004.

Hoyt, Thomas. "The Biblical Tradition of the Poor and Martin Luther King, Jr." *The Journal of the Interdenominational Theological Center,* 4, no. 2 (1977): 12-32.

Huddleston, Darrell Kent. "Biblical Perspectives on World Hunger." D. Min. diss., Boston University School of Theology, 1980.

Huffmon, Herbert B., Frank Anthony Spina, and A. R. W. Green, eds. *Quest for the Kingdom of God: Essays in Honor of George E. Mendenhall.* Winona Lake, IN: Eisenbrauns, 1983.

Huffmon, Herbert B. "The Social Role of Amos' Message." In *Quest for the Kingdom of God: Essays in Honor of George E. Mendenhall.* Edited by Herbert B. Huffmon, Frank Anthony Spina, and A. R. W. Green, 109-16. Winona Lake, IN: Eisenbrauns, 1983.

Humbert, Paul. *"Le mot biblique 'ebyon.'"* Revue d'histoire et de philosophie religieuses 32 (1952): 1-6.

Hyatt, J. Philip. *Commentary on Exodus.* New Century Bible. London: Oliphants, 1971.

Iliffe, John. *The African Poor: A History.* African Studies Series 58. Cambridge, New York, New Rochelle, Melbourne, Sydney: Cambridge University Press, 1987.

————. *Famine in Zimbabwe: 1890-1960.* Zambeziana Vol. XX. Gweru: Mambo Press, 1990.

————. "Poverty and Transvaluation in Nineteenth-Century Yorubaland." *Journal of African History* 3 (1991): 495-506.

Janzen, Waldemar. *Old Testament Ethics: A Paradigmatic Approach.* Louisville, KY: Westminster / John Knox Press, 1994.

Jenkins, David Edward. "The Power of the Powerless." *Risk* 6, no. 3 (1970): 35-38.

Jenni, Ernst. "Day of the Lord." In *The Interpreter's Dictionary of the Bible.* Vol. 1. Edited by George Arthur Buttrick, 784-85. New York, Nashville: Abingdon Press, 1962.

Jenni, Ernst, and Claus Westermann. *Theologisches Handworterbuch zum alten Testament.* Vols. I and II. Munich: Chr. Kaiser, 1978 and 1979.

Jobling, David, Peggy L. Day, and Gerald T. Sheppard, eds. *The Bible and the Politics of Exegesis: Essays in Honor of Norman K. Gottwald on his Sixty-Fifth Birthday.* Cleveland, Ohio: The Pilgrim Press, 1991.

Jones, Douglas Rawlinson. *Jeremiah.* New Century Bible Commentary. Grand Rapids, MI: William B. Eerdmans Publishing Company, 1992.

Kaiser, Otto. *Isaiah 1-12: A Commentary.* 2d ed. Old Testament Library. Philadelphia: Fortress Press, 1983.

Kaiser, Walter C. *Toward Old Testament Ethics.* Grand Rapids, MI: Zondervan Publishing House, 1983.

————. "The Old Testament Promise of Material Blessings and the Contemporary Believer." *Trinity Journal* 9 (Fall 1988): 151-70.

Kalilombe, Patrick A. "Cry of the Poor in Africa." *African Ecclesial Review* 29 (August 1987): 202-13.

Kalmin, Richard. "Levirate Law." In *The Anchor Bible Dictionary.* Vol. 4. Edited by David Noel Freedman, 296-97. New York, London, Toronto, Sydney, Auckland: Doubleday, 1992.

Kaminsky, Joel S. *Corporate Responsibility in the Hebrew Bible.* Journal for the Study of the Old Testament Supplement Series 196. Sheffield: Sheffield Academic Press, 1995.

Kamya, Hugo A. "The Interrelationship of Stress, Self-Esteem, Spiritual Well-Being and Coping Mechanisms among African Immigrants." Ph.D. diss., Boston University, 1994.

Kandathil, Joseph. "Oppression / Liberation Experience of Israel in Exodus." *Jeevadhara* 17 (1987): 438-50.

Kaniarakath, George P. "Liberation in the Old Testament." *Bible Bhashyam* 9, no. 3 (1983): 5-16.

Kantzer, Kenneth S., ed. *Applying the Scriptures.* Grand Rapids, MI: Academic Books, 1987.

Kaufman, Stephen A. "A Reconstruction of the Social Welfare System of Ancient Israel." In *In the Shelter of Elyon: Essays on Ancient Palestinian Life and Literature in Honor of G. W. Ahlström.* Edited by W. Boyd Barrick and John R. Spencer, 277-86. Sheffield, England: JSOT Press, 1984.

Keck, Leander E. "Poor." In *The Interpreter's Dictionary of the Bible.* Supplementary Volume. Edited by Keith Crim, 672-75. Nashville: Abingdon Press, 1976. Ninth Printing, 1990.

————, ed. *The New Interpreter's Bible.* Vol. 1. Nashville: Abingdon Press, 1994.

Kee, Alistair. "Amos and Affluence." *The Furrow* 38, no. 1 (1987): 151-61.

Kellermann, Diether. *"gûr; gēr; gērûth; mĕghûrîm."* In *Theological Dictionary of the Old Testament.* Vol. 2. Rev. ed. Edited by G. Johannes Botterweck and Helmer Ringgren. Translated by John T. Willis, 439-49. Grand Rapids, MI: Eerdmans, 1977.

Kittel, R. ed. *Biblia Hebraica Stuttgartensia.* Stuttgart: Deutsche Bibelgesellschaft, 1984.

Klein, Ralph W. *Textual Criticism of the Old Testament: The Septuagint after Qumran.* Guides to Biblical Scholarship. Edited by Gene M. Tucker. Philadelphia: Fortress Press, 1974. 3d Printing, 1981.

Koch, Klaus. *The Prophets.* Vol. 1. Philadelphia: Fortress Press, 1982. 3d Printing, 1987.

————. *The Prophets.* Vol. 2. Philadelphia: Fortress Press, 1984.

Koehler, Ludwig, and Walter Baumgartner. *Lexicon in Veteris Testamenti libros.* Vols. I and II. Grand Rapids, MI: Wm. B. Eerdmans Publishing Company / Leiden: E. J. Brill, 1951 and 1953.

Koehler, Ludwig, and Walter Baumgartner. *The Hebrew and Aramaic Lexicon of the Old Testament.* Vols. I-III. Revised by Walter Baumgartner and Johann Jakob Stamm. Translated and edited under the supervision of M. E. J. Richardson. Leiden, New York, Cologne: E. J. Brill:1994-1996.

Koehler, Ludwig, and Walter Baumgartner. *Hebraisches und Aramaisches Lexicon zum Alten Testament.* Vols. I-VI. Leiden: E. J. Brill, 1967-1996.

Kottackal, Joseph. "Jubilee in the Old Testament." *Bible Bhashyam* 9, no. 3 (1983): 157-67.

Kovacks, Brian. "Is There a Class-Ethic in Proverbs?" In *Essays in Old Testament Ethics.* Edited by James L. Crenshaw and John T. Willis, 173-89. New York: Ktav Publishing House, 1974.

Kuhrt, Amelie. "Non-Royal Women in the Late Babylonian Period: A Survey." In *Women's Earliest Records: From Ancient Egypt and Western Asia.* Proceedings of the Conference on Women in the Ancient Near East held at Brown University, Providence RI 5-7 November 1987. Edited by Barbara S. Lesko, 215-43. Atlanta, GA: Scholars Press, 1989.

Kutsch, E. *"ybm; yābām; yĕbāmâ."* In *Theological Dictionary of the Old Testament.* Vol. V. Edited by G. Johannes Botterweck and Helmer Ringgren. Translated by David E. Green, 367-73. Grand Rapids, MI: William B. Eerdmans Publishing Company, 1986.

Krass, Alfred C. "Blessing of Poverty." *Frontier* 13 (August 1970): 189-193.

Lambert, W. G. *Babylonian Wisdom Literature.* Oxford: The Clarendon Press, 1960.

Lang, Bernhard. "The Social Organization of Peasant Poverty in Biblical Israel." *Journal for the Study of the Old Testament* 24 (1982): 47-63.

————, ed. *Anthropological Approaches to the Old Testament.* Philadelphia: Fortress Press / London: SPCK, 1985.

Lappé, Frances Moore. "Who Benefits; Who Has the Power to Decide? The Cause and Relief of Poverty." *Currents in Theology and Mission* 7 (October 1980): 277-87.

———. *World Hunger: Twelve Myths.* New York: Gore Place, 1986.

Larkin, William J. "The Ethics of Inflation: A Biblical Critique of the Causes and Consequences." *Grace Theological Journal* 3, no. 1 (1982): 89-105.

Larue, Gerald. *Sex and the Bible.* Buffalo, NY: Prometheus Books, 1983.

Lebacqz, Karen. *Justice in an Unjust World: Foundations for a Christian Approach to Justice.* Minneapolis: Fortress Press, 2007.

Lee, Jong Keun. "The Theological Concept of Divine Ownership of the Land in the Hebrew Bible." Th.D. diss., Boston University, 1993.

Lemche, Neils Peter. "The 'Hebrew Slave': Comments on the Slave Law. Ex. xxi 2-11." *Vetus Testamentum* 25, no. 2 (1975): 129-44.

———. "The Manumission of Slaves—Fallow Year—The Sabbatical Year—The Jobel Year." *Vetus Testamentum* 26, no. 1 (1976): 38-59.

Le Roux, Jurie. "God Also Loves the Rich: An Allegorical Reading of the Old Testament." In *Plutocrats and Paupers: Wealth and Poverty in the Old Testament.* Edited by Hendrik L. Bosman, I. G. P. Gous, and Izak J. J. Spangenberg, 85-94. Pretoria: J. L. van Schaik, 1991.

Lesko, Barbara S., ed. *Women's Earliest Records: From Ancient Egypt and Western Asia.* Proceedings of the Conference on Women in the Ancient Near East held at Brown University, Providence RI 5-7 November 1987. Atlanta, GA: Scholars Press, 1989.

Leslie, Joanne, and Michael Paolisso, eds. *Women, Work, and Child Welfare in the Third World* Boulder, CO: Westview Press, 1989.

Levenson, Jon D. "Poverty and the State in Biblical Thought." *Judaism* 25 (Spring 1976): 230-41.

Lichtheim, Miriam. *Ancient Egyptian Literature: A Book of Readings.* Vols. I-III: Berkeley, Los Angeles, London: University of California Press, 1973-1980.

Liddell, Henry G., and Roger Scott. *A Greek-English Lexicon.* Oxford: Clarendon Press, 1968.

Limburg, James. *The Prophets and the Powerless.* Atlanta: John Knox Press, 1977.

———. *Hosea-Micah.* Interpretation. Atlanta: John Knox Press, 1988.

Lindberg, Carter, "Through a Glass Darkly: A History of the Church's Vision of the Poor and Poverty." *The Ecumenical Review* 33, no. 1 (1981): 37-52.

———. *Beyond Charity: Reformation Initiatives for the Poor.* Minneapolis: Fortress Press, 1993.

———. "The Liturgy after the Liturgy: Welfare in the Early Reformation." In *Through the Eye of a Needle: Judeo-Christian Roots of Social Welfare.* Edited by Emily Albu Hanawalt and Carter Lindberg, 177-92. Kirksville, MO: The Thomas Jefferson University Press at Northeast Missouri State University, 1994.

Linnenbrink, Gunther. "Solidarity with the Poor: The Role of the Church in the Conflict on Development." *The Ecumenical Review* 27 (July 1975): 270-75.

Lohfink, Norbert. "*ḥopšî; ḥupšâ; ḥopšît.*" In *Theological Dictionary of the Old Testament.* Vol. V. Edited by G. Johannes Botterweck and Helmer Ringgren. Translated by David E. Green, 114-18. Grand Rapids, MI: William B. Eerdmans Publishing Company, 1986.

———. *Option for the Poor: The Basic Principle of Liberation Theology in Light of the Bible.* Translated by Linda M. Maloney. Edited by Duane L. Christensen. Berkeley, CA: Bibal Press, 1987.

———. "Poverty in the Laws of the Ancient Near East and of the Bible." *Theological Studies* 52 (March 1991): 34-50.

Lukas, Jozsef. "The Problem of Poverty and the Poor in Catholic Social Teaching: A Marxist Perspective." In *Official Catholic Social Teaching.* Edited by Charles E. Curran and Richard McCormick, 301-12. New York, Mahwah: Paulist Press. 1986.

MacPherson, Stewart. *Five Hundred Million Children: Poverty and Child Welfare in the Third World.* Sussex, UK: Wheatsheaf Books / New York: St. Martin's Press, 1987.

Mafico, Temba Levi Jackson. "The Relevance and Appeal of the Old Testament to the Ndau People of Rhodesia, Based on a Form-Critical Analysis of the Patriarchal and Covenantal Historical Narratives Recorded in Genesis 12-35 and Exodus 1-24." Th.M. Thesis. Harvard University, 1973.

———. "A Study of the Hebrew Root *Špt* With Reference to Yahweh." Ph.D. diss., Harvard University, 1979.

———. "Ethics (Old Testament)." In *The Anchor Bible Dictionary.* Vol. 2. Edited by David Noel Freedman, 645-52. New York, London, Toronto, Sydney, Auckland: Doubleday, 1992.

———. "Judge, Judging." In *The Anchor Bible Dictionary.* Vol. 3. Edited by David Noel Freedman, 1104-1106. New York, London, Toronto, Sydney, Auckland: Doubleday, 1992.

———. "Just, Justice." In *The Anchor Bible Dictionary.* Vol. 3. Edited by David Noel Freedman, 1127-29. New York, London, Toronto, Sydney, Auckland: Doubleday, 1992.

———. *Yahweh's Emergence as "Judge" among the Gods: A Study of the Hebrew Root Špṭ.* Lewiston, Queenston, Lampeter: The Edwin Mellen Press, 2006.

Mair, Lucy P. *Welfare in the British Colonies.* London: The Royal Institute of International Affairs, 1944.

Malchow, Bruce. "Social Justice in Wisdom Literature." *Biblical Theology Bulletin* 12 (1982): 120-24.

———. "Social Justice and the Israelite Law Codes." *Word & World* 4 (Summer 1984): 299-306.

———. "Poverty in the Laws of the Ancient Near East and of the Bible." *Theological Studies* 52 (March 1991): 34-50.

———. *Social Justice in the Hebrew Bible: What is New and What is Old.* Collegeville, Minnesota: The Liturgical Press, 1996.

March, W. Eugene. "Psalm 86: When Love is not Enough." *Austin Seminary Bulletin: Faculty Edition* 105 (Spring 1990): 17-25.

Mason, John D. "Biblical Teaching and Assisting the Poor." *Transformation* 4, no. 2 (1987): 1-14.

Massey, James L. "Reading the Bible from Particular Social Locations: An Introduction." In *The New Interpreter's Bible*. Vol. 1. Edited by Leander E. Keck, 150-53. Nashville: Abingdon Press, 1994.

Matthews, Victor H., and Don C. Benjamin. *Social World of Ancient Israel, 1250-587 BCE*. Peabody, MA: Hendrickson Publishers, 1993.

Matthews, Victor H. *Social World of the Hebrew Prophets*. Peabody, MA.: Hendrickson Publishers, 2001.

Mauch, Theodor M. "Sojourner." In *The Interpreter's Dictionary of the Bible*. Vol. 4. Edited by George Arthur Buttrick, 397-99. New York, Nashville: Abingdon Press, 1962.

Mauchline, John. *1 and 2 Samuel*. New Century Bible. London: Oliphants, 1971.

Mays, James Luther. *Amos: A Commentary*. Old Testament Library. Philadelphia: The Westminster Press, 1969.

———. *Micah: A Commentary*. Old Testament Library. London: SCM, 1976.

———. "Justice: Perspectives from the Prophetic Tradition." *Interpretation* 37 (1983): 5-17.

———. *Psalms*. Interpretation. Louisville: John Knox Press, 1994.

Mays, James Luther, and Paul J. Achtemeier, eds. *Interpreting the Prophets*. Philadelphia: Fortress Press, 1987.

Mbiti, John S. *African Religions and Philosophy*. 2d ed., rev. and enl. Oxford and Portsmouth, NH: Heinemann, 1990.

———. *Introduction to African Religion*. 2d ed., rev. London: Heinemann, 1991.

McAffe, R. *Unexpected News: Reading the Bible with Third World Eyes*. Philadelphia: Westminster Press, 1984.

McCarter, P. Kyle. *I Samuel: A New Translation with Introduction, Notes, and Commentary*. Anchor Bible 8. Garden City, NY: Doubleday & Company, 1980.

———. *II Samuel: A New Translation with Introduction, Notes, and Commentary*. Anchor Bible 9. Garden City, NY: Doubleday & Company, 1984.

McKenzie, John L. *Second Isaiah: Introduction, Translation and Notes*. 1st ed. Garden City, NY: Doubleday, 1968.

McKane, William. *Proverbs: A New Approach*. Old Testament Library. Philadelphia: Westminster Press, 1970.

McPolin, James. "Psalms as Prayers of the Poor." In *Back to the Sources: Biblical and Near Eastern Studies in Honor of Demot Ryan*. Edited by Kevin J. Cathcart and John F. Healey, 79-103. Dublin: The Glendale Press, 1989.

Mendelsohn, Isaac. *Slavery in the Ancient Near East: A Comparative Study of Slavery in Babylonia, Assyria, Syria, and Palestine from the Middle of the Third Millennium to the End of the First Millennium*. New York: Oxford University Press, 1949.

———. "Slavery in the OT." In *The Interpreter's Dictionary of the Bible*. Vol. 4. Edited by George Arthur Buttrick, 383-91. New York, Nashville: Abingdon Press, 1962.

Mendenhall, George E. *Law and Covenant in Israel and the Ancient Near East*. Pittsburgh, Pennsylvania: The Biblical Colloquium, 1955.

———. "The Hebrew Conquest of Palestine." *Biblical Archaeologist* 25 (1962): 66-87. Reprinted in *The Biblical Archaeologist Reader*. Vol. 3. Edited by E. F. Campbell and David Noel Freedman, 100-120. Garden City: Doubleday, 1970.

————. *The Tenth Generation: The Origins of the Biblical Tradition*. Baltimore: Johns Hopkins University, 1973.

————. "Social Organization in Early Israel." In *Magnalia Dei: The Mighty Acts of God: Essays on the Bible and Archaeology in Memory of George Ernst Wright*. Edited by Frank Moore Cross, Werner E. Lemke, and Patrick D. Miller, 132-51. Garden City, New York: Doubleday, 1976.

————. "Migration Theories versus Cultural Changes as an Explanation for Early Israel." *Society of Biblical Literature Seminar Papers*, 135-43. Missoula, Montana: Scholars Press, 1976.

Meyers, Carol L., and M. O'Connor, eds. *The Word of the Lord Shall Go Forth: Essays in Honor of David Noel Freedman in Celebration of His Sixtieth Birthday*. Winona Lake, IN: Eisenbrauns, 1983.

Meyers, Carol. "Women in the Domestic Economy of Early Israel." In *Women's Earliest Records: From Ancient Egypt and Western Asia*. Proceedings of the Conference on Women in the Ancient Near East held at Brown University, Providence RI 5-7 November 1987, Edited by Barbara S. Lesko, 265-81. Atlanta, GA: Scholars Press, 1989.

Miller, Patrick D. *Deuteronomy*. Interpretation. Louisville: John Knox Press, 1990.

Miscall, Peter Darwin. "The Concept of the Poor in the Old Testament." Ph.D. diss., Harvard University, 1972.

Morgenstern, Julian. "Sabbatical Year." In *The Interpreter's Dictionary of the Bible*. Vol. 4. Edited by George Arthur Buttrick, 141-44. Nashville, New York: Abingdon Press, 1962.

————. "Jubilee, Year of." In *The Interpreter's Dictionary of the Bible*. Vol. 2. Edited by George Arthur Buttrick, 1001-1002. Nashville, New York: Abingdon Press, 1962.

Mosala, Itumeleng J. "Good News for the Poor: A Black African Biblical Hermeneutics." *Epworth Review* 20 (September 1993): 85-91.

Mott, Stephen Charles. *Biblical Ethics and Social Change*. New York/Oxford: Oxford University Press, 1982.

Mowinckel, Sigmund. *The Psalms in Israel's Worship*. Vols. 1-2. Translated by D. R. AP-Thomas. Nashville, New York: Abingdon Press, 1962.

Moyo, Sam, Nelson P. Moyo, and Rene Lowenson. "The Root Causes of Hunger in Zimbabwe: An Overview of the Nature, Causes, and Effects of Hunger, and Strategies to Combat Hunger." In Zimbabwe Institute of Development Studies Working Papers, No. 4, 1-89. Harare: ZIDS, 1985.

Murphy, Seamus. "The Work of Justice and the Option for the Poor." *SEDOS Bulletin* 25 (January 1993): 19-22.

Muthengi, Julius K. "The Culture of Poverty: Implications for the Urban Ministry." *Africa Journal of Evangelical Theology* 11, no. 2 (1992): 90-104.

Nafziger, Wayne E. *Inequality in Africa: Political Elites, Proletariat, Peasants and the Poor*. Cambridge: Cambridge University Press, 1988.

Nash, Ronald H. "Poverty and Wealth." *Concordia Journal* 14 (April 1988): 198-99.

————. *Poverty and Wealth: The Christian Debate over Capitalism*. Westchester, IL: Crossway Books, 1986.

Neal, Marie Augusta. *The Just Demands of the Poor: Essays in Socio-Theology.* Mahwah, NY: Paulist Press, 1987.

Nebechukwu, Augustine. "Solidarity with the Poor: Christian Response to Poverty." *African Ecclesial Review* 32 (August 1990): 96-111.

Nelson, Richard D. *First and Second Kings.* Atlanta: John Knox Press, 1987.

Nessan, Craig L. "Poverty: The Biblical Witness and Contemporary Reality." *Currents in Theology and Mission* 13 (August 1986): 236-38.

Neuhaus, Richard John, ed. *The Preferential Option for the Poor.* Grand Rapids, MI: Eerdmans, 1988.

Newsom, Carol A. "Women and the Discourse of Patriarchal Wisdom: A Study of Proverbs 1-9." In *Gender and Difference in Ancient Israel.* Edited by Peggy L. Day, 142-60. Minneapolis: Fortress Press, 1989.

Noble, Paul R. "The Literary Structure of Amos: A Thematic Analysis." *Journal of Biblical Literature* 114 (1995): 209-26.

Nolan, Albert. "The Option for the Poor in South Africa." In *Resistance and Hope: South African Essays in Honor of Beyers Naude.* Edited by Charles Villa-Vicencio and John W. De Grunchy, 189-98. Grand Rapids, MI: Wm. B. Eerdmans Publishing Company, 1985. Reprinted in *SEDOS Bulletin* 87 (March 1987): 90-97.

North, Robert. *Sociology of the Biblical Jubilee.* Rome: Pontifical Biblical Institute, 1954.

Noth, Martin. *Uberlieferungsgeschichtliche Studien. Die sammelnden und bearbeitenden Geschichtswerke in alten Testament.* Tubingen: Max Niemeyer, 1943.

———. *The History of Israel.* 2d ed. New York: Harper & Row, 1960.

———. *Exodus: A Commentary.* Old Testament Library. Philadelphia: The Westminster Press, 1962.

———. *Leviticus: A Commentary.* Old Testament Library. Philadelphia: Westminster Press, 1965.

———. *The Deuteronomistic History.* Journal for the Study of the Old Testament Supplement 15. Sheffield: University of Sheffield, 1981.

Nurnberger, Klaus, ed. *Affluence, Poverty and the Word of God: An Interdisciplinary Study Program of the Missiological Institute, Mapumulo.* Durban, South Africa: Lutheran Publishing House, 1978.

———. "What Do We Actually Mean when We Speak of Affluence and Poverty?" In *Poverty, Affluence and the Word of God: An Interdisciplinary Study-Program of the Missiological Institute, Mapumulo.* Edited by Klaus Nurnberger, 27-34. Durban, South Africa: The Lutheran Publishing House, 1978.

———. "The Affluent Centre and the Poor Periphery: Structural Aspects of Urban and Rural Development in Southern Africa." In *Poverty, Affluence and the Word of God: An Interdisciplinary Study-Program of the Missiological Institute, Mapumulo.* Edited by Klaus Nurnberger, 57-66. Durban, South Africa: The Lutheran Publishing House, 1978.

———. "The Message of the O.T. Prophets during the Eighth Century B.C. concerning Affluence and Poverty." In *Poverty, Affluence and the Word of God: An Interdisciplinary Study-Program of the Missiological Institute, Mapumulo.* Edited by Klaus Nurnberger, 141-52. Durban, South Africa: The Lutheran Publishing House, 1978.

Nyathi, Andrew, and John Hoffman. *Tomorrow is Built Today: Experiences of War, Colonialism and the Struggle for Collective Co-Operatives in Zimbabwe.* Harare: Anvil Press, 1990.

O'Brien, John. *Theology and the Option for the Poor.* Dublin: Columbia Press/Collegeville, MN: Liturgical Press, 1992.

O'Donovan, O. M. T. "Toward an Interpretation of Biblical Ethics." *Tyndale Bulletin* 27 (1976): 54-78.

O'Hagan, Angelo P. "Poverty in the Bible." *Australian Biblical Review* 12 (December 1964): 1-9.

Oakman, Douglas E. "The Ancient Economy in the Bible." *Biblical Theology Bulletin* 21, no. 1 (1991): 34-39.

Oates, Wayne E. "Ethics of Poverty." *Pastoral Psychology* 20 (November 1969): 30-44.

Olley, John W. "'Righteous' and Wealthy? The Description of the *saddiq* in Wisdom Literature." *Colloquium: The Australian and New Zealand Theological Society* 22 (May 1990): 38-45.

Osiek, Carolyn. "Rich and Poor in the Shepherd of Hermas: An Exegetical Social Investigation." Th.D. diss., Harvard University, 1978.

Osthathios, Geevarghese Mar. "Mission in the Context of Endemic Poverty and in Situations of Affluence." *Mission Studies* 3, no. 1 (1986): 43-50.

Page, Hugh R. Jr., gen. ed. *The Africana Bible: Reading Israel's Scriptures from Africa and the African Diaspora.* Minneapolis: Fortress Press, 2010.

Pantelis, Jorge. "The Bible as the Memory of the Poor." *Apuntes* 10, no. 1 (1990): 9-14.

Parker, Simon B. *The Pre-Biblical Narrative Tradition: Essays on the Ugaritic Poems Keret and Aqhat.* Society of Biblical Literature Resources for Biblical Study 24. Atlanta, GA: Scholars Press, 1989.

Patrick, Dale. "The Rights of the Underprivileged." *Society of Biblical Literature Seminar Papers* 1 (1975): 1-6.

———. *Old Testament Law.* Atlanta: John Knox Press, 1985.

Patterson, Richard D. "The Widow, the Orphan, and the Poor in the Old Testament and the Extra-Biblical Literature." *Bibliotheca Sacra* 130 (July-September 1973): 223-34.

Paul, Shalom M. *Amos.* Hermenia. Minneapolis: Fortress Press, 1991.

Pedersen, Johs. "Note on the Hebrew *ḥofšī*." *Journal of the Palestine Oriental Society* 6 (1926): 103-105.

———. *Israel: It's Life and Culture.* Vols. I-II. London: Oxford University Press, 1926.

———. *Israel: It's Life and Culture.* Vols. 3-4. London: Oxford University Press, 1940.

Perdue, Leo G., Bernard B. Scott, and William J. Wiseman, eds. *In Search of Wisdom: Essays in Memory of John G. Gammie.* Louisville, KY: Westminster / John Knox Press, 1993.

Petersen, David L. *The Prophetic Literature: An Introduction.* Louisville, London: Westminster John Knox Press, 2002.

Petersen, Paul D., and Ruth F. Frazer, eds. *Poverty, Hunger, and Religion: A Bibliography Selected from the American Theological Library Association Religion Database.* 2d ed., rev. Chicago, IL: ATLA, 1984.

Phan, Peter C. "Overcoming Poverty and Injustice: The Response of Liberation Theology to Evil." *Dialogue and Alliance* 8 (Fall-Winter 1994): 47-64.

Phillips, Anthony. *Ancient Israel's Criminal Law: A New Approach to the Decalogue.* Oxford: Basil Blackwell, 1970.

Pickering, John. *A Comprehensive Lexicon of the Greek Language.* Boston: Wilkins, Carter, and Company, 1849.

Pieris, Aloysius. "Religion and the Liberation of the Oppressed." *Dialogue* 15, nos. 1-3 (1988): 101-110.

Pilgrim, Walter E. *Good News to the Poor: Wealth and Poverty in Luke-Acts.* Minneapolis, MN: Augsburg Publishing House, 1981.

Pinnock, Clark H. "Pursuit of Utopia, Betrayal of the Poor." *Crux* 23 (December 1987): 5-14.

Pixley, George V. "People of God: Popular Majorities in the Bible." *Foundations* 23 (October December 1980): 368-79.

———. "The Poor Evangelize Biblical Scholarship." *American Baptist Quarterly* 2 (June 1983): 157-67.

———. "Micah—A Revolutionary." In *The Bible and the Politics of Exegesis: Essays in Honor of Norman K. Gottwald on His Sixty-Fifth Birthday.* Edited by David Jobling, Peggy L. Day, and Gerald T. Sheppard, 53-60, 308. Cleveland, Ohio: The Pilgrim Press, 1991.

———. "A Latin American Perspective: The Option for the Poor in the Old Testament." In *Voices from the Margin: Interpreting the Bible in the Third World.* Edited by R. S. Sugirtharajah, 229-40. London: SPCK, 1991.

Pixley, George V., and Clodovis Boff. *The Bible, the Church, and the Poor.* Translated by Paul Burns. Maryknoll, NY: Orbis Books, 1989.

Pleins, J. David. "Poverty in the Social World of the Wise." *Journal for the Study of the Old Testament* 37 (1987): 61-78.

———. "Poor, Poverty (Old Testament)." In *The Anchor Bible Dictionary.* Vol. 5. Edited by David Noel Freedman, 402-14. New York, London, Toronto, Sydney, Auckland: Doubleday, 1992.

———. *The Social Visions of the Hebrew Bible: A Theological Introduction.* Louisville, KY: Westminster John Knox Press, 2001.

Pobee, John S. *Toward an African Theology.* Nashville: Abingdon, 1979.

———. *Who are the Poor? The Beatitudes as a Call to Community.* Geneva: World Council of Churches, 1987.

Pobee, John S., and Barbel von Wartenberg-Potter, eds. *New Eyes for Reading: Biblical and Theological Reflections by Women from the Third World.* Geneva: World Council of Churches, 1986.

Pope, Marvin. *Job.* Anchor Bible. Garden City, NY: Doubleday & Company, 1965.

Pope, Stephen J. "Proper and Improper Partiality and the Preferential Option for the Poor." *Theological Studies* 54 (June 1993): 242-71.

————. "Christian Love for the Poor: Alms-giving and the Preferential Option." *Horizons* 21 (Fall 1994): 288-312.

Porter, Joshua Roy. *The Extended Family in the Old Testament.* London: Edutext, 1967.

Potaro, Sam A. "Is God Prejudiced in Favor of the Poor?" *The Christian Century* 102 (April 1985): 404-405.

Premnath, D. N. "Latifundialization and Isaiah 5:8-10." *Journal for the Study of the Old Testament* 40 (1988): 49-60.

Pritchard, James B., ed. *Ancient Near Eastern Texts Relating to the Old Testament.* 3d ed. Princeton, NJ: Princeton University Press, 1969.

Prusak, Bernard P., ed. *Raising the Torch of Good Hope: Catholic Authority and Dialogue with the World.* Lanham, MD: University Press of America / The College Society, 1988.

Rempel, Kaye. "Women and Poverty: What is the Church's Role?" *The Conrad Grebel Review* 10 (Winter 1992): 59-65.

Rendtorff, Rolf. *The Old Testament: An Introduction.* Translated by John Bowden. Philadelphia: Fortress Press, 1991.

Reverentlow, Henning Graf, and Yair Hoffman, eds. *Justice and Righteousness: Biblical Themes and their Influence.* Journal for the Study of the Old Testament Supplement Series 137. Sheffield, England: JSOT Press, 1994.

Riddell, Roger C., and Peter S. Harris. *The Poverty Datum Line as a Wage-Fixing Standard: An Application to Rhodesia.* Gwelo: Mambo Press, 1975.

Ringgren, Helmer. *"yātôm."* In *Theological Dictionary of the Old Testament.* Vol. VI. Edited by G. Johannes Botterweck and Helmer Ringgren. Translated by David E. Green, 477-81. Grand Rapids, MI: William B. Eerdmans Publishing Company, 1990.

Roberts, J. J. M. "Isaiah in Old Testament Theology." In *Interpreting the Prophets.* Edited by James Luther Mays and Paul J. Achtemeier, 62-74. Philadelphia: Fortress Press, 1987.

Roberts, W. Dayton. "Liberation Theologies: Looking at Poverty from the Underside." *Evangelical Review of Theology* 10 (April 1986): 110-14.

Rodrigo, Michael. "Bible and the Liberation of the Poor." *Dialogue* (Colombo) 15, nos. 1-3 (1988): 61-83.

Rosner, Dov. "The Balance of Economic Security and Income According to the Mosaic Law (The Torah)." In *Poverty, Affluence and the Word of God: An Interdisciplinary Study-Program of the Missiological Institute, Mapumulo.* Edited by Klaus Nurnberger, 135-40. Durban, South Africa: The Lutheran Publishing House, 1978.

Ross, Jerome C. *The History of Ancient Israel and Judah: A Compilation.* Pittsburgh, PA.: Dorrance Publishing Co., 2003.

Rostagno, Sergio. "Is an Interclass Reading of the Bible Legitimate?" *Communio Viatorum* 17, nos. 1-2 (1974): 1-14.

Roth, Martha T. "Marriage and Matrimonial Prestations in First Millennium B. C. Babylon." In *Women's Earliest Records: From Ancient Egypt and Western Asia.* Proceedings of the Conference on Women in the Ancient Near East held at Brown University, Providence RI 5-7 November 1987. Edited by Barbara S. Lesko, 245-60. Atlanta, GA: Scholars Press, 1989.

Roth, Wolfgang. *Isaiah*. Knox Preaching Guides. Atlanta: John Knox Press, 1988.

Rowe, Douglas. "Social Injustice and Liberation in Light of Exodus." *Bible Bhashyam* 7 (1981): 55-59.

Rowland, Christopher. "In Dialogue with Itumeleng Mosala: A Contribution to Liberation Exegesis." *Journal for the Study of the New Testament* 50 (June 1993): 43-57.

Rowley, H. H. *Job*. The Century Bible. Ontario, Trinidad: Nelson, 1970.

Russell, Letty M., ed. *Feminist Interpretations of the Bible*. Philadelphia: The Westminster Press, 1985.

Rylaarsdam, Coert. "Poverty and the Poor in the Bible." *Pastoral Psychology* 19, no. 182 (1968): 13-24.

Sabath, Bob. "Bible and the Poor." *Post American* 3 (February-March 1974): 4-5.

Sachs, Jeffrey D. *The End of Poverty: Economic Possibilities for Our Time*. New York: Penguin Books, 2005.

Sacks, Jonathan. *Wealth and Poverty: A Jewish Analysis*. London: Social Affairs Unit, 1984.

Sadowsky, James. *The Christian Response to Poverty: Working with God's Economic Laws*. London: Social Affairs Unit, 1985.

Scaria, K. J. "Social Justice in the Old Testament." *Bible Bhashyam* 4, no. 3 (1978): 163-92.

Schifferdecker, Kathryn. *Out of the Whirlwind: Creation Theology in the Book of Job*. Harvard Theological Studies 61. Cambridge, MA: Harvard University Press, 2008.

Schlemmer, Lawrence. "The Two Significant Income Gaps in South Africa." In *Poverty, Affluence and the Word of God: An Interdisciplinary Study-Program of the Missiological Institute, Mapumulo*. Edited by Klaus Nurnberger, 49-56. Durban, South Africa: The Lutheran Publishing House, 1978.

Schlossberg, Herbert, Pierre Berthoud, Clark H. Pinnock, and Marvin Olasky, eds. *Freedom Justice, and Hope: Toward a Strategy for the Poor and the Oppressed*. Westchester, IL: Crossway Books, 1988.

Schottroff, Willy, and Wolfgang Stegemann, eds. *God of the Lowly: Socio-Historical Interpretations of the Bible*. Translated by Matthew J. O'Connell. Maryknoll, NY: Orbis Books, 1984.

Schottroff, Willy. "The Prophet Amos: A Socio-Historical Assessment of His Ministry." In *God of the Lowly: Socio-Historical Interpretations of the Bible*. Edited by Willy Schottroff and Wolfgang Stegemann. Translated by Matthew J. O'Connell, 27-46. Maryknoll, NY: Orbis Books, 1984.

Schüssler Fiorenza, Elisabeth. *In Memory of Her: A Feminist Theological Reconstruction of Christian Origins*. New York: Crossroad, 1983.

Schüssler Fiorenza, Elisabeth, and Anne Carr, eds. *Women, Work and Poverty*. Edinburgh: T. & T. Clark, 1987.

Scott, R. B. Y. *Proverbs. Ecclesiastes*. Anchor Bible. Garden City, NY: Doubleday and Company, 1965.

Seitz, Christopher R., ed. *Reading and Preaching the Book of Isaiah*. Philadelphia: Fortress Press, 1988.

———. "Introduction: The One Isaiah // The Three Isaiahs." In *Reading and Preaching the Book of Isaiah*. Edited by Christopher R. Seitz, 13-22. Philadelphia: Fortress Press, 1988.

————. "Isaiah 1-66: Making Sense of the Whole." In *Reading and Preaching the Book of Isaiah.* Edited by Christopher R. Seitz, 105-126. Philadelphia: Fortress Press, 1988.

Shanks, Hershel, William G. Dever, Baruch Halpern, and P. Kyle McCarter. *The Rise of Ancient Israel.* Symposium at the Smithsonian Institution 26 October 1991, Sponsored by the Resident Associate Program. Washington, DC: Biblical Archaeology Society, 1992.

Shanks, Hershel. "Defining the Problem: Where We Are in the Debate." In *The Rise of Ancient Israel.* By Hershel Shanks, William G. Dever, Baruch Halpern, and P. Kyle McCarter. Symposium at the Smithsonian Institution 26 October 1991, Sponsored by the Resident Associate Program, 1-25. Washington, DC: Biblical Archaeology Society, 1992.

Sheppard, Lancelot C. "Poverty." *The Downside Review* 73 (1955): 395-97.

Shourie, Chandrakat. "Poverty is Powerlessness." *Evangelical Review of Theology* 11 (July 1987): 254-60.

Sider, Ronald J. "Is God Really on the Side of the Poor?" *Sojourners* 6 (October 1977): 11-14.

————, ed. *Cry Justice!: The Bible Speaks on Hunger and Poverty.* New York: Paulist Press, 1980.

————, ed. *Lifestyle in the Eighties: An Evangelical Commitment to Simple Life.* Philadelphia: The Westminster Press, 1982.

————. *Rich Christians in an Age of Hunger: A Biblical Study.* Rev. and exp. Downers Grove, IL: Intervarsity Press, 1984.

Simpson, William Kelly, ed. *The Literature of Ancient Egypt: An Anthology of Stories, Instructions, and Poetry.* New Edition. New Haven and London: Yale University Press, 1973.

Siwo-Okundi, Elizabeth J. A. "Listening to the Small Voice: Toward an Orphan Theology," *Harvard Divinity Bulletin,* Vol. 37, Number 2 & 3 (Spring/Summer 2009): 33-43.

Skillen, James W., ed. *The Problem of Poverty.* Washington, DC: The Center for Public Justice / Grand Rapids, MI: Baker Book House, 1991.

Skotte, Phil. "The Problem of Poverty in the Old Testament." *The Bible Today* 26 (1988): 87-93.

Sobrino, Jon. *The True Church and the Poor.* Maryknoll, NY: Orbis Books, 1985.

Sowada, John. "Let Justice Surge Like Water...." *The Bible Today* 19 (1981): 301-305.

Spangenberg, Izak. "'The Poor Will Always Be with You': Wealth and Poverty in a Wisdom Perspective." In *Plutocrats and Paupers: Wealth and Poverty in the Old Testament.* Edited by Hendrik L. Bosman, I. G. P. Gous, and Izak J. J. Spangenberg, 228-46. Pretoria: J. L. van Schaik, 1991.

Spencer, John R. "Sojourner." In *The Anchor Bible Dictionary.* Vol. 6. Edited by David Noel Freedman, 103-104. New York, London, Toronto, Sydney, Auckland: Doubleday, 1992.

Spina, Frank Anthony. "Qoheleth and the Reformation of Wisdom." In *The Quest for the Kingdom of God: Studies in Honor of George E. Mendenhall.* Edited by

Herbert B. Huffmon, Frank Anthony Spina, and A. R. W. Green, 267-79. Winona Lake, IN: Eisenbrauns, 1983.

———. "Israelites as *gērîm,* 'Sojourners,' in Social and Historical Context." In *The Word of the Lord Shall Go Forth: Essays in Honor of David Noel Freedman in Celebration of His Sixtieth Birthday.* Edited by Carol L. Meyers and Michael O'Connor, 321-35. Winona Lake, IN: Eisenbrauns, 1983.

Sprinkle, Joe M. *The Book of the Covenant: A Literary Approach.* Journal for the Study of the Old Testament Supplement Series 174. Sheffield: JSOT Press, 1994.

Stackhouse, Max L. "What Then Shall We Do?: On Using Scripture in Economic Ethics." *Interpretation* 41 (October 1987): 382-97.

Stager, Lawrence E. "The Archaeology of the Family in Ancient Israel." *Bulletin of the American Schools of Oriental Research* 260 (Fall 1985): 1-35.

Stegemann, Wolfgang. *The Gospel and the Poor.* Translated by Dietlinde Elliott. Philadelphia: Fortress Press, 1984.

Steindorff, George, and Keith C. Seele. *When Egypt Ruled the East.* Chicago and London: The University of Chicago Press, 1957.

Stek, John H. "Salvation, Justice, and Liberation in the Old Testament." *Calvin Theological Journal* 13 (November 1978): 133-65.

Storøy, Solfrid. "On Proverbs and Riddles. Polar Word Pairs and Other Poetic Devices, and Words for 'Poor and Needy' in the Book of Proverbs." *Scandinavian Journal of the Old Testament* 7, no. 2 (1993): 270-84.

Stuhlmueller, Carroll. "Justice Toward the Poor." *The Bible Today* 24 (November 1986): 385-90.

Sugirtharajah R. S. "'For You Always Have the Poor with You': An Example of Hermeneutics of Suspicion." *Asia Journal of Theology* 4, no. 1 (1990): 102-107.

———, ed. *Voices from the Margin: Interpreting the Bible in the Third World.* London: SPCK, 1991.

Sumithra, Sunard, ed. "Prosperity, Property and Poverty." *Evangelical Review of Theology* 11 (July 1987): 195-272.

Sutherland, John R. "Usury: God's Forgotten Doctrine." *Crux* 18 no. 1 (1982): 9-14.

Talmon, Shemaryahu. *"midbār; 'ārābâ."* In *Theological Dictionary of the Old Testament.* Vol. VIII. Edited by G. Johannes Botterweck, Helmer Ringgren, and Heinz-Josef Fabry. Translated by Douglas W. Stott, 87-118. Grand Rapids, MI / Cambridge, UK: William B. Eerdmans Publishing Company, 1997.

Tamez, Elsa. *Bible of the Oppressed.* Translated by Matthew J. O'Connell. Maryknoll, NY: Orbis Books: 1987.

———. "Reading the Bible from the Eyes of the Poor: For Women, It's Not Enough." *The Other Side* 24, no. 6 (1988): 24-25.

Terrien, Samuel. *Till the Heart Sings: A Biblical Theology of Manhood and Womanhood.* Philadelphia: Fortress Press, 1985.

Thagale, Buti, and Itumeleng Mosala, eds. *Hammering Swords into Ploughshares: Essays in Honor of Archbishop Mpilo Desmond Tutu.* Johannesburg: Skataville Publishers,1986 / Grand Rapids, MI: Eerdmans, 1987.

Tinker, George E. "Blessed are the Poor: A Theology of Solidarity with the Poor in the Two-Thirds World." *Church and Society* 84 (March-April 1994): 45-55.

Townsend, T. P. "The Poor in Wisdom Literature." *Bible Bhashyam* 14 (1988): 5-25.

Tucker, Gene M. "Prophetic Speech." In *Interpreting the Prophets.* Edited by James Luther Mays and Paul J. Achtemeier, 27-40. Philadelphia: Fortress Press, 1987.

Tutu, Desmond M. "How Can You Say You Love God whom You Have Not Seen when You Hate Your Brother whom You Have Seen?" *Engage/Social Action* 13, no. 11 (1985): 18-19.

Van De Laar, A. J. M. *The World Bank and the Poor.* Boston: MA: Nijhoff, 1980.

Van Houten, Christiana de Groot. *The Alien in Israelite Law.* Journal for the Study of the Old Testament Supplement Series 107. Sheffield: JSOT Press, 1991.

Van Leeuwen, Raymond C. "Wealth and Poverty: System and Contradiction in Proverbs." *Hebrew Studies* 33 (1992): 25-36.

Van Selms A. "Jubilee, Year of." In *The Interpreter's Dictionary of the Bible.* Supplementary Volume. Ninth Printing. Edited by Keith Crim, 496-98. Nashville: Abingdon Press, 1990.

Verhey, Allen D. "Poverty." In *The International Standard Bible Encyclopedia.* Vol. 3. Edited by Geoffrey W. Bromiley, 921-26. Grand Rapids, MI: William B. Eerdmans Publishing Company, 1986.

Vijayakumar, J. "Factors Causing Poverty and Oppression in 8th-Century Israel and the Prophetic Response." Diss. Abst. *Bangalore Theological Forum* 15 (January-April 1983): 59-60.

Vogels, Walter. "Biblical Theology for the 'Haves' and the 'Have-Nots.'" *Science et esprit* 39, no. 2 (1987): 193-210.

Vogels, Walter, A. Loiselle, R. Roach, G. Bourgeault, J. Lemarier, M. Boyer, S. Beauchamp, and C. Lefebvre. *Attentive to the Cry of the Needy.* Domum Dei Series No. 19. Ottawa, Canada: Canadian Religious Conference, 1973.

Vogels, Walter. "The Social Dimension of the Bible's Teaching." In *Attentive to the Cry of the Needy.* Donum Dei Series No. 19. By Walter Vogels, A. Loiselle, R. Roach, G. Bourgeault, J. Lemarier, M. Boyer, S. Beauchamp, and C. Lefebvre, 11-26. Ottawa, Canada: Canadian Religious Conference, 1973.

Von Rad, Gerhard. *Studies in Deuteronomy.* Studies in Biblical Theology 9. London: SCM, 1953.

―――. *Old Testament Theology: The Theology of Israel's Historical Traditions.* Vol. I. Translated by D. M. G. Stalker. New York, Hagerstown, San Francisco, London: Harper & Row, 1962.

―――. *Old Testament Theology: The Theology of Israel's Prophetic Traditions.* Vol. II. Translated by D. M. G. Stalker. San Francisco, New York, Grand Rapids, Philadelphia, St. Louis, London, Singapore, Sydney, Tokyo, Toronto: Harper & Row, 1965.

―――. *The Message of the Prophets.* Translated by D. M. G. Stalker. New York: Harper &Row Publishers, 1965.

―――. *Deuteronomy: A Commentary.* Old Testament Library. Philadelphia: The Westminster Press, 1966.

―――. *Wisdom in Israel.* Nashville, New York: Abingdon Press, 1972.

Von Waldow, H. E. "Social Responsibility and Social Structure in Early Israel." *Catholic Biblical Quarterly* 32 (April 1970): 182-204.

Wafawanaka, Robert. "Preaching in the Context of Poverty, Economic Marginaliza-
tion, and the Ideal of Social Justice." In *Born to Preach: Essays in Honor of the
Ministry of Henry & Ella Mitchell*. Edited by Samuel K. Roberts, 40-54. Valley
Forge, PA: Judson Press, 2000.

———. "African Perspectives on Poverty in the Hebrew Law Codes." In *The Bible
in Africa: Transactions, Trajectories, and Trends*. Edited by Gerald O. West and
Musa W. Dube, 490-97. Leiden, The Netherlands, Boston, Koln: Brill Publishers,
2000.

———. "Amos' Attitude toward Poverty: An African Perspective." In African *Journal of Biblical Studies*. Edited by David Tuesday Adamo. Vol. XIX /2 (November
2003): 97-109.

———. "Poverty in the Old Testament in African Perspective." In *Biblical Interpretation in African Perspective*. Edited by David Tuesday Adamo, 223-58. Lanham,
Boulder, New York, Toronto, Oxford: University Press of America, 2006.

Walchoder, Ben Zion. "Sabbatical Year." In *The Interpreter's Dictionary of the Bible*.
Supplementary Volume. Ninth Printing. Edited by Keith Crim, 762-63. Nashville:
Abingdon Press, 1990.

Walker, David S. "Preferential Option for the Poor in Evangelical Theology: Assess-
ments and Proposals." *Journal of Theology for Southern Africa* 79 (June 1992):
53-62.

Wallis, Jim. "Poverty is a Scandal." *Sojourners* 14, no. 10 (1985): 4-5.

Ward, James M. *Thus Says the Lord: The Message of the Prophets*. Nashville: Abingdon, 1991.

Washington, Harold C. *Wealth and Poverty in the Instruction of Amenemope and the
Hebrew Proverbs*. Society of Biblical Literature Dissertation Series 142. Atlanta,
Georgia: Scholars Press, 1994.

Weber, Max. *Ancient Judaism*. Translated and edited by Hans H. Gerth and Don
Martindale. Glencoe, IL: The Free Press, 1952.

Wee, Paul A. "Biblical Ethics and Lending to the Poor." *The Ecumenical Review* 38
(October 1986): 416-30.

Weinfeld, Moshe. *Deuteronomy and the Deuteronomic School*. Oxford: The Clarendon Press, 1972.

———. "Freedom Proclamation in Egypt and in the Ancient Near East." In *Pharaonic Egypt: The Bible and Christianity*. Edited by Sarah Israelit-Groll, 317-27.
Jerusalem: The Magnes Press, 1985.

———. *Social Justice in Ancient Israel and the Ancient Near East*. Jerusalem: The
Magnes Press / Minneapolis: Fortress Press, 1995.

Weir, J. Emmette. "The Poor Are Powerless: A Response to R. J. Coggins." *The
Expository Times* 100 (October 1988): 13-15.

Weiser, Artur. *The Psalms*. Old Testament Library. Philadelphia: The Westminster
Press, 1962.

West, Charles. "The Sharing of Resources: A Biblical Reflection." *The Ecumenical
Review* 38 (October 1986): 357-69.

Westbrook, Raymond. *Studies in Biblical and Cuneiform Law*. Cahiers De La Revue
Biblique 26. Paris: J. Gabalda, 1988.

————. *Property and the Family in Biblical Law.* Journal for the Study of the Old Testament Supplement Series 113. Sheffield, England: JSOT Press, 1991.

Westermann, Claus. *Basic Forms of Prophetic Speech.* Translated by Hugh Clayton White. Philadelphia: Westminster Press, 1967.

————. *Isaiah 40-66: A Commentary.* Philadelphia: Fortress Press, 1969.

————. *Praise and Lament in the Psalms.* Translated by Keith R. Crim and Richard N. Soulen. Atlanta: John Knox Press, 1981.

Westhues, Kenneth. "The Option for (and Against) the Poor." *Grail* 3, no. 1 (1987): 23-38.

Whitelam, Keith W. "Israelite Kingship. The Royal Ideology and its Opponents." In *The World of Ancient Israel: Sociological, Anthropological and Political Perspectives: Essays by Members of the Society for Old Testament Study.* Edited by R. E. Clements, 119-39. Cambridge, New York, New Rochelle, Melbourne, Sydney: Cambridge University Press, 1989.

Whiteman, Darrel. "Good News for the Poor?" *Missiology* 17 (October 1989): 387-464.

Whybray, Roger N. "Some Literary Problems in Proverbs I-IX." *Vetus Testamentum* 16 (1966): 482-496.

————. *Isaiah 40-66.* New Century Bible. London: Oliphants, 1975.

————. "The Social World of the Wisdom Writers." In *The World of Ancient Israel: Sociological, Anthropological and Political Perspectives: Essays by Members of the Society for Old Testament Study.* Edited by R. E. Clements, 227-50. Cambridge, New York, New Rochelle, Melbourne, Sydney: Cambridge University Press, 1989.

————. "Poverty, Wealth, and Point of View in Proverbs." *The Expository Times* 100 (June 1989): 332-36.

————. *Ecclesiastes.* New Century Bible Commentary. Grand Rapids, MI: Wm. B. Eerdmans Publishing Company, 1989.

————. *Wealth and Poverty in the Book of Proverbs.* Sheffield, England: JSOT Press, 1990.

————. *Proverbs.* New Century Bible Commentary. Grand Rapids, MI: William B. Eerdmans Publishing Company, 1994.

Wigglesworth, Chris. "Evangelical Views of the Poor and Social Ethics Today." *Tyndale Bulletin* 35 (1984): 161-84.

Williams, David T. "The Heresy of Prosperity Teaching: A Message for the Church in its Approach to Need." *Journal of Theology for Southern Africa* 61 (December 1987): 33-44.

————. "Poverty: An Integrated Christian Approach." *Journal of Theology for Southern Africa* 77 (December 1991): 47-57.

Williams, Oliver F., and John W. Houck, eds. *The Common Good and US Capitalism.* Lanham, MD: University Press of America, 1987.

Williamson, H. G. M. "The Old Testament and the Material World." *Evangelical Quarterly* 57, no. 1 (1985): 5-22.

Wilson, Harold. *The War on World Poverty: An Appeal to the Conscience of Mankind.* London: Gollancz, 1953. Reprint, New York: Kraus, 1969.

Wilson, Robert R. *Prophecy and Society in Ancient Israel.* Philadelphia: Fortress Press, 1980.

Wittenberg, G. H. "The Message of the Old Testament Prophets during the Eighth Century B.C. concerning Affluence and Poverty." In *Affluence, Poverty and the Word of God: An Interdisciplinary Study-Program of the Missiological Institute, Mapumulo.* Edited by Klaus Nurnberger, 141-52. Durban, South Africa: Lutheran Publishing House, 1978.

———. "The Lexical Context of the Terminology for 'Poor' in the Book of Proverbs." *Scriptura* S2 (1986): 40-85.

———. "The Situational Context of Statements concerning Poverty and Wealth in the Book of Proverbs." *Scriptura* 21 (1987): 1-23.

Wolf, C. Umhau. "Poor." In *The Interpreter's Dictionary of the Bible.* Vol. 3. Edited by George Arthur Buttrick, 843-44. New York, Nashville: Abingdon Press, 1962. 11th Printing, 1990.

———. "Poverty." In *The Interpreter's Dictionary of the Bible.* Vol. 3. Edited by George Arthur Buttrick, 853-54. New York, Nashville: Abingdon Press, 1962. 11th Printing, 1990.

Wolff, Hans Walter. *"Das Kerygma des deuteronomistischen Geschichtswerkes." Zeitschrift fur die alttestamentliche Wissenschaft* 73 (1961): 171-86.

———. "The Kerygma of the Deuteronomic Historian." In *The Vitality of Old Testament Traditions.* Edited by Walter Brueggemann and Hans Walter Wolff, 83-100. Atlanta: John Knox Press, 1975.

———. *Joel and Amos: A Commentary on the Books of the Prophets Joel and Amos.* Translated by Waldemar Janzen and S. Dean McBride. Hermenia. Philadelphia: Fortress Press, 1977.

———. *Micah the Prophet.* Translated by Ralph D. Gehrke. Philadelphia: Fortress Press, 1981.

Wolterstorff, Nicholas P. "The Moral Significance of Poverty." *Perspectives* 6 (Fall 1991): 8-11.

Wortman, Julie A. "Family Values: Only for the Privileged?" *The Witness* 77 (December 1994): 11-13.

Wright, George Ernst. "The Literary and Historical Problem of Joshua 10 and Judges 1." *Journal of Near Eastern Studies* 5 (1946): 105-11.

———. *Biblical Archaeology.* 2d ed. Philadelphia: Westminster, 1962.

Wright, Christopher J. H. *An Eye for An Eye: The Place of Old Testament Ethics Today.* Downers Grove, IL: Intervarsity Press, 1983.

———. *God's People in God's Land: Family, Land, and Property in the Old Testament.* Grand Rapids, MI: William B. Eerdmans Publishing Company/Exeter: The Paternoster Press, 1990.

———. "Family." In *The Anchor Bible Dictionary.* Vol. 3. Edited by David Noel Freedman, 761-69. New York, London, Toronto, Sydney, Auckland: Doubleday, 1992.

———. "Jubilee, Year of." In *The Anchor Bible Dictionary.* Vol. 3. Edited by David Noel Freedman, 1025-30. New York, London, Toronto, Sydney, Auckland: Doubleday, 1992.

———. "Sabbatical Year." In *The Anchor Bible Dictionary.* Vol. 5. Edited by David Noel Freedman, 857-61. New York, London, Toronto, Sydney, Auckland: Doubleday, 1992.

Young, Edward J. *The Book of Isaiah.* The New International Commentary on the Old Testament. Grand Rapids, MI: William B. Eerdmans Publishing Company, 1969.

Yuzon, Lourdino A. ed. *Mission in the Context of Endemic Poverty.* Papers of a Consultation on Mission in the Context of Poverty and in Situations of Affluence, Manila, Philippines, December 10-14, 1982. Toa Payoh, Singapore: Christian Conference of Asia, 1983.

Zimmerli, Walther. "Slavery in the OT." In *The Interpreter's Dictionary of the Bible.* Supplementary Volume. Edited by Keith Crim, 829-30. Nashville: Abingdon Press, 1976. Ninth Printing, 1990.

Index of Authors

Index of Subjects

'almānâ, 46, 131-32, 146n12, 147n28, 150n52, 159

Amos, 82, 84, 90-97, 158; book of, 115n46; as champion of the poor, 96; conflict with Amaziah, 90; on cows of Bashan, 92-93; credentials and occupation of, 90; debt slavery in, 91, 95; justice in, 94, 109; market practices in, 95-96; pledge garments in, 92; the poor in, 91-96

'ănāwîm, 50-51, 91-92, 95, 101, 103, 116n47, 122n117, 132-34, 138

'ānî, 50-51, 55-58, 66n15, 73n125, 76n153, 77n163, 101-3, 105-6, 116n47, 122n117, 123n136, 128-34, 136-41, 146n12, 147nn27-28, 148n38, 149n44, 150n52, 157-58

'ăniwwê-'āreṣ, 130

annual tithe, 63, 147n28, 150n52

'āšîr, 50-51, 85-86, 105, 132, 135-36, 147n28

Aqhat, tale of, 47

Baal, 120n99

"Babylonian Theodicy," 54

biblical mandate, xix-xxi, 3-17; as call to action, 9; 52, 54, 59, 62, 81-82, 89, 99, 105, 109, 110-11, 127, 142-44, 155-56, 158-59; challenge of, 164; vision of, 164

boundary markers, 63

brother's (sister's) keeper, concept of, xix-xxi; 111, 155, 159, 164

Cain and Abel, xix

clan, 26

Code of Hammurabi, on release of slaves, 29; compared with Hebrew law, 29; 33, 35, 45, 54, 89

Code of Ur-Nammu, 45, 118n81

Covenant Code. *See* legal codes

culture of poverty, 145n5

dal, 50, 55-56, 66n15, 73n125, 74n130, 77n163, 84-87, 91-93, 95, 101-3, 116n47, 122n117, 123n136, 124n147, 129-34, 136, 138, 140-41, 146n12, 147nn27-28, 148n38, 150n52, 157-58

dallâ, 50-51, 123n136

dallaṯ 'am-hā'āreṣ, 86, 124n143

dallaṯ hā'āreṣ, 86

dallîm, 92, 95, 103, 106, 116n47, 130, 132-33

David, and Bathsheba, 86

Day of the Lord, 89, 94

debt reduction / cancellation, 53-54, 60-61, 63, 163-64

Index of Scripture References

About the Author

Robert Wafawanaka is assistant professor of Biblical Studies and Old Testament/Hebrew Bible at the Samuel DeWitt Proctor School of Theology of Virginia Union University. He holds the ThM and MTS degrees from Harvard University Divinity School and the ThD degree from Boston University School of Theology.